Art and Eth
Criticism

New Directions in Aesthetics
Series editors: Dominic McIver Lopes, University of British Columbia, and Berys Gaut, University of St Andrews

Blackwell's New Directions in Aesthetics series highlights ambitious single- and multiple-author books that confront the most intriguing and pressing problems in aesthetics and the philosophy of art today. Each book is written in a way that advances understanding of the subject at hand and is accessible to upper-undergraduate and graduate students.

Art and Ethical Criticism

Edited by Garry L. Hagberg

WILEY-BLACKWELL

A John Wiley & Sons, Ltd., Publication

This paper edition first published 2011
© 2011 John Wiley & Sons, Inc
except for editorial material and organization © 2011 Garry L. Hagberg

Edition history: Blackwell Publishing Ltd (hardback, 2008)

Blackwell Publishing was acquired by John Wiley & Sons in February 2007. Blackwell's
publishing program has been merged with Wiley's global Scientific, Technical, and Medical
business to form Wiley-Blackwell.

Registered Office
John Wiley & Sons Ltd, The Atrium, Southern Gate, Chichester, West Sussex, PO19 8SQ,
United Kingdom

Editorial Offices
350 Main Street, Malden, MA 02148-5020, USA
9600 Garsington Road, Oxford, OX4 2DQ, UK
The Atrium, Southern Gate, Chichester, West Sussex, PO19 8SQ, UK

For details of our global editorial offices, for customer services, and for information about how
to apply for permission to reuse the copyright material in this book please see our website at
www.wiley.com/wiley-blackwell.

The right of Garry L. Hagberg to be identified as the author of the editorial material in this
work has been asserted in accordance with the UK Copyright, Designs and Patents Act 1988.

All rights reserved. No part of this publication may be reproduced, stored in a retrieval system,
or transmitted, in any form or by any means, electronic, mechanical, photocopying, recording
or otherwise, except as permitted by the UK Copyright, Designs and Patents Act 1988,
without the prior permission of the publisher.

Wiley also publishes its books in a variety of electronic formats. Some content that appears in
print may not be available in electronic books.

Designations used by companies to distinguish their products are often claimed as trademarks.
All brand names and product names used in this book are trade names, service marks,
trademarks or registered trademarks of their respective owners. The publisher is not associated
with any product or vendor mentioned in this book. This publication is designed to provide
accurate and authoritative information in regard to the subject matter covered. It is sold
on the understanding that the publisher is not engaged in rendering professional services.
If professional advice or other expert assistance is required, the services of a competent
professional should be sought.

Library of Congress Cataloging-in-Publication Data

Art and ethical criticism / edited by Garry L. Hagberg.
    p. cm. — (New directions in aesthetics)
    Includes bibliographical references and index.
    ISBN 978-1-4051-3483-5 (hardcover: alk. paper)
    ISBN 978-1-4443-3787-7 (paperback: alk. paper)
1. Aesthetics. 2. Aesthetics—Moral and ethical aspects. 3. Art—Philosophy.
I. Hagberg, Garry, 1952–
    BH39.A6855 2008
    111'.85—dc22
                                                                    2007046033

A catalogue record for this book is available from the British Library.

Set in 10/12.5pt Galliard by Graphicraft Limited, Hong Kong
Printed in Malaysia by Ho Printing (M) Sdn Bhd

01   2011

CONTENTS

NOTES ON
CONTRIBUTORS

Noël Carroll is the Andrew W. Mellon Professor of the Humanities at Temple University. His most recent published book is *The Philosophy of Motion Pictures* in Blackwell's Foundations of the Philosophy of the Arts series. His next book is *On Criticism* for the Routledge Thinking in Action series, slated for 2008. He is past President of the American Society for Aesthetics.

David Davies is Associate Professor in the department of philosophy at McGill University. He is the author of *Art as Performance* and *Aesthetics and Literature*, and co-editor of *Contemporary Readings in the Philosophy of Literature*. He has published articles on issues in the philosophies of film, photography, literature, and the visual arts, and has also published on topics in metaphysics, philosophy of mind, philosophy of language, and philosophy of science. He is currently editing a collection of papers on the cinema of Terrence Malick, and working on a book on the philosophical foundations of the performing arts.

Stephen Davies teaches philosophy at the University of Auckland. His books include *The Philosophy of Art*, *Philosophical Perspectives on Art*, *Definitions of Art*, *Musical Meaning and Expression*, *Musical Works and Performances*, and two volumes of collected essays, *Themes in the Philosophy of Art* and *Themes in the Philosophy of Music*. He is President of the American Society for Aesthetics.

Ivan Gaskell is Margaret S. Winthrop Curator at the Fogg Art Museum, Harvard University, where his faculty appointment is in the History Department. Among his publications are *Vermeer's Wager: Speculations on Art History, Theory, and Art Museums* and six books edited with the late Salim Kemal in the Cambridge University Press series of which they were joint general editors, Cambridge Studies in Philosophy and the Arts, beginning with *The Language of Art History* and concluding with *Politics and Aesthetics in the Arts.* In 2007 he edited (with Jeffrey Quilter) and contributed to *Museums – Crossing Boundaries*, a special issue of *Res: Anthropology and Aesthetics* on relations between art museums and anthropology museums.

Mitchell Green is the Cavaliers' Distinguished Teaching Professor at the University of Virginia. His research focuses on the philosophy of language, aesthetics, and the philosophy of mind. He co-edited *Moore's Paradox: New Essays on Belief, Rationality and the First Person* with John Williams, and his book *Self-Expression* appeared with Oxford University Press in 2007.

Paul Guyer is the Florence R. C. Murray Professor in the Humanities at the University of Pennsylvania. He has worked on all aspects of the philosophy of Kant as well as on the history of modern aesthetics. His works on Kant's aesthetics include *Kant and the Claims of Taste, Kant and the Experience of Freedom*, and *Values of Beauty*, as well as new translations of the *Critique of the Power of Judgment* and Kant's early "Observations on the Feeling of the Beautiful and the Sublime." He has also published extensively on Kant's theoretical and practical philosophy. He is currently working on a history of modern aesthetics from Shaftesbury and Addison through Danto and Cavell.

Garry L. Hagberg presently holds a Chair in the School of Philosophy at the University of East Anglia, Norwich, and has for some years served as the James H. Ottaway, Jr., Professor of Philosophy and Aesthetics at Bard College. Author of *Meaning and Interpretation: Wittgenstein, Henry James, and Literary Knowledge* and *Art as Language: Wittgenstein, Meaning, and Aesthetic Theory*, his *Describing Ourselves: Wittgenstein and Autobiographical Consciousness* was published by Oxford University Press in 2008. He is joint editor, with Denis Dutton, of the journal *Philosophy and Literature* and co-author, with Howard Roberts, of the three-volume *Guitar Compendium: Technique, Improvisation, Musicianship, Theory*. He guest-edited a special issue of the *Journal of Aesthetics and Art Criticism* on improvisation in the arts.

Carolyn Korsmeyer is Professor of Philosophy at the University at Buffalo, State University of New York. Her research interests include aesthetics and emotion theory, and she is particularly interested in philosophical treatments of the senses. She is the author and editor of a number of books, among them *Making Sense of Taste: Food and Philosophy*, *Gender and Aesthetics*, *Aesthetics in Feminist Perspective*, and *The Taste Culture Reader: Experiencing Food and Drink*. She is a past President of the American Society for Aesthetics.

Joshua Landy is Associate Professor of French at Stanford University, where he co-directs Stanford's Initiative in Philosophy and Literature. He is the author of *Philosophy as Fiction: Self, Deception, and Knowledge in Proust* and editor, with Claude Bremond and Thomas Pavel, of *Thematics: New Approaches*. He is currently working on a second collection, *The Re-Enchantment of the World: Secular Magic in a Rational Age* (co-edited with Michael Saler), and on a second book, *Formative Fictions: Literary Structure and the Life Well Lived*.

Paisley Livingston is Chair Professor and Head of the Department of Philosophy at Lingnan University (Hong Kong). He has held teaching and research positions at the University of Michigan, Ann Arbor, McGill University, l'École Polytechnique (Paris), Siegen University, the University of Aarhus, Roskilde University Center, the University of Copenhagen, and Zinbin (Kyoto). His publications include *Ingmar Bergman and the Rituals of Art*, *Literary Knowledge*, *Literature and Rationality*, *Models of Desire*, and *Art and Intention*. He co-edited *The Creation of Art* with Berys Gaut, and is currently co-editing *The Routledge Companion to Philosophy and Film* with Carl Plantinga.

Robert C. Solomon (1942–2007) was Quincy Lee Centennial Professor of Philosophy and Business at the University of Texas at Austin. Over the course of his career he also taught at numerous other places, including Princeton, the University of Pennsylvania, the University of Pittsburgh, UCLA, the University of California Riverside, Simon Fraser University, the University of British Columbia, and the University of Auckland. He was the author of over 40 books, in addition to numerous textbooks. Among these are *The Passions*, *About Love*, *A Defense of Sentimentality*, *Ethics and Excellence*, *The Joy of Philosophy*, and *Spirituality for the Skeptic*. He also wrote numerous articles on diverse topics, including aesthetics, ethics, emotion, nineteenth and twentieth century continental philosophy, history of philosophy, and humor. He had an international career as a consultant in business ethics. He also appeared as the existentialism professor in Richard Linklater's film *Waking Life*.

Catherine Wilson is currently Professor of Philosophy at the Graduate Center of the City University of New York, having held positions and visiting positions in the United States, Canada, the United Kingdom, and Germany. She has written widely on the history of philosophy and on issues in meta-ethics and moral and political philosophy. She is the author most recently of *Moral Animals: Ideals and Constraints in Moral Theory*, and she is preparing a separate essay on Bernard Williams for *Twelve Analytical Philosophers*, scheduled to appear from Blackwell in 2008.

FOREWORD

Ludwig Wittgenstein famously delivered early in his philosophical life the gnomic utterance "Ethics and aesthetics are one." That, as stated, is perhaps too general a claim to be judged true or false. The proof would of course be in the particulars (as indeed Wittgenstein was to go on to show in his later philosophical work). And it is just such particulars into which the authors in this collection descend (it should be said, for most of them, without any part of Wittgenstein's philosophy in tow).

Ethical criticism – the task of elucidating the ethical content of the arts, the character and viability of our ethical responses to them, and the nature of the moral benefit provided by a serious engagement with literature, the visual arts, and music – is pursued here under five headings. They are: (Part I) the historical precedents and groundings of the very idea of ethical criticism (Guyer); (Part II) ways of describing ethical content in the arts and the ways in which that content is delivered (Carroll, Landy, Green); (Part III) demonstrations of the value of literary case-studies – in these discussions Virginia Woolf, J. M. Coetzee, and Albert Camus – for moral understanding (Livingston, Wilson, Solomon); (Part IV) distinct ethical issues that arise in connection with our viewing and handling of visual art, artifacts, photography, and architecture (Korsmeyer, D. Davies, Gaskell); and (Part V) the significance of – and some of the telling complexities of – moral relations as they are both depicted and exemplified in music and its performance (S. Davies, Hagberg).

Taken together, the essays offered herein show that ethics and aesthetics aren't in any generic sense one – but nor are they two. These explorations suggest, rather, that the connections between art and morality are, as an intricate web or complex network of relations, more intricate, complex, subtle, and indeed more interesting, than any over-generalized account of *the* relation could accommodate. And, taken together, they show that it is within particularized contexts of usage that our aesthetic descriptions, and our ethically resonant aesthetic predicates in particular, assume the precise meanings they do – it is here that such words *work*. (It was J. L. Austin who gave us the sometimes fair remark that over-generalization would be an occupational hazard in philosophy if it weren't the occupation.)

Because this volume is the work of a dozen pairs of hands, with the authors working from their individual philosophical "backstories," a close reading will show that they do not agree on all points; a few of these are matters of substance and many are matters of emphasis. For a collection devoted to a descent into the instructive particularities and contextually nuanced details of aesthetics-ethics connections, this is just as it should be: each author casts certain issues, considerations, concerns, and interests into higher relief while backgrounding others. It is hoped that the collection, taken *in toto* as a kind of conceptual mosaic, will afford both an enriching multifaceted view and an awareness of the significance of fairly wide-ranging particular cases that might escape full articulation in the hands of a single author. Such, in any case, was the editorial aspiration motivating the project, and I am extremely grateful to each of the contributors for responding to the invitation to participate in the undertaking with such alacrity and enthusiasm.

I am also very grateful to Berys Gaut and Dom Lopes, who invited the volume for their series and who provided expert advice in the form-ative stage, and to Jeff Dean at Blackwell, for doing so much to make this book a reality. Jeanette McDonald at Bard College has once again proved invaluable in assembling and preparing the manuscript, and we are all indebted to Claire Creffield for her meticulous and sensitive copy-editing.

I would also like to express how saddened we all were to learn, as this book was in preparation, of the death of Bob Solomon. His contribution displays his rare combination of acute discernment, cultural breadth, and profound human concern that we will all very much miss. The contri-butors and I are of one mind in wishing to dedicate our collective work in this volume to his memory.

G. H.

Part I
Historical Foundations

1

IS ETHICAL CRITICISM A PROBLEM? A HISTORICAL PERSPECTIVE

Paul Guyer

1 Is There a Problem about Ethical Criticism?

In recent discussion, the question whether "ethical criticism" of art is possible and appropriate has been understood as the question whether ethical merits or flaws in works of art, but especially the latter, are themselves also aesthetic merits or flaws of those works, again typically the latter, or only merits or flaws of those works considered from some non-aesthetic point of view, not *qua* works of art.[1] Noël Carroll has written that "philosophers from Plato through Hume supposed that the pertinence of ethical criticism to art was unproblematic. It is only since the late eighteenth century that the view took hold that the aesthetic realm and the ethical realm are each absolutely autonomous from the other."[2] This correctly assumes that there cannot even be a question about whether an ethical criticism of a work is also an aesthetic criticism unless the ethical and the aesthetic are considered to be separate dimensions of value in our experience and its objects, and suggests that the separation between the ethical and the aesthetic that underlies the contemporary discussion was made only in the late eighteenth century. Presumably Carroll supposes that the decisive event that made this separation in the late eighteenth century was Kant's insistence in his 1790 *Critique of the Power of Judgment* that judgments of taste are disinterested, while moral judgments express the interest of pure practical reason. What I want to argue here is that while the idea of the disinterestedness of aesthetic judgment may have been an eighteenth-century innovation, it was only later adapters of the idea, in the late nineteenth century and again in the second half of the twentieth century, who thought that it makes ethical criticism of works of art problematic; neither Kant himself nor those of his predecessors who first introduced the idea of the disinterestedness of judgments of beauty, namely Anthony Ashley Cooper, the third Earl of Shaftesbury, and Francis Hutcheson, thought that the disinterestedness of judgments of taste in general precluded the centrality of ethical issues to works of art in particular, and thus the appropriateness of ethical criticism of such works. Moreover, I believe, they were right to think that there is no problem about ethical criticism, although I will not attempt to defend this position independently. Carroll himself does so quite ably.

Before turning to details, two comments are in order. First, it may be useful to distinguish between two different issues that have been central both in eighteenth-century discussions of the relations between art and morality and in recent discussions, although they have not always been distinguished. One of these issues is what has come to be called the issue of ethical criticism; the other is what might be called, adopting an eighteenth-century term, the issue of aesthetic education. The former is the question of whether an ethical dimension can be essential to a work of art *qua* work of art, so that an ethical criticism of the work is also an aesthetic criticism of it, not an independent criticism. The second is the question of whether the experience of works of art and the cultivation of the skills and sensibilities necessary to the full and proper appreciation and enjoyment of (at least some kinds of) works of arts is advantageous for the development of moral sensitivity, judgment, or even commitment, thus whether aesthetic education makes a contribution to moral development. In the most general terms, the former question is thus whether the ethical makes a contribution to the aesthetic, and the latter is whether the aesthetic makes a contribution to the ethical. Both of these questions were extensively discussed in the eighteenth century, and both have figured in the recent discussion of the relation between aesthetics and morality as well.[3] But because of the focus of the present volume, my discussion in this paper will focus on the topic of ethical criticism rather than aesthetic education.

My second preliminary point is that although the idea of the disinterestedness of judgments of taste and therefore of a significant distinction between the aesthetic and the ethical was certainly one major development in eighteenth-century aesthetics, that century was a period of intense activity in aesthetics, with a wide array of theories on offer, and the line of thought that leads from Hutcheson to Kant – or more precisely, from Hutcheson to one element emphasized in Kant's initial analysis of pure judgments of taste in general, but hardly mentioned in his analysis of the creation and reception of works of fine art in particular, a distinction that will become important as I proceed – was hardly the only approach in eighteenth-century aesthetics or even the predominant one. On many eighteenth-century accounts of art and our experience of it, ethical criticism would have seemed even less problematic than I will argue it was for Kant and other theorists of disinterestedness. For many eighteenth-century theorists, art was defined as the communication of truths and emotions, and in particular morally significant truths and emotions, through media accessible to our senses and imaginations, and our enjoyment of art was essentially connected to our appreciation of both the form and the content of such communication. On theories such as this, there could be no question that ethical criticism is apposite to the criticism of art *qua* art.

2   The Sensible Representation of the Moral

I will briefly illustrate this kind of aesthetic theory, which if anything was the dominant kind of theory in the eighteenth century, before turning to the theories emphasizing disinterestedness, which have seemed to recent writers to create a problem about ethical criticism.

German aesthetics before Kant was dominated by Wolffians, including Alexander Gottlieb Baumgarten, Georg Friedrich Meier, Moses Mendelssohn, and Johann Georg Sulzer. Christian Wolff himself did not use the term "aesthetic" – that would be introduced by Baumgarten in 1735[4] – but ascribed the pleasure of what we would call aesthetic response to the sensible, or clear but indistinct, cognition of perfection; the aesthetic qualities of an object, conversely, would be its perfections insofar as they are suitable for sensible cognition and are so perceived. Thus, "Beauty consists in the perfection of a thing, insofar as it is suitable for producing pleasure in us" by means of the sensory cognition of that perfection.[5] Wolff defined perfection, very abstractly, as the harmony or concordance of the parts of an object with one another and with the aim of an object.[6] In the case of representational arts such as painting, the aim of the object is representation, and the perfection of representation is similarity,[7] but what is represented should also be a perfection, and moral perfections are certainly among the perfections that can be represented by such art. In this case, the moral significance of what is represented thus makes an essential contribution to the overall perfection of the object, and ethical criticism of the content of the work of art would be part of the criticism of it as a work of art. Baumgarten placed greater emphasis than Wolff on the perfection of the representation itself rather than of the represented content when he transformed Wolff's formula that beauty is the sensible

6 *Paul Guyer*

cognition of perfection into the definition of beauty as "the perfection of sensible cognition as such."[8] But Baumgarten's enumeration of the specific perfections of representational art include not only such formal features as "wealth," "truth," "clarity," and "liveliness" (*ubertas, veritas, claritas*, and *vita cognitionis*), but also "magnitude" (*magnitudo*), which is typically the *moral* magnitude of that which is represented. Baumgarten made it clear that art typically represents morally significant content in a number of passages in his classroom lectures on the *Aesthetica*. He said that "Everything that we are to think beautifully must be aesthetically great . . . For this it is requisite that the objects of thought be great, and then that the thoughts of the object be made equal or proportionate, and that finally both not be without important consequences, but must rather be fruitful and touching."[9] Even more explicitly, he said that "nothing can be beautiful that is not moral, because insofar as I would think beautifully I must think morally and virtuously."[10] Likewise, Baumgarten's disciple Meier said that "For a sensible representation to enjoy the greatest possible beauty," it must have formal merits such as "wealth," and thus for example "A beautiful cognition must represent a great variety in a single image," but it must also possess "The magnitude of cognition, the noble, the sublime, etc. For the sake of this beauty sensible cognition must not only represent great, suitable, important, noble objects, and so on, but must represent them in a way that is suitable and proportionate to their magnitude."[11] This makes it clear that both the moral quality of what is represented by a work of art and the way in which it is represented contribute to the beauty of the work, and thus that criticism of the moral content of a work is just as much a part of the criticism of it as a work of art as is criticism of the way in which the content is presented.

Moses Mendelssohn's aesthetics of "mixed emotions," developed in the later 1750s, thus at the same time as the work of Meier's just cited, remains within the same general framework. Mendelssohn recognized the possibility of beautiful representations of morally negative or disturbing content, because he held that the activity of representing is itself an "affirmative determination of the soul" and thus something we take pleasure in, so that while

> We cannot perceive a good action without approving it, without feeling inside a certain enjoyment of it, nor can we perceive an evil action without disapproving of the action itself and being disgusted by it[, y]et recognizing an evil action and disapproving it are affirmative features of the soul, expressions of the mental powers in knowing and desiring, and

elements of perfection which, in this connection, must be gratifying and enjoyable . . . [Thus,] considered as a representation, a picture within us that engages the soul's capacities of knowing and desiring, the representation of what is evil is itself an element of the soul's perfection and brings with it something quite pleasant that we by no means would prefer not to feel than to feel.[12]

Thus for Mendelssohn the fact that the content of art typically has moral significance does not mean that beautiful art can represent only what is morally good. But the moral status of the content interacts with the more formal merits of the artistic representation in forming our overall response, and certainly the moral demerits of the work can outweigh its other merits; thus moral assessment of the content of a work is certainly relevant to the assessment of its beauty or aesthetic merit as a whole.

Johann Georg Sulzer also recognized that art aims to produce pleasure both by setting our cognitive powers into activity through the formal features of its object and by arousing our deepest feelings. Thus he wrote that "the essence" of art "consists in the fact that it impresses the objects of our representation with sensible force, its end is the lively affection of our minds, and in its application it aims at the elevation of the spirit and the heart," and that "The fine arts also use their charms in order to draw our attention to the good and to affect us with love for it. Only through this application does it become important to the human race and deserve the attention of the wise and the support of regents."[13] Sulzer recognized that the arts could "affect us with love for" the good through their depiction of the ugly, including the morally ugly, as well as through their depiction of the good,[14] and thus like Mendelssohn he did not assume that morally valuable art can represent only what is morally valuable. But he firmly held that the vivification of our moral sentiments is a proper, indeed perhaps the central, aim of fine art as such, and thus that moral criticism of the effect of a work is a proper part of the criticism of it as a work of art.

These writers represented the mainstream of German aesthetics before Kant, and for all of them ethical criticism was clearly part of the criticism of art as such, not a separate and alternative form of criticism. None of them emphasized or even discussed the idea of the disinterestedness of judgments of taste. Kant would introduce that idea to German aesthetic discourse, having appropriated it from British aesthetics. Even so, we will see, he did not take the disinterestedness of aesthetic judgment to make ethical criticism entirely separate from the criticism of art as such. Before we turn to Kant and other theorists of disinterestedness, however, let us take a brief look at exemplary French and British writers for whom, like the Germans we have just considered, it was patent that the affection of our moral feelings was central to the aims of art and thus that ethical criticism was part and parcel of aesthetic judgment.

Among the major contributors to aesthetics in eighteenth-century France, Denis Diderot is an interesting case, because some of his theoretical writings espouse what could be the basis for a separation between ethical and aesthetical values in works of art that is, however, clearly belied by his own extensive critical practice. In his essay on beauty in the *Encyclopédie*, published in 1752, Diderot locates our sense of beauty in the contemplation of such formal properties as "order, relation, arrangement, symmetry, propriety, impropriety, etc.," and says that "I therefore term 'beautiful,' independently of my existence, everything that contains the power of awakening the notion of relation in my mind."[15] If "beauty" stands in for a general category of aesthetic qualities, this seems to limit such qualities to formal qualities of objects that are not obviously moral in nature. And if such relations as "propriety" and "impropriety" might seem to be moral in nature, thereby immediately subtending the ethical under the aesthetic category of beauty, Diderot seems explicitly to reject such a supposition by clearly separating a moral species of beauty from other, properly aesthetic, species of beauty. Thus he writes:

> Either we consider the relations apparent in men's actions, and we have *moral beauty*; or in works of literature, and we have *literary beauty*; or in musical compositions, and we have *musical beauty*; or in the works of nature; and we have *natural beauty*; or in the mechanical creations of man, and we have the *beauty of artifice*; or in the likenesses provided by works of art or of nature, and we have *imitative beauty*.[16]

This suggests that while there might be grounds for distinguishing among literary, musical, natural, artificial, and imitative beauty, they are all genuinely aesthetic sorts of beauty, while moral beauty is something else altogether. Further, Diderot seems to lend support to such a position when he illustrates his conception of "propriety" as a relation in a specific work of art, Pierre Corneille's play *Horace*. His argument is that our response to the beauty of a character's action or statement is not a direct response to his expression of a moral quality, but rather a response to the "propriety" or relation *between* the agent's moral character and his manner of expression. Thus, the beauty of propriety does not seem to be ethical, but rather aesthetic, and our pleasure in it seems to be independent of a purely moral judgment.

However, in his more mature critical practice, Diderot strongly suggests that it is an aim of art *qua* art to arouse our emotions by appealing to our moral sensibilities, and thus that it would be an entirely apposite criticism of a work of art as such that it in some way expressed a morally defective rather than appropriate moral attitude or quality: that would directly interfere with its goal as a work of art. Thus in an essay "On Dramatic Poetry" from 1758, he writes that

> The poet, the novelist, and the actor make their way into our hearts by indirect means. They touch our souls all the more strongly and the more surely because we are relaxed, because we offer ourselves to the blow. The sufferings with which they move me are imaginary, I agree, but they move me all the same. Every line rouses an impulse of concern in me for the misfortunes of virtue and moves me to expend my tears on them. What could be more pernicious than an art that instilled in me a feeling of complicity with an evil man? But, by the same token, what art could be more precious than the one that imperceptibly makes me feel concern for the fate of a good man, that draws me out of the quiet and comfortable situation I myself enjoy in order to accompany him . . . ?[17]

And in the "Notes on Painting" appended to his review of the Salon of 1765, he says that "One should inscribe over the door of one's studio: Here the unfortunate will find eyes that will weep for them. To make virtue attractive, vice odious, and ridicule effective: such is the project every upstanding man who takes up the pen, the brush, or the chisel should make his own."[18] Both of these statements suggest that the arousal of morally significant and appropriate emotions by the vivid and engaging depiction of characters is an essential aim of art, and thus that the criticism that a work of art "that instilled in me a feeling of complicity with an evil man" is "pernicious" is an entirely proper judgment of it *as a work of art*, not an independent judgment of the object under some non-aesthetic category. However Diderot's abstract definition of beauty should be understood, he seems far from seeing ethical criticism of art as alternative to aesthetic criticism of it.

Among writers on aesthetics in mid-eighteenth-century Britain, the most influential was no doubt Henry Home, Lord Kames, the Scottish lawyer who published *Essays on the Principles of Morality and Natural Religion* in 1751 and the *Elements of Criticism* in 1762, a book that remained continuously in print well into the nineteenth century and was quickly translated into other European languages. (I will return to the earlier British writers Shaftesbury and Hutcheson in Section 3 below.) The 1751 *Essays* contain an important criticism of Hutcheson's and Hume's attempt to found all of moral philosophy on our natural approbation of benevolence, among other riches, but its interest here is its initial chapter on "Our Attachment to Objects of Distress," Kames's contribution to the great eighteenth-century debate about the paradox of our pleasure in tragedy. Kames's argument here is based on the premise "that naturally we have a strong desire to be acquainted with the history of others. We judge of their actions, approve or disapprove, condemn or acquit; and in this the busy mind has a wonderful delight."[19] The pleasure that we take in judging of the actions and, as it turns out, the feelings of others, is central to our experience of art as well, because "whatever may be the physical cause, one thing is evident, that [the] aptitude of the mind of man to receive impressions from feigned as well as from real objects, contributes to the noblest purposes of life."[20] Thus, not only history but also novels and plays are "the most universal and favourite entertainments," because in them we "enter deep into the concerns" and "partake of [the] joys and distresses" of other human beings. In particular tragedy, a "feigned history," "imitation or representation of human characters and actions," "commonly makes a stronger impression than what is real; because, if it be a work of genius, incidents will be chosen to make the deepest impressions; and will be so conducted as to keep the mind in continual suspense and agitation, beyond what commonly happens in real life."[21] We enjoy this, according to Kames, because the experience of even painful events, whether real or feigned, as in art, is not itself necessarily painful:

> Thus the moral affections, even such of them as produce pain, are none of them attended with any degree of aversion . . . Sympathy in particular attaches us to an object in distress so powerfully as even to overbalance self-love, which would make us fly from it. Sympathy accordingly, though a painful passion, is attractive; and in affording relief, the gratification of the passion is not a little pleasant.[22]

Because of this fact, "tragedy is allowed to seize the mind with all the different charms which arise from the exercise of the social passions,"[23] and indeed the *point* of tragedy as a paradigmatic form of art is precisely to so "seize the mind." Anything about a tragedy that would stand in the way of our sympathetic response to its characters, including anything morally inappropriate in their depiction, would thus block the intended effect of the tragedy, as a work of art, and an ethical criticism of the characters and actions of the tragedy would thus be an aesthetic criticism of it.

Kames's theory of art in the *Elements of Criticism* is based on the premises that "A man while awake is conscious of a continued train of perceptions and ideas passing in his mind,"[24] that "we are framed by nature to relish order and connection" in such trains of perceptions and ideas,[25] and that "Every work of art that is conformable to the natural course of our ideas, is so far agreeable; and every work of art that reverses that course, is so far disagreeable."[26] Our pleasure in art is based in the way that our experience of it facilitates, or, as the earlier discussion of tragedy suggests, intensifies, this natural course of ideas and perceptions in the mind. This does not mean that works of art must necessarily represent or imitate the order of objects and events in nature, but that the flow of our ideas and perceptions in *response* to works of art must be natural in the appropriate sense. Kames then argues that central, if indeed not foremost, among the "ideas and perceptions" that are to be put into a natural flow by works of arts are our emotions and passions, and thus that it is central to the success of art that it arouse these responses and let or make them flow in a natural way. "Passions, as all the world knows, are moved by fiction as well as truth" even though man is a creature "so remarkably addicted to truth and reality."[27] Kames does not see a paradox here that needs to be resolved, but an empirically obvious fact about human nature. His theory is that verbal descriptions as well as pictorial representations can produce "ideal presence," or sensory imagery so rich and yet distinct "that I perceive the thing as a spectator; and as existing in my presence; which means not that I am really a spectator, but only that I conceive myself to be a spectator, and have a perception of the object similar to what a real spectator hath."[28] And since perceptions can lead directly to emotions and passions, that means that ideal presence can produce emotions and passions just as forceful as those created by the perception of real objects. Ideal presence, in turn, can be created by "speech, by writing, or by painting," because "A lively and accurate description of an important event, raises in me ideas no less distinct than if I had originally been an eye-witness; I am insensibly transformed into a spectator; and have an impression that every incident is passing in my presence." And "in idea we perceive persons acting and suffering, precisely as in an original survey: if our sympathy be engaged by the latter, it must also in some degree be engaged by the former, especially if the distinctness of ideal presence approach to that of real presence."[29] Whatever in a work of art would prevent the engagement of our emotions, then, would be a defect in it as a work of art. If moral defects in the characters depicted or in the expression of an author's attitude toward such characters would stand in the way of such engagement of our emotions, that would be an artistic failure in the work, something standing in the way of the work's achieving that which makes art valuable for us. An ethical criticism of a work of art is therefore a criticism of it as a work of art.

3   The Theory of Disinterestedness

For a large number of writers who are very much in the mainstream of eighteenth-century aesthetics, then, art aims to engage our emotions and passions, and anything that would stand in the way of that engagement would be an artistic failure. For such writers, ethical criticism, that is, criticism of the ethical attitudes depicted or expressed in a work, would not be independent of aesthetic criticism, because the flaws so criticized would prevent the work from having the effect that is central to its value as art. The mainstream of eighteenth-century aesthetics cannot be seen as anticipating the rigid separation between aesthetic and ethical domains on which the more recent assumption that there may be a problem about ethical criticism has been based. Let us now consider whether the theorists of disinterestedness who have been so central to recent conceptions of eighteenth-century aesthetics actually raise a problem about ethical criticism of the arts.

The identification of disinterestedness as a criterion of the aesthetic has been traced back to Anthony Ashley Cooper, third Earl of Shaftesbury.[30] In a famous passage in "The Moralists," first published in 1709 and then included in his *Characteristicks of Men, Manners, Opinions, Times* in 1711, Shaftesbury wrote that the idea that one should require "the *Property* or *Possession* of the Land" for "*Enjoyment* of the Prospect" of, for example, "this delicious *Vale* we see beneath us" is "absurd," that the idea that "the *Beauty* of . . . *Trees*" is connected to "some certain relish by which [their] *Acorns* or *Berrys* . . . become as palatable as the *Figs* or *Peaches* of the Garden" is "sordidly luxurious," and that the "set of eager *Desires, Wishes* and *Hopes*" that "certain powerful FORMS in *Human* Kind" draw after themselves are in "no-way sutable . . . to your rational and refin'd Contemplation of *Beauty*."[31] Shaftesbury did not actually apply the term "disinterested" to the "contemplation of beauty" that he distinguished in these ways from those pleasures that are dependent upon possession and use or consumption of their objects. He did, however, use the term "disinterestedness" in another of his writings, namely "Sensus communis: An Essay on the Freedom of Wit and Humor," also first published in 1709, in order to contrast a "mercenary" and self-regarding attitude in which moral rules are observed only for fear of punishment or hope of reward with a truly virtuous attitude in which virtue is perceived to be "a *good* and *right* Inclination" "of it-self," something with "Intrinsick Worth or Value." Being virtuous for the sake of an extrinsic reward is what would leave "no room" for "*Disinterestedness.*"[32] Insofar as Shaftesbury sought to characterize the contemplation of beauty as disinterested, what he meant was that our pleasure in it is independent of the fulfillment of hunger or sexual desire in the same way in which virtue is independent of the enjoyment of a reward or the avoidance of punishment. But that does not mean that beauty, in particular the beauty of art, has nothing to do with moral goodness. On the contrary, Shaftesbury's separation of the contemplation of beauty from the fulfillment of desire and of true virtue from mercenary and self-regarding interest was meant precisely to open the way for the recognition that at bottom beauty and moral goodness are closely connected, thus "That *Beauty* and *Good* are still the same."[33] And since the good is just what is harmonious, and harmony is the true nature of the universe, beauty, goodness, and truth are just different ways in which symmetry and order are presented. Thus, in arts like architecture, beauty not only can but must be connected to utility, and in imitative arts such as painting and literature beauty is inextricably connected to the truthful depiction of both the outward features and the inner characters of its subjects. So Shaftesbury wrote that "*Beauty* and *Truth* are plainly join'd with the Notion of *Utility* and *Convenience*, even in the Apprehension of every ingenious Artist, the *Architect*, the *Statuary*, or the *Painter*."[34]

> AND thus, after all, the most natural Beauty in the World is *Honesty*, and *Moral Truth*. For all *Beauty* is TRUTH. *True* Features make the Beauty of a Face; and true Proportions the Beauty of Architecture; as *true* Measures that of Harmony and Musick. In Poetry, which is all Fable, *Truth* still is the Perfection. And whoever is scholar enough to read the antient Philosopher, or his modern Copists, upon the nature of a Dramatick and Epick Poem, will easily understand this account of *Truth*.[35]

For Shaftesbury, the disinterestedness of the aesthetic did not separate it from the ethical, but connected it to the latter.

This philosophical position was reflected in Shaftesbury's critical writing. His most extended piece of criticism, "A Notion of the Historical Draught of Hercules" (1713), was not a direct criticism of an actual work of visual art, but rather based upon a literary description of the choice of Hercules by the sophist Prodicus, as recounted in Xenophon's *Socratic Memoribilia* (2.1.21), a description that gave rise to many subsequent paintings. In the chapter of this essay (to which he devoted much effort in the waning months of his life) that considers ornament, and in a passage that considers in particular the proper balance between non-human and human figures in an illustration that has a human situation like the choice of Hercules as its central subject, Shaftesbury wrote:

> But if . . . the human species be that which first presents itself in a picture; if it be the intelligent life, which is set to view; it is the other species, the other life, which must then surrender and become subservient. The merely natural must pay homage to the historical or moral. Every beauty, every grace must be sacrificed to the real beauty of this first and highest order. For nothing can be more deformed than a confusion of many beauties: and the confusion becomes inevitable, where the subjection is not complete.[36]

This passage argues specifically that in a painting or other work of art the depiction of that which does not have direct moral significance must be subordinated to the depiction of that which does. But more generally it implies that *every* beauty or grace in a work must be consonant with the conditions of moral beauty and grace. This does not mean, to be sure, that art must depict only that which is morally beautiful or graceful; after all, a depiction of the choice of Hercules will include a figure representing vice as well as one representing virtue, and makes its point only by depicting vice as well as virtue. But it does mean that in the judgment of a work of art that has a moral subject at all, the judgment of its moral content is as much of a judgment of it as a work of art as is the judgment of any more purely formal merits, and indeed that in the work itself and thus in a proper judgment of it the formal merits must be subordinated to its moral merits. In other words, a separation between ethical and aesthetic criticism was the furthest thing from the thought of the founder of the theory of aesthetic disinterestedness.

The first Treatise of Francis Hutcheson's *Inquiry into the Original of our Ideas of Beauty and Virtue* (1725), the inquiry *Concerning Beauty, Order, Harmony, Design*, defines the response to beauty as "a Sense, because of its Affinity to the other Senses in this, that the Pleasure does not arise from any Knowledge of Principles, Proportions, Causes, or of the Usefulness of the Object,"[37] and thus seems to separate aesthetic response from all consideration of utility and/or moral value. But the title page of the first edition of Hutcheson's work proudly stated that in it "The Principles of the late Earl of SHAFTESBURY are explain'd and defended, against the Author of the *Fable of the Bees*,"[38] and Hutcheson's characterization of aesthetic response as like a sense rather than an intellectual judgment was meant to prepare the way for his characterization of moral judgment too as a form of sense, not to separate the aesthetic and the moral. The paragraph immediately following Hutcheson's claim that aesthetic "Perception is justly called a Sense" makes it clear that, like Shaftesbury, he intended to argue only that aesthetic response and judgment should be independent of any mercenary considerations of *self*-interest, not independent of the moral in general:

> And further, the Ideas of Beauty and Harmony, like other sensible Ideas, are necessarily pleasant to us, as well as immediately so; neither can any Resolution of our own, nor any Prospect of Advantage or Disadvantage, vary the Beauty or Deformity of an Object: For as in the external Sensations, no View of Interest will make an Object grateful, nor View of Detriment, distinct from immediate Pain in the Perception, make it disagreeable to the Sense; so propose the whole World as a Reward, or threaten the greatest Evil, to make us approve a deform'd Object, or disapprove a beautiful one; Dissimulation may be procur'd by Rewards or Threatnings, or we may in external conduct abstain from any pursuit of the Beautiful, and pursue the Deform'd; but our Sentiments of the Forms, and our Perceptions, would continue inevitably the same.[39]

This distinction of our genuine response to beauty from any prospect of advantage or expectation of reward does not mean that a response to moral qualities is not part and parcel of our response to beauty. On the contrary, Hutcheson observes in his discussion of "Original or Absolute Beauty," that is, beauty in non-representational objects, typically objects of nature, that the "most powerful Beauty in Countenances, Airs, Gestures, Motion" of human beings "arises from some imagin'd Indication of morally good Dispositions of Mind,"[40] although, in light of the previous section, these must be dispositions to which we respond immediately, thus as if it were sensorily, rather than through any judgment of our own advantage or otherwise. And in the case of representational art, our response to what Hutcheson calls "Relative or Comparative Beauty" likewise involves an immediate response to moral qualities. Here Hutcheson argues that we take pleasure in an "exact Imitation" that is independent of the beauty of the content that the imitation represents, but also that "the Imitation of absolute Beauty may indeed in the whole make a more lovely piece."[41] He then argues explicitly that works of art need not depict only morally admirable characters or actions, but at the same time that in our response to a work of art our moral responses are inextricably intertwined with what might be thought to be our responses to its more purely formal features:

The same Observation holds true in the Descriptions of the Poets either of natural Objects or Persons; and this relative beauty is what they should principally endeavour to obtain, as the peculiar Beauty of their Works. By the *Moratae Fabulae*, or the ηθη of Aristotle, we are not to understand virtuous Manners in a moral Sense, but a just Representation of Manners and Characters as they are in Nature; and that the Actions and Sentiments be suited to the Characters of the Persons to whom they are ascrib'd in Epick and Dramatick Poetry. Perhaps very good Reasons may be suggested from the Nature of our Passions, to prove that a Poet should not draw his Characters perfectly Virtuous; these Characters indeed abstractly consider'd might give much more Pleasure, and have more Beauty than the imperfect ones which occur in Life with a mixture of Good and evil: But it may suffice at present to suggest against this Choice, that we have more lively Ideas of imperfect Men with all their Passions, than of morally perfect Heroes, such as never really occur to our Observation; and of which consequently we cannot judge exactly as to their Agreement with the Copy. And further, thro' Consciousness of our own State, we are more nearly touch'd and affected by the imperfect Characters; since in them we see represented, in the Persons of others, the Contrasts of Inclinations, and the Struggles between the Passions of Self-Love and those of Honour and Virtue, which we often feel in our own Breasts. This is the Perfection of Beauty for which Homer is justly admir'd, as well as for the Variety of his Characters.[42]

What is crucial about this passage is that it makes manifest Hutcheson's unquestioning assumption that the point of a work of art is to engage our passions of "Honour and Virtue," although to do this requires the depiction of morally imperfect as well as perfect characters, but in a proper light. On this assumption, the failure of a work of art to engage our moral sensibilities because of an imbalance between its morally less perfect and more perfect characters or for any other moral reason would be its failure *as a work of art*. Again, there is no suggestion in Hutcheson's account of the sense of beauty that ethical criticism is distinct from aesthetic criticism, or the criticism of a work of art as a work of art.

But in recent discussions the paradigm theorist of the disinterestedness and thus the autonomy of the aesthetic is always Kant, and my argument that the authors of the theory of disinterestedness did not intend to make a problem for the ethical criticism of art can only be made convincing by means of an analysis of Kant's theory of fine art. I say Kant's theory of *fine art* because the heart of my argument will be that Kant clearly intended to show that our experience and judgment of fine art are more complicated than the case of the pure judgment of beauty with which he begins the exposition of his theory of taste, and that it is the moral content of art that makes our experience and judgment of it complicated.

Kant is of course famous for two claims: the claim that "The satisfaction that determines the judgment of taste is without any interest"[43] in the existence of its object, the beautiful, unlike our pleasure in either the useful or the good; and the claim that the beautiful "pleases universally without a concept."[44] Both of these claims are to be explained by the theory that our pleasure in the beautiful arises from the "animation of [the] faculties [of] the imagination and the understanding to an activity that is indeterminate but yet, through the stimulus of the given representation, in unison, namely that which belongs to a cognition in general," and thus a "sensation whose universal communicability" can be "postulated by the judgment of taste." That is, our pleasure in a beautiful object is caused by a free yet harmonious play of the imagination that is not determined by any concept, and therefore not by any concept of the practical use or moral value of an object that could reflect or generate an interest in its existence, but which, precisely because it does involve cognitive faculties shared by all normal human beings, can be imputed to all as the response they too would have to the object, at least under optimal circumstances. These are the claims with which Kant opens the "Analytic of the Beautiful" of the "Critique of the Aesthetic Power of Judgment," which is in turn the first half of the *Critique of the Power of Judgment*. Or as Kant puts his position in the Introduction to the whole work, employing more of the technical terminology that he develops for his conjoined exposition of his aesthetics and his reconstruction of traditional teleology,[45]

If pleasure is connected with the mere apprehension of the form of an object of intuition without a relation to a concept for a determinate cognition, then the representation is thereby related not to the object, but solely to the subject, and the pleasure can express nothing but its suitability to the cognitive faculties that are in play in the reflecting power of judgment, insofar as they are in play, and thus merely a subjective formal purposiveness of the object. For that apprehension of forms in the imagination can never take place without the reflecting power of judgment, even if unintentionally, at least comparing them to its faculty for relating intuitions to concepts. Now if in this comparison the imagination (as the faculty of *a priori* intuitions) is unintentionally brought into accord with the understanding, as the faculty of concepts, through a given representation and a feeling of pleasure is thereby aroused, then the object must be regarded as purposive for the reflecting power of judgment. Such a judgment is an aesthetic judgment on the purposiveness of the object, which is not grounded on any available concept of the object and does not furnish one.[46]

Precisely because in aesthetic response so explained the power of judgment is "independent of concepts and sensations that are related to the determination of the faculty of desire and could thereby be immediately practical," Kant observes that the feeling of pleasure generated in this way possesses a kind of autonomy.[47] In this way Kant can reasonably be thought to have argued for the autonomy of the pleasure in the beautiful from all concepts, *a fortiori* from moral concepts, and thereby to have argued for the autonomy of the aesthetic vis-à-vis the ethical.[48]

But it would be a mistake to infer from this thus far reasonable conclusion that Kant has argued for the autonomy of *art* and the judgment of it from all ethical concerns and criticism. For what Kant has been analyzing in the theses thus far considered is the case of *pure* aesthetic response and judgment, which occur in response to objects of natural beauty like flowers, birds, or crustacea, works of decorative art such as wallpapers and borders, and what are, at least for Kant, marginal cases of fine art such as musical fantasias (without a theme)[49] – but not in response to what are for Kant paradigmatic cases of fine art, such as works of literature or representational painting. For Kant, our response to fine art *as such* is much more complicated than the simple case of pure aesthetic response and judgment with which he begins for expository purposes, and centrally involves a moral aspect. Kant does not develop a theory of criticism, but it is only natural to assume that since on his account a moral aspect is central to our experience of fine art, criticism of works of art on ethical grounds will not be extraneous to criticism of them as works of art but part and parcel of such criticism of them.

No doubt simplifying somewhat, we can think of Kant's analysis of our experience and judgment of fine art as being developed by the addition of four points to his initial analysis of "pure" aesthetic judgment. (Kant's account of our experience of the sublime also adds an ineliminable moral element to his picture of aesthetic experience, but since he thinks of the experience of the sublime as paradigmatically a response to nature rather than to art, and the recent debate about ethical criticism has clearly been a debate about the place of such criticism in the criticism of art only, I will not discuss Kant's account of the sublime here.)[50]

The concept of adherent beauty

The first step comes in Kant's addition of the concept of "adherent beauty" to his initial conception of "free beauty." Free beauty is beauty that "presupposes no concept of what the object ought to be," while adherent beauty "does presuppose such a concept and the perfection of the object in accordance with it." As examples of adherent beauty, Kant mentions "the beauty of a human being (and in this species that of a man, a woman, or a child), the beauty of a horse, of a building (such as a church, a palace, an arsenal, or a garden house)," and says that in cases of such objects the intended purpose of the object and the concept which reflects that purpose place certain constraints on the forms that we can find beautiful in those objects:

> One would be able to add much to a building that would be pleasing in the intuition of it if only it were not supposed to be a church; a figure could be beautified with all sorts of curlicues and light but regular tattooing, if only it were not a human being; and the latter could have much finer features and a more pleasing, softer outline to its facial structure if only it were not supposed to represent a man, or even a warrior.[51]

There are several points to be noted here. First, although Kant does say that strictly speaking in an object with adherent beauty "perfection does not gain by beauty, nor does beauty gain by perfection,"[52] thereby suggesting that the judgment of an object's perfection in light of some practical or moral concept and the judgment of its beauty are two separate judgments about a single object, as the modern theorist who would strictly distinguish ethical from aesthetic criticism of a work of art supposes, Kant belies this claim by his acceptance of adherent beauty as a species of beauty rather than simply a contrast to it. Although the response to and judgment of adherent beauty does involve a determinate concept of what the object is supposed to be, Kant does not deny that adherent beauty is a kind of beauty at all, only that it is not the *same* as free beauty. But if it is to be a kind of beauty at all, then we must suppose that our response to it does involve a free play of the imagination and understanding, not just a subsumption of the object under a determinate concept, although, as the last quotation suggests, that free play must take place *within* certain boundaries set by the concept associated with the intended purpose of the object. Thus, for example, while the concept of church – let's take the case of a cathedral church, with its requisite cruciform floor plan – does place certain constraints on what forms we can find beautiful in a church, it cannot by itself determine what form a beautiful church must have; the difference between a beautiful church and an indifferent one must consist in the fact that the former but not the latter stimulates a free play of imagination and understanding within the boundaries determined by the concept of a church.[53] Second, although Kant emphasizes cases in which the intended purpose of an object merely places a limit on what forms we could find beautiful in it, his own examples also suggest that there will be cases of adherent beauty in which we feel that there is a harmony *between* those aspects of the form of the object that are determined by its concept and those that are not – thus, an especially beautiful church will be one in which we have a sense of unusual harmony between the mandatory features of its floor plan and other, optional features of its design and decoration; a beautiful arsenal will be one which does not merely have strong walls and secure openings, but whose overall form somehow freely and harmoniously expresses the ideas of strength and security, and so on.[54] Finally, although Kant does not directly apply his conception of adherent beauty to the case of representational *fine* art – on standard eighteenth-century analyses, architecture, which involves considerations of utility but not representational content, is a *mixed* art[55] – Kant's analysis of fine art is clearly along similar lines to his analysis of adherent beauty: in fine art, the intended purpose of a work as well as its intended content clearly both constrain the form of the object but also enter into free play with the form and matter of the object, in such a way that ethical considerations do not remain external to the work's character as a work of art but become part and parcel of it. If that is so, then responses to the ethical content or significance of a work are not separable from the response to it as a work of art, and ethical criticism is thus part of aesthetic criticism, or the criticism of a work as a work of art, not independent from it.

Kant's theory of fine art

So let us now turn to the second step in what we can take to be Kant's argument for rather than against ethical criticism of art, namely his theory of fine art proper. We need not consider every step of Kant's exposition, but can focus on several main points. First, in his distinction of fine art from mere handicraft, Kant emphasizes that works of fine art must both follow certain rules of their medium or genre yet also leave room for the free play of our cognitive powers:

> It is not inadvisable to recall that in all liberal arts there is . . . required something compulsory, or, as it is called, a mechanism, without which the spirit, which must be free in the art and which alone animates the work, would have no body at all and would entirely evaporate (e.g., in the art of poetry, correctness and richness of diction as well as prosody and meter), since many modern teachers believe that they can best promote a liberal art if they remove all compulsion from it and transform it from labor into mere play.[56]

This already makes it clear that our response to and judgment of a work of art as such, like our response to and judgment of adherent beauty, will be mixed, not simple or pure, involving both the satisfaction of rules and the free play of imagination and understanding. Second, Kant tries to explain that beautiful or fine art has the somewhat paradoxical purpose of producing that free state of mind that is characterized precisely by not being (at least fully) determined by a concept: "Beautiful art . . . is a kind of representation that is purposive in itself and, though without an end, nevertheless promotes the cultivation of the mental powers for social communication," which means that the pleasure we take in fine art as such "must not be a pleasure of enjoyment from mere sensation, but one of reflection; and thus aesthetic art, as beautiful art, is one that has the reflecting power of judgment and not mere sensation as its standard."[57] This means that while fine art is produced both in accordance with certain determinate rules that flow from its medium and genre and in accordance with the aim of pleasing, it must find a way to stimulate the free play of imagination and understanding that is consistent with those constraints. Next, Kant emphasizes that paradigmatic works of artistic genius have content, indeed typically moral content, yet that such moral content does not merely set boundaries within which the work may stimulate the free play of our mental powers, but rather is part of what the mind plays with in responding to the work, or something that enters into harmony with the form and matter of the work. This is the gist of Kant's theory of "aesthetic ideas" as the source of the "spirit" that is essential to a work of genius. He defines an aesthetic idea as a "representation of the imagination that occasions much thinking though without it being possible for any determinate thought, i.e., concept, to be adequate to it, which, consequently, no language fully attains or can make intelligible." An aesthetic idea has intellectual and indeed typically moral content:

> One can call such representations of the imagination ideas: on the one hand because they at least strive toward something lying beyond the bounds of experience, and thus seek to approximate a presentation of concepts of reason (of intellectual ideas), which gives them the appearance of an objective reality

(but presents that content in a way that cannot be determinate and mechanical, but must be part of a free play of the imagination, understanding, and, now, reason);

> on the other hand, and indeed principally, because no concept can be fully adequate to them, as inner intuitions. The poet ventures to make sensible

rational ideas of invisible beings, the kingdom of the blessed, the kingdom of hell, eternity, creation, etc., as well as to make that of which there are examples in experience, e.g., death, envy, and all sorts of vices, as well as love, fame, etc., sensible beyond the limits of experience, with a completeness that goes beyond anything of which there is an example in nature, by means of an imagination that emulates the precedent of reason in attaining to a maximum.[58]

Kant then concludes that in a work of art, its content, again typically moral content, does not merely constrain the work, but is "enlarged" by the work:

Now if we add to a concept a representation of the imagination that belongs to its presentation, but which by itself stimulates so much thinking that it can never be grasped in a determinate concept, *hence which aesthetically enlarges the concept itself in an unbounded way*, then in this case the imagination is creative, and sets the faculty of intellectual ideas (reason) into motion, that is, at the instigation of a representation it gives more to think about than can be grasped and made distinct in it (although it does, to be sure, belong to the concept of the object).[59]

The free play of the imagination in response to a work of art is thus a free play *with* its content, which Kant assumes to be moral content, rather than a play *within* the bounds set by that concept. Kant also assumes the essentiality of content to the experience of art in his scheme for the division of the fine arts, which is based on "the analogy of art with the kind of expression that people use in speaking in order to communicate to each other." This analogy leads us to classify the arts as arts of either word, gesture, or tone ("articulation, gesticulation, and modulation"), and on this basis to divide the fine arts into "the arts of speech, pictorial art, and the art of the play of sensations."[60] This classification would make no sense if content were not part of what fine art plays with.

Since content thus enters into the free play of imagination, understanding, and reason stimulated by paradigmatic cases of artistic genius, and Kant takes it to be self-evident that such content will typically consist of moral ideas, our response to those ideas in that context must be part of our response to such works as works of art, and criticism of their moral content, at least insofar as that content does bear on the free play of our mental powers, will be part of the criticism of such works as works of art.

Constraints on beautiful representation of the ugly

Finally, let us consider two further points on Kant's view of the relation between the aesthetic and the ethical. First, in a section somewhat misleadingly entitled "On the relation of genius to taste," Kant takes a position in the eighteenth-century discussion of the possibility of beautiful artistic representations of ugly or tragic objects. Because "A beauty of nature is a beautiful thing" but "the beauty of art is a beautiful representation of a thing,"[61] he argues, it is quite possible for a beautiful work of art to represent something that is not itself beautiful. Indeed it may even be the case that "Beautiful art displays its excellence precisely by describing things that in nature would be ugly or displeasing," such as "The furies, diseases, devastations of war." Presumably this means that fine art can also provide beautiful depictions of that which is morally ugly, so the mere fact that a work of art represents something that would be liable to ethical criticism is not itself necessarily a ground for criticism of the work as a work of art. Kant limits the possibility for beautiful representation of the ugly, however, by stating that "one kind of ugliness cannot be represented in a way adequate to nature without destroying all aesthetic satisfaction, hence beauty in art, namely, that which arouses loathing" (*Ekel*).[62] He does not define what he means by "loathing" in this context; since this restriction on the scope of beautiful representation was in fact a commonplace,[63] perhaps he felt no need to do so. Kant uses the term several times in his handbook of anthropology, however. In one place he uses it to connote the feeling of nausea caused by something that powerfully offends the outer senses of taste or smell,[64] but in another place he uses it to connote the emotional character of our response to arrogant excess in luxury and debauchery.[65] In the latter case loathing is clearly a moral sentiment. On Kant's account, then, we would be incapable of responding to beauty in a work of art that represented something morally loathsome, and such a work could be criticized on that ground.

Moral content as a source of enduring and self-sustaining interest

A contemporary defender of "autonomism," that is, the view that ethical and aesthetic criticism are two separate forms of criticism even when they have the same object, could, however, argue that all that Kant has shown here is that an ethical defect in a work sufficient to arouse loathing could *prevent* any aesthetic response to it at all, but not that such an ethical defect is itself an aesthetic defect. However, a further observation that Kant makes could justify a claim that moral content is necessary for the enduring interest of a work of art, and thus that criticism of the ethical power of a work of art is criticism of its success as a work of art. In a subsequent section "On the combination of the beautiful arts in one and the same product," where Kant takes initial steps toward a conception of complex arts, such as opera, as *Gesamtkunstwerken*, he says that even though what is "essential" in all beautiful art "consists in the form, which is purposive for observation and judging," nevertheless the pleasure produced by such form "is at the same time culture and disposes the spirit to ideas, hence makes it receptive to several sorts of pleasure and entertainment." Truly successful art produces pleasure through more than the mere "matter of sensation (the charm or emotion), where it is aimed merely at enjoyment, which leaves behind it nothing in the idea, and makes the spirit dull, the object by and by loathsome (*anekelnd*), and the mind, because it is aware that its disposition is contrapurposive in the judgment of reason, dissatisfied with itself and moody." From this Kant concludes that "If the beautiful arts are not combined, whether closely or at a distance, with moral ideas, which alone carry with them a self-sufficient satisfaction, then the latter," that is, becoming loathsome and making reason dissatisfied with itself, "is their ultimate fate."[66] Even if Kant must allow that pure aesthetic judgment of the free beauty in the form of an object is an *autonomous* source of pleasure in it, independent of any practical or moral foundation, a pleasure that may first pique our interest in the object, he is not prepared to allow that our pleasure in a work of art can be *enduring* or *self-sustaining* unless that work has some moral content sufficient to sustain our satisfaction in it. But if it is part of the intention in producing or experiencing a work of art that it sustain our pleasure in it, then the criticism that it contains no ethical content sufficient to do so would be a criticism of its success *as a work of art*, and in this way ethical criticism would become part of aesthetic criticism.

It could well be argued that Kant has gone too far here. In his theory of fine art he has argued that a truly satisfying response to a work of art must ultimately be a free play involving not only imagination and understanding but also reason, the faculty of ideas. He could now be taken to have argued that reason must be engaged by a work in order for it to sustain our satisfaction with it and with ourself for being pleased by it. But for Kant himself reason can be theoretical as well as practical, so he ought to allow that a work might sustain our interest and satisfaction by adequately engaging either our theoretical or our practical reason in a free play with our imagination and understanding. And indeed it would seem plausible to suppose that some works of art, for example Bach's *Art of the Fugue*, do sustain our interest by engaging our theoretical rather than practical faculties. But widening Kant's point in this way would not undermine his assumption that many works of art do aim to sustain our interest by bringing moral ideas into play with their more purely formal features, and that criticism of a work of art that attempts to do this for failing to succeed in doing so, either because of the inadequacy or defect of its moral content or because of its failure to put that moral content into a pleasing play with its formal features, would be criticism of it for failing to achieve its goal as a work of art. Criticism of a work for failing to have moral content adequate to engage us or for having moral content that prevents us from being engaged by it would then be just as much of a criticism of it as a work of art as criticism of it for failing to present an engaging moral content in an engaging way.

For Kant, then, ethical criticism can certainly be part of the criticism of a work of art, or of aesthetic criticism as that concept is now understood. Failure to see this can only be due to failure to see that for Kant the response to and judgment of fine art is more complex than the pure aesthetic response to and judgment of a free beauty of nature. Thus, enlisting Kant in support of the contemporary position of autonomism would be anachronistic, even if it might be correct that *later interpretations* of Kant have led to this contemporary position.

4 Coda: The Beautiful as that which is Complete in itself

At this point, we have reached the conclusion that one broad stream in eighteenth-century aesthetics took it to be obvious from the outset that the aim of art is to move our moral sentiments through the vivid means of sensible representation, and that while the theory of disinterestedness that culminated in Kant may have begun with a conception of pure aesthetic judgment, separate from all moral considerations, the theory of *art* that this approach developed also concluded that art must always or at least often have engaging moral content if it is to generate an enduring and satisfying response. On either approach, ethical criticism cannot be separated from the criticism of the success of works of art as such; rather, the criticism of a work of art that it has content that leaves us ethically indifferent or repulsed would be criticism of its success *as art*. We could conclude our capsule history here. However, let us instead conclude with a quick look at another eighteenth-century aesthetician who in fact has a much better claim than Kant himself to be the author of the idea of "art for art's sake," and thus of the position of autonomism that has recently been supposed to raise a problem for the ethical criticism of art. This is Karl Philipp Moritz.

Moritz published a brief "Essay on the unification of all fine arts and sciences under the concept of that which is complete [or perfect, *Vollendeten*] in itself" in the *Berlinische Monatsschrift* in March 1785 (in the same issue as that in which Kant published his essay "On the Volcanoes on the Moon," so certainly Moritz's essay did not escape Kant's attention). In this essay, Moritz argued that a beautiful work of art "does not have its end outside of itself, and does not exist on account of the perfection of something else, but only on account of its internal perfection. One does not contemplate it in order to use it, rather one uses it only insofar as one can contemplate it."[67] He thus claimed that a beautiful work of art does not please because it satisfies any independent interest of its audience or its artist; rather it pleases us because its self-perfection or self-containment "draws our contemplation entirely to it, distracting us from ourself for a while, and causing us to lose ourself in the beautiful object; and just this loss, this forgetting of the self, is the highest degree of the pure and unselfish satisfaction which the beautiful affords us."[68] Here Moritz implies that our pleasure in the beauty of a work of art arises precisely from the fact that it does not engage any of our other interests, moral interests included, thereby producing a state of blissful detachment from our usual preoccupations. This passage, far more than anything in Kant's invocation of disinterestedness, anticipates Schopenhauer's conception of the blissful state of pure will-less, self-less knowing as the essence of the experience of beauty,[69] although in his published works Schopenhauer refers only to Moritz's autobiographical novel *Anton Reiser* in an essay "On the Different Periods of Life."[70] And through Schopenhauer, Moritz's view of the inner perfection of the beautiful rather than the conception of disinterestedness in Shaftesbury, Hutcheson, and Kant would have led to the late nineteenth-century conception of art for art's sake and the recent conception of autonomism.

But even for Moritz, this view of the inner perfection of beautiful art proved too simple, and in a more extended essay "On the pictorial [*bildende*] imitation of the beautiful" published in 1788, three years after the previous essay, he offered a further analysis of beauty that connects it more closely with moral qualities, thereby opening the way for the position that our response to the moral qualities suggested by a work are part of our response to it as a work of art, not independent of that response, in turn opening the way to a defense of ethical criticism. In this essay Moritz argues that the beautiful must be distinguished from the *useful*, but that in this regard it is like the *noble*, and indeed that it *is* the noble insofar as it "*strikes our senses* or can *be grasped by our imagination*."[71] Moritz does not reach this conclusion by simply forgetting or rejecting his earlier conception of beauty, but rather by conceiving of the noble as well as the beautiful as a form of internal, self-contained perfection that is contrasted to the merely useful: the concept of the noble is a "concept of the non-useful [*Unnützen*], insofar as it has no end, no aim outside of itself for why it exists," and thus "is connected most closely with the concept of the beautiful, insofar as that too *needs* no final end, no aim outside of itself for why it is, but rather has its entire value and the final end of its existence within itself."[72] Perhaps Moritz's conception of the noble was influenced by the conception of the good will as unmotivated by any desire for an object other than itself that Kant had promulgated in the *Groundwork for the Metaphysics of Morals*, which had appeared in 1785 a few months after Moritz's earlier essay; in any case, in the present essay he uses this conception of the noble to link the beautiful and the morally good more closely than Kant himself had ever done. Ultimately, he arrives at a neo-Shaftesburian (and thus neo-neo-Platonic) position that the beautiful and the good are virtually the same, the former just being the latter in a sensory guise. Thus he can conclude that "Every beautiful *action* must necessarily also be noble,"[73] and thus that every beautiful imitation must be an imitation of something noble. On this account, of course, a criticism of the moral quality represented or exemplified by a work of art will certainly be a criticism of its aesthetic quality.

My argument has been, then, that many eighteenth-century aestheticians assumed from the outset that at least one of the central functions of art is to make moral truths vivid to us and arouse our moral sentiments, and that they would have regarded anything in a work of art that would prevent that as a failure of it as a work of art, thus in our terms as a proper object of aesthetic criticism; that those theorists who emphasized the disinterestedness of aesthetic response meant only to emphasize that our pleasure in beauty is not mercenary and self-regarding, and that when they came to the case of art in particular they shared with their contemporaries the assumption that moral content is central to art, and thus that criticism of the moral content of a work or of its effect would be part of the criticism of it as a work of art; and that even the one eighteenth-century writer who did clearly anticipate the later idea of "art for art's sake" which is the source of the contemporary doubt about ethical criticism of the arts could not himself sustain such a conception, but instead associated beauty so closely with nobility that he too could not maintain a rigid separation between aesthetic and ethical criticism. I have no doubt that this overarching eighteenth-century assumption that for many works of art ethical criticism is a proper part of the criticism of works of art as such could be defended, even for much contemporary art, but I trust that I can leave that task to other contributors to this volume.

Notes

1   See for example Berys Gaut, "The Ethical Criticism of Art," in Jerrold Levinson, ed., *Aesthetics and Ethics: Essays at the Intersection* (Cambridge: Cambridge University Press, 1998), pp. 182–203, at pp. 182–3; Berys Gaut, "Art and Ethics," in Berys Gaut and Dominic McIver Lopes, eds., *The Routledge Companion to Aesthetics*, 2nd edn. (London: Routledge, 2005), pp. 431–43, at p. 432. Gaut has defended the position that ethical flaws are at least sometimes *pro tanto* aesthetic flaws; that is, aesthetic flaws but ones that may sometimes be outweighed by other aesthetic merits in a work. The position that ethical flaws are not intrinsically aesthetic flaws, dubbed "autonomism," has been defended by, among others, Daniel Jacobson, in e.g., "In Praise of Immoral Art," *Philosophical Topics* 25 (1997): 155–99.

2   Noël Carroll, "Art and Ethical Criticism: An Overview of Recent Directions of Research," *Ethics* 110 (January, 2000): 350–87, p. 350.

3   Of course I have borrowed the name "aesthetic education" from Friedrich Schiller's *Letters on the Aesthetic Education of Humankind* (1795), but Schiller's work was his distinctive contribution to a discussion that had been going on throughout the century, not the innovation of a new topic. In recent literature, the question of aesthetic education has been especially associated with Martha Nussbaum and Noël Carroll; see especially Carroll's essay "Art and the Moral Realm," in Peter Kivy, ed., *The Blackwell Guide to Aesthetics* (Malden, MA, and Oxford: Blackwell, 2004), pp. 126–51, where his discussion of "epistemic arguments" (pp. 129–40), which is the most extensive part of his discussion, actually concerns what we can learn from the experience of art that contributes to our moral education and development.

4   See Alexander Gottlieb Baumgarten, *Meditationes philosophicae de nonnullis ad poema pertinentibus*, §116; translated as *Reflections on Poetry* by Karl Aschenbrenner and William B. Holther (Berkeley and Los Angeles, CA: University of California Press, 1954), p. 78.

5   Christian Wolff, *Psychologia empirica*, new edn. (1738; reprint, Hildelsheim: Georg Olms, 1968), §404, p. 344.

6   For example, Christian Wolff, *Philosophia prima sive ontologia*, new edn. (1736; reprint, ed. Jean Ecole, Hildesheim: Georg Olms, 1962), §503, p. 390.

7   Christian Wolff, *Vernünfftige Gedancken von Gott, der Welt, und der Seele des Menschen* (German Metaphysics), new edn. (Halle: Renger, 1751), §404; cited from Christian Wolff, *Metafisica Tedesca*, ed. Raffaele Ciafardone (Milan: Bompiani, 2003), p. 344. This is a bilingual German-Italian edition.

8   Alexander Gottlieb Baumgarten, *Aesthetica*, §14; cited from Hans Rudolf Schweizer, *Ästhetik als Philosophie der sinnlichen Erkenntnis: Eine Interpretation der "Aesthetica" A. G. Baumgartens mit teilweiser Wiedergabe der lateinischen Textes und deutscher Übersetzung* (Basel: Schwabe, 1973), p. 115.

9   Cited from Bernhard Poppe, *Alexander Gottlieb Baumgarten: Seine Bedeutung und Stellung in der Leibniz-Wolffischen Philosophie und seine Beziehungen zu Kant: Nebst Veröffentlichung einer bisher unbekannten Handschrift der Ästhetik Baumgartens* (Borna-Leipzig: Robert Noske, 1907), §177, p. 154.

10   Baumgarten, cited from Poppe, *Alexander Gottlieb Baumgarten*, §182, p. 156.

11   Georg Friedrich Meier, *Betrachtungen über den ersten Grundsatz aller schönen Künste und Wissenschaften* (Considerations on the first principle of all fine arts and sciences) (Halle: Carl Hermann Hemmerde, 1757), §22; reprinted in Meier, *Frühe Schriften zur ästhetischen Erziehung der Deutschen*, ed. Hans-Joachim Kertscher and Günter Schenk (Halle: Hallescher Verlag, 1999), vol. 3, pp. 170–206, at pp. 192–3.

12   Moses Mendelssohn, *Rhapsody or Additions to the Letters on Sentiments*, from his *Philosophische Schriften*, part 2 (Berlin: Voss, 1761), translated in Mendelssohn, *Philosophical Writings*, ed. Daniel O. Dahlstrom (Cambridge: Cambridge University Press, 1997), pp. 131–68, at pp. 133–4.

13   Johann Georg Sulzer, "Künste; Schöne Künste," in his *Allgemeine Theorie der schönen Künste*, enlarged 2nd edn., ed. Friedrich von Blankenburg (Leipzig: Weidmann, 1792–4), vol. 3, pp. 72–95, at pp. 75–6.

14   See Sulzer, "Häßlich," in *Allgemeine Theorie*, vol. 2, pp. 457–9.

15   Denis Diderot, "On the Origin and Nature of the Beautiful," in *Diderot's Selected Writings*, ed. Lester G. Crocker, trans. Derek Coltman (New York: Macmillan, 1966), pp. 53–4.

16   Diderot, "On the Beautiful," p. 55.

17   Diderot, "On Dramatic Poetry," in *Diderot's Selected Writings*, p. 104.

18   Diderot, "Notes on Painting," in *Diderot's Selected Writings*, p. 225.

19   Henry Home, Lord Kames, *Essays on the Principles of Morality and Natural Religion*, ed. Mary Catherine Moran (Indianapolis, IN: Liberty Fund, 2005), p. 17.

20   Ibid., p. 18.

21   Ibid., p. 17.

22   Ibid., p. 20.

23   Ibid.

24   Henry Home, Lord Kames, *Elements of Criticism*, ed. Peter Jones, (Indianapolis, IN: Liberty Fund, 2005), vol. 1, p. 21.

25   Ibid., p. 26.

26   Ibid., p. 27.

27   Ibid., p. 66.

28   Ibid., p. 68.

29   Ibid., p. 69.

30   Most famously by Jerome Stolnitz, "On the Origins of 'Aesthetic Disinterest'," *Journal of Aesthetics and Art Criticism* 20 (1961): 131–43; and "On the Significance of Lord Shaftesbury in Modern Aesthetic Theory," *Philosophical Quarterly* 11 (1961): 97–113.

31   Anthony Ashley Cooper, third Earl of Shaftesbury, "The Moralists," in Anthony Ashley Cooper, *Characteristicks of Men, Manners, Opinions, Times*, ed. Philip Ayres (Oxford: Clarendon Press, 1999), vol. 2, pp. 102–3.

32   Shaftesbury, "Sensus communis," *Characteristicks*, vol. 1, pp. 55–6.

33   Shaftesbury, "The Moralists," *Characteristicks*, vol. 2, p. 112; see also vol. 2, p. 104.

34   Shaftesbury, "Miscellaneous Reflections," *Characteristicks*, vol. 2, p. 215.

35   Shaftesbury, "Sensus communis," *Characteristicks*, vol. 1, p. 77.

36   Anthony Ashley Cooper, third Earl of Shaftesbury, "A Notion of the Historical Draught or Tablature of the Judgment of Hercules," in Anthony Ashley Cooper, *Second Characters or the Language of Form*, ed. Benjamin Rand (1914; reprint, Bristol: Thoemmes Press, 1999), p. 53. Rand provides Xenophon's account of Prodicus's description of the choice of Hercules in a footnote at pp. 30–32.

37   Francis Hutcheson, *An Inquiry into the Original of our Ideas of Beauty and Virtue in Two Treatises*, ed. Wolfgang Leidhold (Indianapolis, IN: Liberty Fund, 2004), 1.1.13, p. 25.

38   See Francis Hutcheson, *An Inquiry concerning Beauty, Order, Harmony, Design*, ed. Peter Kivy (The Hague: Martinus Nijhoff, 1973), p. 3. The author of the *Fable of the Bees*, of course, was Bernard Mandeville, who argued that private vices can become public virtues, that is, that selfishness rather than virtuousness can be the source of a thriving economy and polity that is beneficial to all.

39   Hutcheson, *An Inquiry into the Original of our Ideas of Beauty and Virtue*, 1.1.14, p. 25.

40   Ibid., 1.2.9, p. 33.

41   Ibid., 1.4.1, p. 42.

42   Ibid., 1.4, p. 43.

43   Immanuel Kant, *Critique of the Power of Judgment*, ed. Paul Guyer, trans. Paul Guyer and Eric Matthews (Cambridge: Cambridge University Press, 2000), §2, 5:204.

44   Ibid., §9, 5:219.

45   For the latter, which I will not discuss here, see Paul Guyer, *Kant's System of Nature and Freedom: Selected Essays* (Oxford: Clarendon Press, 2005), chapters 11–13, pp. 277–372; and Paul Guyer, *Kant* (London and New York: Routledge, 2006), chapter 10, pp. 335–59.

46   Kant, *Critique of the Power of Judgment*, Introduction, §7, 5:189–90.

47   Ibid., §9, 5:196–7.

48　The passages cited in this paragraph should make it clear that Kant, like his predecessors Shaftesbury and Hutcheson, did not mean to make the disinterestedness of aesthetic response the *cause* of its pleasurableness, as is suggested by Gordon Graham in *Philosophy of the Arts: An Introduction to Aesthetics*, 2nd edn. (London and New York: Routledge, 2000), p. 169; disinterestedness is a property *of* aesthetic pleasure, which allows judgments about it to be universally valid.

49　Kant, *Critique of the Power of Judgment*, §16, 5:229.

50　I have discussed Kant's account of the sublime in *Kant and the Experience of Freedom* (Cambridge: Cambridge University Press, 1993), chapter 6, pp. 187–228, and *Values of Beauty: Historical Essays in Aesthetics* (Cambridge: Cambridge University Press, 2005), chapters 8–9, pp. 190–241.

51　Kant, *Critique of the Power of Judgment*, §16, 5:230.

52　Ibid., 5:231.

53　Gordon Graham defends such a view of the relation between function and beauty in architecture in *Philosophy of the Arts*, pp. 146–7.

54　For further analysis of the variety of kinds of adherent beauty that are possible, see my "Free and Adherent Beauty: A Modest Proposal," *British Journal of Aesthetics* 42 (2002): 357–66; reprinted in *Values of Beauty*, chapter 5, pp. 129–40.

55　See, for example, Charles Batteux, *Les Beaux-Arts réduit à un même principe*, ed, Jean-Remy Mantion (Paris: Aux Amateurs de Livres, 1989), p. 82, or, in the version Kant may have known, Charles Batteux, *Einschränkung der Schönen Künste auf einen einzigen Grundsatz, aus dem Französichen übersetzt, und mit verschiedenen eignen damit verwandten Abhandlungen begleitet von Johann Adolf Schlegel*, 3rd edn. (Leipzig: Weidmanns Erben und Reich, 1770), pp. 21–2.

56　Kant, *Critique of the Power of Judgment*, §43, 5:304.

57　Ibid., §44, 5:306.

58　Ibid., §49, 5:314.

59　Ibid., §49, 5:315; emphasis added.

60　Ibid., §51, 5:320–21.

61　Ibid., §48, 5:311.

62　Ibid., 5:312.

63　See Johann Adolf Schlegel's comment, in a footnote to his translation of Batteux, that "Only *loathing* (*der Ekel*) is excluded from those disagreeable sentiments the nature of which may be transformed by imitation. Here art would waste all its effort." In Batteux, *Einschränkung der schönen Künste*, p. 111n.

64　Kant, *Anthropologie in pragmatischer Hinsicht*, §21, 7:157.

65　Ibid., 7:249–50.

66　Kant, *Critique of the Power of Judgment*, §52, 5:326.

67　Karl Philipp Moritz, "Über den Begriff des in sich selbst Vollendeten," in Moritz, *Werke*, ed. Horts Günther, 2nd edn. (Frankfurt am Main: Insel Verlag, 1993), vol. 2, p. 544.

68   Ibid., p. 545.
69   See Arthur Schopenhauer, *The World as Will and Representation*, trans. E. F. J. Payne (Indian Hills, CO: The Falcon's Wing Press, 1958), book 3, §41; vol. 1, p. 209.
70   See Arthur Schopenhauer, *Parerga and Parlipomena*, trans. E. F. J. Payne (Oxford: Clarendon Press, 1974), vol. 1, p. 482.
71   Karl Philipp Moritz, "Über die bildende Nachahmung des Schönen," in Moritz, *Werke*, ed. Horts Günther, 2nd edn. (Frankfurt am Main: Insel Verlag, 1993), vol. 2, p. 558.
72   Ibid., p. 556.
73   Ibid., p. 554.

Part II
Conceptions of Ethical Content

2

NARRATIVE AND THE ETHICAL LIFE

Noël Carroll

In recent years, the conjunction of "narrative" and "ethics" has become increasingly frequent. There are even books with titles like *Narrative Ethics*.[1] In this article, I will not attempt anything as ambitious as the construction of a narrative ethics. Rather I will explore certain relations between these two practices, focusing especially on the ways in which various recurring structures of typical narratives can abet some of the purposes of our ethical lives.

For more than a decade, some philosophers, perhaps most notably Martha Nussbaum, have drawn a contrast between the quality of moral insight to be had from ethical theory (and the reasoning it enjoins) and that available from narrative. In this comparison, narrative is often said to win. Without flying to establish that one of these modes is superior, across the board, to the other, in this chapter, I will examine several of the kinds of contributions that (some) typical narratives – in virtue of specific structural features – can make to ethical understanding and deliberation.

I will begin by sketching the advantages certain typical narratives have over ethical theorizing when it comes to promoting clear and often convergent moral understanding; this advantage has to do primarily, I maintain, with the emotive resources at the disposal of typical narratives. Next I will investigate what it is structurally about some typical narratives that make them particularly suitable for educating readers, listeners, and viewers about virtue (and vice) – that is, for improving our understanding of the virtues (and the vices) and our ability to recognize them when we encounter them face to face. Lastly, I will consider how narrative plays a role in moral deliberation both at the local level of how to act and also in the more comprehensive sense of designing a meaningful life.

1   The Narrative Advantage

In *Tales of Good and Evil, Help and Harm,* Philip Hallie writes:

> General principles, like John Stuart Mill's greatest happiness (which makes
> an action good insofar as it tends to create more pleasure than pain) or
> Immanuel Kant's categorical imperative (which makes an action good if the
> idea behind it can be made into a universal Law without conflicting
> with itself), do not make the goodness in helping as clear to me as do the
> stories of The Good Samaritan or Father Damien. At their best Kant's and
> Mill's philosophies are ingenious generalizations about particular people
> and doing particular things. I can understand their principles only insofar
> as I can understand a story that embodies them. If there were no stories to
> illuminate their principles, I would not understand the principles at all. They
> would be words about words.[2]

In this quotation, Hallie is drawing a contrast between moral theories,
which he refers to in terms of general principles, and narratives; and he
is claiming that narratives have certain advantages that moral theories do
not. Specifically, they have a greater power to clarify moral issues than
do theories. In conversation, Hallie also often said to me that it was his
experience that when teaching ethics, he found that students were more
likely to converge in their moral judgments when exposed to a typical
narrative – a narrative composed of developed characters and particularized situations – than they would if left to negotiate an issue equipped
with moral theories and the deductive type of reasoning they recommend.[3]
In fact, disagreement, he claimed, was more likely to eventuate where only
the latter were deployed. Hallie's sentiments in this matter are not
uncommon. In this section, I would like to explore the question of whether
there is anything about typical narratives – about their structure – that
would lend credence to such a view.

Hallie himself suggested one reason why typical narratives might have
the power that he attributes to them. He writes: "It has been said that
God dwells in detail; be that as it may, it is plain that good and evil and
help and harm dwell in detail, or they dwell nowhere else."[4] Poetically
put, this observation suggests that what typical narratives possess and
general moral theories lack is detail, particularity, and concreteness.
Moreover, this is a frequently repeated conjecture. Whether fictional
(like *Great Expectations*) or non-fictional (like Plutarch's *Lives*), typical
narratives are more fleshed out than the steps in a deductive argument
that employs abstract moral principles (for example, citing general rules,
duties, and obligations) and thin descriptions of particular situations.

Among other things, the concreteness ascribed to typical narratives involves the fact that typical narratives are, comparatively speaking, richer in terms of their contextualization. We have a better idea of who the characters are (of their motivations, commitments, thoughts, reasons, desires, and feelings), of what (often moral) problems they confront, and of what options are practically available to them. We are problem-solving animals and, in this regard, typical narratives get our pragmatic juices flowing. Because typical narratives are concrete, they function to engage us in grappling with the situated problems they show forth in a way that enables us to find moral clarity. That is, the greater detail found in a typical narrative gives the mind more to work with and elicits greater understanding because it encourages a quotient of active problem solving on one's own part from the reader, viewer, or listener as she contemplates the predicaments of the agents in the story.

It seems reasonable to believe that this might be part of the story. It is certainly said often enough to count as a truism. But it cannot be the whole story for two reasons. First, ordinary experience is detailed, particular, and concrete, but no one would allege that it is a source of moral clarity. Indeed, quite the opposite seems to be the case. And second, there is nothing in the concreteness hypothesis that satisfactorily explains why at least many typical narratives are very frequently able to elicit convergent moral judgments for example, that Claggart, in Herman Melville's *Billy Budd*, is evil.

In order to deal with observations like these, it is necessary to supplement the concreteness hypothesis by noting that in addition to being concrete, typical narratives are also abstract. They are patently more abstract than ordinary events, since the detail they afford has always been selected from an indefinitely larger array of further potential details. Moreover, it is probable that whatever advantages typical narratives possess for enlisting roughly convergent responses is highly dependent on the principles of selectivity or abstraction (abstraction as extraction or distillation) that operate as a necessary condition of narrativity.[5]

So the advantage that typical narratives possess relative to general moral principles and to actual experience is that they are both complex *and* simplified, rich *and* compact, concrete *and* abstract. However, this sounds less like an explanation and more like an invitation to inconsistency. Perhaps it only appears to be an explanation because everything follows from a contradiction.

The philosopher of history Peter Munz thinks of narratives as concrete universals, echoing Hegel's characterization of artworks in general.[6] Maybe because the phrase "concrete universal" has a distinguished lineage and has been repeated sufficiently often, it strikes us as less offensive logically than alternatives like "concrete abstraction." But it is still paradoxical. Nevertheless, rather than discarding it peremptorily, I would like to probe the possibility that it can be interpreted, at least with respect to typical narratives, in a way that may elucidate what it is about such narratives that make them more useful for certain moral purposes than other modes of presentation.[7]

Both Munz and Hegel connect their concrete universals to purposes that they take to be connected to universal historical processes. The images and stories that concern them are parts of larger stories, ultimately of the story of History writ large. This is not a way that we can understand the phrase, however, both because we are skeptical of the notion that there is a story of History writ large and because it is improbable to suppose that every typical narrative can be nested neatly inside such an overarching tale anyway. And yet it does seem plausible to construe narratives as having a dimension of particularity or concreteness along with a dimension, if not of universality, then at least of generality. The real problem here is showing how these dimensions fit together in straightforward and non-paradoxical fashion, and then going on to show how this specific constellation of features has something to do with the power of typical narratives to clarify moral understanding and even to encourage converging moral judgments.

Undoubtedly, it is easiest to start with the particularity side of this relationship. Typical narratives – narratives with moderately worked-out characters, circumstances, problems, options, and so forth – are concrete insofar as they recount singular events by means of detailed descriptions and/or depictions. Whether alluding to fictional worlds or to the actual world, they are usually primarily concerned with individuals. This seems uncontroversial. But where does generality enter the picture?

At least one avenue – and one of especial interest to us – is the way in which those particular persons, places, things, states of affairs, actions, and events are framed emotively. The inhabitants of narratives are not only described and/or depicted in terms of their physical and psychological characteristics. Most frequently, particularly when we are speaking of the major players in our narratives, an emotional stance – whether explicitly or more often implicitly – toward the character is also part of the description. The stature, fortitude, and strength of the hero are not merely described; the hero is described admiringly in a manner that is intended to elicit admiration from us. Events and actions in narratives are also standardly described or depicted through an emotive perspective that the reader, listener, or viewer is invited to share; and even places and objects are frequently subjected to what we might call affective coloration. This is true of typical narratives, both fictions and non-fictions alike.

But what does this undeniable feature of affective coloration have to do with the generality component of typical narratives? Let us pause to recall the nature of what are called cognitive or garden-variety emotions, the sort of emotions most comprehensively pertinent to typical narratives, especially written ones.

Certain emotions – like pity, fear, anger, horror, admiration, awe, indignation, outrage, sorrow, joy, and so on – (emotions often at the very heart of typical narratives) have a cognitive component. This involves the subsumption, often automatic, of the particulars toward which the emotions in question are directed under the pertinent emotion-category in virtue of specific, necessary criteria of application. To be angry, for example, I must regard the object of my mental state to be someone or something that has wronged me or mine. To be angry, in other words, is to be in a cognitive state – to believe, or to construe, or to entertain a thought, or to somehow otherwise cognize the object of my anger under the category of perceived injury (or affront) either to myself or to some person, affiliation, cause, or even thing to which I am allied. Thus, the "universal" figures in an emotional state inasmuch as that state is governed by certain *necessary* criteria of application.

Emotions, that is, are comprised of, among other things, a generality component – garden-variety emotions or cognitive emotions involve concepts, concepts whose general criteria of application must be perceived or cognized to obtain with respect to the particular object of the emotion before the emotion, if we are not malfunctioning, can take off. Or, more simply, in order to be enraged at the particular pickpocket who filched my wallet, I must categorize his action under the concept of a wrongness done to me; if I conceptualized it as a favor, I would not be angry.

But what does this have to do with typical narratives? Typical narratives elicit or are intended to elicit emotional responses from audiences. This may be achieved by blatantly stating the intended emotional stance outright. But more often than not the relevant emotion is called forth or *proponed* by the way in which the persons, places, things, events, and actions are portrayed. Specifically: they are portrayed in such a way that certain features of the situation are foregrounded or made salient. The monster in the horror novel is arrestingly described in terms of those features that emphasize what is slimy and noxious about it, on the one hand, and what is life-threatening, on the other hand.

These descriptions may be routed through the mind of a character via what literary theorists call focalization.[8] Or these properties of the monster may be called to mind by an omniscient narrator. Either way, they focus attention on the monster in virtue of certain attributes rather than others. Which attributes? Those that satisfy the categories of the impure and the harmful, the disgusting and the fearsome. Why? Because those are the categories that are constitutive of horror, the emotional state the author hopes to engender in readers. By saliently describing the monster in light of those general properties that satisfy the criteria of the mental state of horror, the author disposes the reader to subsume, usually automatically, the particular monster in the text under the concept of the horrific and, thereby, the author hopes to jumpstart the appropriate response in the reader. And once in such a state, the reader will search out, albeit with the help of the author, further details in the descriptions and ongoing story that will reinforce the prevailing state of horror.

That is, once the emotional state is aloft, it will guide the subject cognitively, inclining her to track further details in the narrative that are relevant to the presiding emotional condition. The reader, with the author's assistance, will gestalt or configure the fictional state of affairs under the rubric of horror, or, less prosaically, will be horrified. This state, moreover, is not a punctal eruption. Once alerted by its outburst to the horrific variables in the description, the reader's horizons of expectation continue to be shaped by the forward-looking emotion, disposing her to attend to incoming variables that can be folded or incorporated into her emotive gestalt while overlooking others.

A similar account can be developed for visual narratives. In that case, the director will depict the array in such a fashion that details relevant to the intended emotion are selected for emphasis and given visual prominence in the scenography. Through images rather than words, ideally, the details criterially pertinent to horror will come to dominate what we see and fill our minds, triggering the subsumption of the spectacle under the desired categories, thereby engendering the anticipated emotional state which, in turn, once engaged, will continue to influence the audience's continued scansion and organization of her perceptual field.

I call this structural feature of typical narratives *criterial pre-focusing*:[9] the author or director describes or depicts narrative events in a way that is pre-filtered or emotively predigested in its details so as to promote and then sustain certain emotional responses rather than others. The way in which the relevant details are pre-filtered or pre-focused – that is, selected in the first instance and then made to stand out distinctively – is in accordance with the criteria that govern the activation of the desired emotional state. By addressing the affective system in this manner, ideally, the system is primed and then thrown into gear, inducing how the audience reacts initially and then how it follows, processes and configures subsequent descriptions and depictions.

The objects of the emotions described and depicted in detail in the typical narrative are concrete particulars, but the principles of selection and salience that preside over their representation by the text are generic or general, namely, they are the necessary conditions for the emotions in question which serve to criterially pre-focus the text. Thus, typical narratives are concrete universals in at least this sense: their emotional address involves a concrete individual as the particular object of the wonted state *and*, as well, the operation of universal or necessary conditions – what were once called the formal objects of the emotion – as those play a role in the way the narrative has been pre-focused criterially. The concrete components of the narrative are the particular objects it describes, depicts, and/or displays, while the general component enters in the manner in which the particular object is presented in consilience with the criteria essential to the pertinent emotional state. Or, in other words: the particular is what the typical narrative is about, but its emotive address requires a level of generality – criterial pre-focusing – which pre-focusing belongs to its mode of presentation of whatever it is about. This is one important sense in which a typical narrative possesses both concrete and general dimensions.

Whereas Aristotle drew the contrast between history, poetry, and philosophy in terms of distinctions between what is, what is probable, and what is necessary, I am proposing distinctions between what might be thought of as an unadorned chronicle of a series of events, a typical narrative, and moral theory: where moral theory is concerned with abstraction, unadorned chronicles are concerned with particulars, and typical narratives occupy a middle ground, concerned with abstract particularity or concrete universality – at least in terms of the emotive address characteristic of them due to their criterially pre-focused, particular details.

If we have made some sense of the notion that typical narratives can be called concrete universals, it still remains to be shown what relevance this putative finding might have for moral understanding. *Ex hypothesi*, this admixture of particularity and abstraction provides some advantages, at least for some purposes, for typical narratives vis-à-vis moral theory. But what is the nature of these advantages?

Concreteness and abstraction interact in the typical narrative at the level of emotive address.[10] The play between these factors puts the audience in an emotional state. But emotional states are not merely a matter of bodily feeling states. They are also mechanisms for judging situations and sizing them up, usually automatically. Emotions sift through stimuli, weigh or assign different strengths to pertinent variables, and organize said details quickly and clearly, blinkering some and highlighting others. Moreover, emotions not only structure incoming information, they assess it. Perhaps it might even be said they organize the relevant details by assessing them.

Emotions are fast mechanisms for evaluating things. The emotions are marvels of computing that single out, sort, and weigh a large number of variables in a manner that makes situations pellucid to us. Our emotions "look out" for our concerns and, thereby, embody our values. Emotions put us in touch with our values. They enable us to size up a situation in terms of value. By portraying a situation in terms of an emotive optic, then, an author or director can mobilize some of our most important automatic mechanisms for detecting value and then for comprehending the situations in question under its aegis.

Many of the values embodied in emotions are moral values. As noted already, wrongness is a criterion of anger. Engaging the emotions thus can be morally clarifying; an emotional response to a situation can draw our attention quickly and sharply to the pertinent moral variables involved, weighing them differentially and subtly, thereby enabling us to assess and to understand the situation rapidly and clearly. I suspect that this accounts for Hallie's belief that a typical narrative has the power to make him apprehend what "goodness in helping" is more effectively than moral principles.

The application through deliberation of moral principles to situations is often indeterminate. Judgment is needed to supplement the principles in question. Emotions are a tool for making judgments which do not require reflection on abstract principles, but which size up circumstances automatically. By employing abstraction and concreteness in the ways outlined above, the typical narrative can enlist the emotions in the service of ethical understanding, shaping the situation in a way that makes it morally intelligible, that shows us what is at stake, and how to evaluate it.

In their capacities to detect ethically relevant variables, to weigh them, and to illuminate moral situations, emotions are sensitive and effective mechanisms. How precisely they manage to do all this is, of course, in large part still mysterious. For all intents and purposes, emotions remain a black box. But their function as devices that, among other things, scope out moral situations and render them intelligible seems undeniable. Typical narratives, in virtue of criterial pre-focusing, are capable of clarifying situations and issues morally due to the ways in which they engage the emotive resources of readers, listeners, and viewers; audiences fill in the story with their own emotive responses as those are encouraged by the text. Once activated, our own moral-emotive powers bestow intelligibility on the narrative virtually automatically.

The operation of the emotions is itself clarificatory. It is the function of the emotions to clarify situations for us quickly and in a context-sensitive way where proliferating details might otherwise overwhelm, confuse, or distract. By employing criterial pre-focusing, narrators start the emotional ball moving and, as it gains momentum, our own emotions – our own devices for making sense of situations, especially morally charged ones – swing into action. Thus, by sparking the reader's, listener's, or viewer's natural powers of making sense, the narrator elicits moral understanding.

If typical narratives are concrete universals, then the emotions supply the middle term between the concrete and the abstract. The black box of the emotions sizes up and configures narrative situations with a clarity more legible and comprehensible for most than dispassionately contemplating whether the premises about complex particular situations correspond to abstract moral principles in a deductive argument. This is why, I submit, it is so frequently claimed that typical narratives afford a more dependable source of moral clarity than do moral principles. Moreover, insofar as members of a moral community are, by dint of both nature and nurture, apt to share emotive repertoires, such narratives have the power to provoke convergent moral assessments with regularity, though, of course, not with universality.

One response to the claim that typical narratives possess these advantages in virtue of their emotional address is that, if the preceding observations are the basis for the claim, then it is groundless. For the emotions themselves are suspect as sources of moral understanding. The clarity they may appear to engender is really an illusion. Furthermore, if that supposed clarity is a result of the textual structures I've limned, then so much the worse, since everyone knows that the emotions can be manipulated, and what has been called criterial pre-focusing is just the name of the rhetorical lever that does the manipulating. There is no genuine clarity to be had from typical narratives. At best their distortions are mistaken for clarity as the result of the emotional manipulation of readers, listeners, and viewers.

Two things, however, need to be said here. First, though typical narratives can distort and though the emotions can be manipulated, both can also be reliable. Some typical narratives can mislead, but others can illuminate. Likewise many emotional episodes *are* morally clarifying.

The simple fact that typical narratives avail themselves of an appeal to the emotions does not show that they are never or even only rarely truth-tracking. Furthermore, it should be added that moral theorizing and its application to particular cases can also be defective; there is casuistry (in the bad sense of the word). Neither a typical narrative with respect to moral issues nor a comparable moral argument is self-certifying. We need to evaluate both in terms of broader experience.

In virtue of their fusion of concreteness and abstraction *and* the way in which this involves the emotions, some typical narratives would appear to have differential advantages over moral theory for some purposes. They may be more effective instruments for instilling moral clarity and they may be more likely to promote convergent responses among members of the same moral community. This, of course, is not said in order to advocate the wholesale replacement of moral theory by narrative ethics; it is far more plausible to regard these endeavors as supplemental.

Moreover, the capacity of the relevant sorts of typical narratives to endow situations with moral clarity suggests that they have an important role in moral education – both in the inculcation of moral understanding and in its subsequent refinement and cultivation. Not only do such narratives induct us into a moral culture, awakening and calibrating inborn emotions and harnessing them to the pertinent considerations, but, as we continue to mature, stories are a continued source for exercising our emotions, for keeping them in tune, so to speak, and refining them by presenting us with varied situations in the way that a martial arts devotee practices parrying every sort of different imaginable thrust. That is, we cultivate our moral-emotional responses through exposure to typical narratives which keep us alive to far more diverse problems than most of us are likely to encounter in our routine lives. Furthermore, because the moral sensitivity developed in this manner engages the emotions, its lessons may go more deeply than those tutored simply in terms of moral principles, since experiences enlivened by emotional arousal are more memorable.[11]

2   Recognizing Virtue

Because typical narratives marshal the emotions in their presentations of particulars, it has been claimed that they can invest what they represent with enhanced moral clarity. Perhaps because this speculation is itself an attempt at moral theory, it remains a bit abstract. But maybe some of that abstractness can be relieved by reviewing in a bit more detail a species of moral data that is brought to particular clarity by the typical narratives. Virtue and vice are the data I have in mind. What I would like to explore now are the structural features of typical narratives that are especially advantageous for instructing the moral understanding about virtue and vice. This, of course, involves criterial pre-focusing in ways to be discussed. However, it also involves structural potentials of typical narratives that have so far gone unmentioned.[12]

Virtues and vices, of course, are traits, dispositions to act in certain ways in different situations. In this regard, they are temporally extended properties of persons. They have an outside – the bodily actions, behaviors, and speech acts that issue from them; and, as R. G. Collingwood would say, they have an inside – the thoughts, desires, emotions, attitudes, intentions, beliefs, and so on which give rise to further mental events, like plans and assessments, which issue in actions and behaviors.

Also, the behaviors that result from virtuous and vicious dispositions are not robotic. They can vary immensely from one occurrent episode to the next because the particular situations that summon them into action can diverge wildly. Consequently, in one set of circumstances generosity may require giving, while in another situation it may recommend that we refrain from intervening in any way whatsoever. Sometimes courage mandates speaking out; sometimes it advocates silence. Virtues (and vices) may manifest themselves differently because given the "inside" of the virtue (or vice) in question, the purposes that underwrite that virtue can only be secured by different means as dictated by the exigencies of novel concrete circumstances.

So virtues (and vices) have at least these three properties: they are (1) temporally extended qualities that (2) have insides as well as outsides, and that (3) manifest themselves differentially in different concrete situations. Undoubtedly, the property of differential manifestation is an aspect of the temporally extended dimension of virtue, since differential manifestations need time over which to occur, just as the notion of a disposition or a trait assumes temporal extension in order to accommodate the possibility of recurrence.

This, of course, is hardly a full account of virtue. Nevertheless, it is useful to remind ourselves of these three features of virtue, if we wish to understand why typical narratives are so effective at representing virtue. Obviously, typical narratives are temporal representations. They present sequences of states of affairs and events. Thus, they are perfectly suited

vehicles for displaying virtues (and vices); they can show traits manifesting themselves in successive circumstances and they can also show
those dispositions expressing themselves differentially as conditions vary.

Likewise, typical narratives possess conventions that allow us to enter
the minds of agents – whether fictional characters or real historical actors.
These conventions involve penetrating the minds of agents, quoting their
thoughts directly, or displaying their perceptions (point-of-view shots),
or telling us what they are thinking through what is called free indirect
discourse – that is, the omniscient narrator tells us what characters are
thinking, feeling, seeing, hearing, planning, intending, and so on. Thus,
narrative possesses the means to exhibit both the inside and the outside
of virtues and vices.

Furthermore, access to the inside of the character or historical agent
permits a narrator to connect the character's temporally extended overt
behavior – her repeated, though differential, manifestations of the trait
in question – by relating her actions to the underlying patterns of
thought, belief, feeling, intention, desire, etc. that give rise to it. That is,
the aforesaid features of the typical narrative provide a natural resource
for capturing and portraying virtues and vices as the coherent or connected manifestation or expression of underlying character traits or
dispositions over time.

I call this a natural resource, since the use of stories in this way appears
to be nearly universal; every culture I know of tells stories about exemplary figures as a way of articulating an understanding of the virtues it
holds dear. Christianity tutors believers in mercy by portraying repeated
episodes in which Jesus exhibits it. Moreover, this way of educating
people about applying concepts of virtue and vice appears superior to
handing them definitions of the traits in question. Definitions are too thin
to have traction when it comes to particular circumstances. "Showing" a
virtue by means of a narrative that displays its dynamics by charting the
interplay of the inside and the outside of the virtue over time gives most
a better sense of what the virtue is and a surer means for recognizing
it than "telling" them a definition. This, of course, has to do with
the ways in which the represented behavior in question is criterially pre-
focused in terms of positive or negative emotions. But it also has to do
with the potential of narratives to disclose the disposition over time from
both the inside and the outside and to underscore the connection
between them.

Narratives can provide exemplars of virtue and vice that assist in
recognizing the congruent traits in people we encounter in everyday
ethical life.[13] This is why we often use the names of fictional characters

and famous (and infamous) historical personages to tag our contemporaries. However, narratives are not only an aid to the recognition or perception of virtue (and vice). They also increase our understanding of these phenomena. And they are able to do so because of the way in which they unfold the coherence of the traits by connecting the inside and the outside over time. They reveal the virtues as dynamic and unified; they show how a series of disparate actions arise from a consistent set of purposes, thoughts, desires, emotions, values, and so forth. Through a narrative a virtue or a vice is articulated as an intelligible pattern of activities regulated purposively by governing habits of mind (and, in some cases, of body). Think, for instance, of Kierkegaard's portrait of Don Juan in *Either/Or*, where the moral condition of the character is discernible only in the larger narrative setting within which Don Juan's actions fall into a pattern.

Narratives, then, can improve our command of virtue concepts. Insofar as at least some concepts have theoretical or explanatory elements, narratives can illuminate virtue concepts by displaying the causal relations between the inside and the outside of the virtue as the overt behaviors that belong to the virtue are shown to permutate intelligibly in varying concrete situations. Narratives can illustrate the otherwise hidden connections that obtain between the inside of the virtue and its outward expression. In this way, narratives can alert us to variables we should be on the lookout for when we attribute virtues to people in our own experience.

Narratives can sharpen our capacities for detecting virtues and vices not only by providing exemplars to match with people we meet, but also by giving us an operational sense of how various virtues hang together. Narratives can provide the "sense" of the virtue and not only its "reference." Thus, tutored by informative narratives we can begin to scope out virtues and vices in cases that do not look patently like ones we have seen before. In this, narratives have an important advantage over summary definitions of virtue – such as "justice involves giving everyone her due" – which leave one stymied about how to apply such threadbare formulas to concrete cases.

Virtue and vice concepts have what Wittgensteinians call grammars ("*Essence* is expressed by grammar"[14] to quote the master). A grammar tells one what kind of thing something is; it gives us desiderata pertinent to the application of the concept. In order to employ our concepts successfully we rely on a more or less vague grasp of this grammar. Narratives have the capacity to bring our incipient intuitions about the grammar of virtue and vice concepts into greater articulateness by elucidating through exemplification the network of thoughts, feelings, actions, and their interplay that identify the virtues and vices in question. That is, narratives may function to mark the critical variables that govern the application of the concept. Moreover, again in concert with Wittgenstein, one way in which to mark these grammatical conditions of application is to show them in operation.[15] And this, of course is what narratives can do given the structural resources we have been discussing.

Sometimes we may gain a grasp of certain virtue and vice concepts along with a character in a fiction. We refine our concept of pride along with Darcy in Jane Austen's novel as he comes to see that accurate judgment untempered by humility is a form of arrogance; adjusting our interpretation of a character, like Darcy in relation to pride or Elizabeth Bennet in respect of prejudice, that is, can be a way of coming to grasp the grammar of the relevant concepts.[16] Of course, we need not conduct our grammatical investigations in parallel development with characters; they may exhibit the virtue or vice without evolving in their understanding of it – as does Achilles or Captain Jack Aubrey in *Master and Commander*. Nor need the emotional engagement with the characters, discussed in the previous section, be irrelevant to these grammatical explorations, since the emotions themselves can function as searchlights alerting us to and then leading our attention toward pertinent grammatical variables, especially the ones that are themselves value charged.

Narratives exercise our talents for detecting virtue and vice and applying the concepts thereof. In this, they sophisticate our operational skills in navigating our moral universe. But, in addition, the grammatical skills that narrative-marking augments can also be brought to reflective consciousness, and, indeed, certain narratives seem predicated on doing just this. That is, some narratives, like Yasmina Reza's play *Art*, appear self-consciously to invite and then to guide an examination of the virtue of friendship.[17] In this way, once again, one can think of narrative as a supplement to moral theory.

Robert C. Roberts has astutely observed that talk of narrative ethics has arisen alongside renewed interest in virtue ethics.[18] This is no accident, since, as we have suggested, narrative is an ideal medium for characterizing virtues and vices inasmuch as narrative possesses the structural wherewithal to exhibit perspicuously the structures of the virtues and vices. In this regard, narrative is an ally rather than the rival of a certain approach to moral theory, namely virtue ethics.

One objection to according narrative a place of honor in ethics, however, might be the allegation that the virtues displayed in narratives are too contrived, and, in the case of fictional narratives, they are invented; they do not correspond to reality, so they can be of little educative value. Of course, this generalization is too broad. As an initial response it needs to be pointed out that there is no reason to presume that all the virtues represented in typical narratives are contrived.

But, it must also be added that whether the represented virtues are contrived or invented is really of no moment, if what narrative offers is the opportunity to exercise the operational or practical skill of applying the virtue concepts. Flesh and blood cases are not requisite here; soldiers practice target-shooting by aiming at cut-outs of hostiles rather than real people, but their accuracy improves nonetheless.

Moreover, if the objection is that because real-life instances of virtue and vice are likely to diverge so far from the exemplars found in narratives that the latter are useless, then the argument appears to presuppose illicitly that the narrative exemplars are meant to function as rigid templates applied by rote to actual cases which, the critic adds, they will inevitably fail to fit. But this is not the way in which the narrative exhibition of virtue operates. Rather, by clarifying the grammar of the relevant concepts through practice, the narrative prepares or sensitizes readers, viewers, or listeners to discriminate novel expressions of virtue and vice. The narrative is not simply a mold into which actual cases must be slotted or forced. Narrative instead sharpens and refines our powers of observation and inference relative to discerning virtues and vices in their varied manifestations.

The divergence-from-reality objection would only seem to pertain were we thinking that the virtue shown forth by a narrative were something like an exact model of what we could expect to find in life outside of the story. But instead the skill to be derived from narratives is more a matter of cultivating finesse in being able to discern variations of virtue's manifestations due to our command of the grammar of the virtue in question.[19]

Likewise the objection that the virtues and vices exhibited in narratives are invented has no sting if it is intended to disqualify the use of these examples in reflection upon the concept of virtue, since there is no reason to imagine that such reflection or analysis (conceptual, grammatical, or philosophical) requires actual cases. In fact there is every indication that made-up examples are often more efficacious in the probing and elucidation of concepts than actual cases.[20]

Insofar as narratives are devices for representing changes in state over time – which devices have conventions for portraying the insides and the outsides of actions and the relations thereof – narratives are particularly well adapted to displaying virtues and vices clearly. Commerce with successful narratives of this sort exercises skills in detecting manifestations or expressions of virtue and vice, refines and sharpens sensitivity to often non-obvious variables, can enhance our understanding of virtue and vice by illustrating how the inside and outside of these phenomena hang together, and can even facilitate and guide the reflection upon or analysis of the grammar of the virtues and vices in question. If the definitions of moral theories are like engine diagrams that illustrate the parts of the virtues, then narratives are like motion pictures that show how those parts move and work together. *Pace* enthusiasts for narrative ethics, there is no reason to opt for one of these mediums of moral understanding over the other if we can have both.

3   Deliberating Actions, Constructing Lives

So far we have been concentrating our attention narrowly on the ways in which narrative may provide a service to ethical life in terms of exercising and refining our powers of evaluating situations morally and judging instances of virtue and vice, rather than considering its relation to the deliberation of action, though, perhaps needless to say, the kinds of narratives of virtue, especially of exemplars, discussed in the previous section can provide one with clues, in the form of scenarios, to contemplate how to go about acting in such a way as to cultivate the virtue in question. Nevertheless, in this section, I intend to explore more explicitly some of the ways in which narrative, because of its structures, can contribute to moral deliberation, both at the level of local decisions about how to act and at the more comprehensive level of how to construct a meaningful life.

Narrative, of course, is not only integral to moral deliberation. It is central to deliberation of all sorts. Consequently, before zeroing in on its frequent contribution to moral deliberation, something needs to be said about its role in deliberation *tout court*.

Narrative is a cognitive instrument. It is probably the most pervasive tool that humans have for relating the past to the present and to the future. And it is because narrative functions to relate the past and the present, on the one hand, to the future, on the other hand, that it comes to play a role in deliberating about what we will do and in planning for what is ahead.

Narrative is an awesomely adaptive asset from an evolutionary perspective. It enables humans to think about and communicate information about absent situations. One can imagine – by telling oneself a story – what would happen if one stumbled into the lair of a predator, and then proceed to adjust one's behavior accordingly. Or you might tell a story to the tribe about the land of milk and honey on the other side of the hill as a way of preparing them for the journey. That is, narratives can be informative about situations not being experienced in the here and now and, thus, narratives are expeditious ways of envisioning how things might be counterfactually. The elders can warn children about what might befall them in the swamp by recounting either past disasters or imagined ones. In effect, narratives are a means for running cost-free trial runs in thought of possible courses of action. The trial runs are cost free, since no real alligators pose a clear and present danger to the children. The elders are able to influence the children's thinking about where they will play by telling them stories about where dangers lurk.

Narratives not only connect the past, present, and future; they connect them by showing how the future emerges from the past and the present as a realization of a possibility that belongs to a range of alternative possibilities opened up by earlier events and states of affairs in the narrative. If the narrative concerns a battle, the earlier stages of the story call forth a certain package of possibilities: that one side will win and the other lose, or each side will annihilate the other, or both sides will throw in the towel. As the narrative unfolds, ideally, one of these alternatives will be realized and our expectations of this structure the way that we track the narrative.

Following a narrative with understanding involves being able to assimilate the incoming information from the story in terms of the range of possibilities that preceding portions of the narrative make available. That is, following a narrative with understanding hinges upon mobilizing a horizon of expectations in the audience member who then renders subsequent events in the story intelligible to herself, given her sense of what is possible on the basis of the antecedent narrative. When the story eventuates in one of those possibilities it is assimilated intelligibly, due to the audience's antecedent horizon of expectations. Where the putative story fails to realize any instance of the range of possibilities it propones or where the details in the story are so amorphous that they leave the audience floundering with no horizon of expectations, the example at issue defies being followed and is unintelligible. The successful story, in other words, must structurally engage the audience's capacities to project future possibilities as a condition for finding a story navigable and intelligible. Thus, functioning narratives by dint of their structure of address exercise and sharpen the talent for projecting future possibilities and this, of course, is a *sine qua non* of deliberation in general. Thus it comes as no surprise that traffic with narratives may have consequences for deliberation.

Narratives often structure the audience's horizon of expectations because the events they recount raise inevitable questions in the audience's mind. If we are introduced to two attractive young people, we wonder whether or not they will become lovers, and, if they become lovers, will they be married, and, if parted, will they get back together, and so on. So many of the situations in narratives call forth a matrix of future possibilities that we use to organize the incoming story stream. As well, the essential link between incidents in stories, *the narrative connection*, is causation – whether the earlier events in a story fully determine subsequent events as sufficient conditions or whether they are only, as is more frequently the case, causally necessary conditions (in the sense of J. L. Mackies's INUS conditions) for subsequent events, a degree of causation is necessary before something will count as a narrative.[21] But, of course, providing readers, listeners, and viewers with causes unavoidably invites them to ponder possible effects, just as questions point the mind in the direction of possible answers. Thus, once again we see that narratives, due to their structure, enlist audiences into thinking about future possibilities. And in this light, it seems fair to propose that exposure to narratives hones a talent necessary for practical deliberation of any sort.

Steven Pinker regards exposure to narratives, especially fictions, as a form of training whereby we familiarize ourselves about what to do and what not to do in a variety of situations that we have not yet encountered. Like the chess player who pores over the scenarios of a great many games in order to amass knowledge about what works and doesn't work in a wealth of situations that have not confronted her in her own experience, so we consume narratives, fictional and otherwise, in order to store up a repertoire of possible moves and countermoves in the game of life.[22] Moreover, many psychologists argue that we negotiate much of everyday life by means of mental representations called scripts – essentially narrative flowcharts of how to do things like getting a meal in a restaurant.[23] In both these ways, narrative plays an important role in deciding how to act. But, in addition, there is an even deeper way in which narrative contributes to decision-making, since exposure to narration is a primary site for training people to think about future possibilities, facilitating this skill by putting it to work in the process of following stories.[24]

Of course, we are not merely audiences to the narratives of others. We also construct narratives, both for ourselves and others. The transit from being told narratives to telling them appears to arrive with the maturation of linguistic mastery. To become sensitive storytellers we have to become facile at connecting the past and present elements in the story with the possibilities that lie in the future of the earlier segments. Narrative competence requires that we neither forget to actualize at least one of the possibilities convoked by earlier developments, lest we leave our audience bewildered by what is effectively a narrative *non sequitur*, nor allow the story to wander to the point that the reader, with no notion of where it could be possibly headed, finds it unintelligible. Narrative competence, in other words, requires that we evolve the knack for projecting future possibilities – for tying them to the past and for keeping track of them; and, in fact, producing narratives ourselves, rather than merely consuming the narratives of others, is for most people the primary way of developing that knack.[25]

This latter point is important to underline, moreover, for once we note the intimate relation of narrative competence to projecting future possibilities, it becomes evident that narratives are not only a means for strengthening that ability, they are also a means of expressing it. That is, narration – whether to ourselves or others – is itself a way of projecting future possibilities. Thus, narrative does not merely exercise capacities essential to deliberating about future action. It is itself a way of carrying that deliberation forward.

In part, one frequently deliberates about how to act by telling oneself a story. I think about moving from one city to another by thinking about what possibilities the move will open up for me versus those it will close down; I may imagine two scenarios and then compare them. Or my friends may tell me alternative scenarios, perhaps in the hope of persuading me one way or another, or maybe only in order to help me clarify my decision.

This should not appear as an unfamiliar picture of deliberation. Often we are asked to deliberate politically by being offered different scenarios by opposing factions about what will happen consequent to the adoption of the policies of their side and of the other side. But what happens in political deliberation is merely an echo of deliberation in general which comprises, to a large degree, projecting future possibilities narratively and then thinking about which story, if any, suits one.

If narrative can play a role in all kinds of deliberation, it obviously has a role to play in moral deliberation. But can anything more be said about the role of narrative in moral deliberation? The kinds of narratives that we tell ourselves in the process of moral deliberation are not merely exercises in projecting future possibilities; they belong to a subclass of narratives that we might call *orientational*. That is, they are undertaken in order to find our bearings in relation to future possibilities, where finding our bearings is a matter of determining which future possibilities cohere best with whom one already is.

Narratives connect past events to future outcomes. The earlier parts of the narrative constrain the pertinent future possibilities available to the storyteller. Moral deliberation involves asking whether some action is a future possibility for me. In order to do that, I need to construct a narrative of who I am relevant to the decision at hand in order to assess whether some contemplated action is a genuine possibility. An orientational narrative involves a retrospective moment in which I examine my commitments as they emerge from the narrative pattern or patterns in my life thus far. This then creates a *backstory* which, in addition to the particulars of the present situation generates a forward-looking field of possible actions and responses that I might take in the situation at hand. The question before me then is whether I can prospectively construct a *continuing story* on the basis of the contemplated action that coheres with the retrospective story that I believe best captures who I am. My retrospective story orients my choice of behavior in the present by testing possible actions in terms of whether or not they can be incorporated in a continuation of the story that, so to speak, I've already begun or in which I find myself *in medias res*.

Suppose I know an obscure language that no one else in my field knows and I read an article in that language in a defunct, small-circulation journal by an author who is dead; suppose as well that due to a series of bloody purges there are no scholars left in that far off country – no one who was familiar with the original article is alive; so if I were to plagiarize that article, the likelihood of my being unmasked is infinitesimal. Now, since the idea has crossed my mind, the moral issue is whether or not I should plagiarize the article. I can easily deduce that it is wrong; it would not be a moral question for me if I couldn't. In order to answer this question, I think one of the most natural ways to proceed is to ask whether plagiarizing this article is a continuation of the story I want to tell about myself as a forthright and productive scholar. Does this way of carrying my story forward realize the possibilities the rest of my story indicates to me I value? Or is the ensuing story one of which I say "It's not me; that is not my story, or, at least, the story that I want"? My deliberation over whether or not to plagiarize can be readily staged through the question of how I wish to continue my story or of which continuing story I am willing to endorse, given my own retrospective story. Clearly if the story I want to tell is one in which I am an honest, creative, and resourceful researcher, I would choke on the story where the plagiarism is an episode. The narrative in which the plagiarism plays a role, perhaps because it addresses me emotionally, makes a dramatic contribution to the deliberative process. Nor do I think this example is exceptional. Most cases where we are really pressed to deliberate morally – as opposed to the many moral actions, like not running over pedestrians with our car, that we perform automatically – will elicit orientational narration from us or from our moral advisers. That is, we will use our pre-existing backstories to probe which possible courses of action are most suited to telling the next episode of the story we wish to continue.[26]

In the co-ordination of our retrospective story with future possibilities, a premium is typically placed on conserving as much of the past and the values it evinces as possible, but in telling the backstory sometimes the agent may find contradictions (in the Marxist sense) in it that suggests the need to opt for future possibilities that jettison problematic parts of the retrospective story for a better continuing story. One searches for the best continuing story. Usually this will be the story that coheres best with our retrospective story; where the retrospective story is one we find satisfying, the tendency will be to consider the possibilities that maximize the commitments of the retrospective story as the way of moving the story forward. Since the retrospective story will reflect our moral commitments, if we are moral and take that to be part of who we are, continuing the story by opting for an immoral possibility, like plagiarism, will strike us as cognitively and emotively incoherent and will turn our deliberations against it. At the same time, it may happen that in constructing my backstory I find disturbing anomalies in it which lead me to elect a possibility that cancels offending parts of the retrospective story and uses the remaining fragments to start a new story. Undoubtedly, the latter course is less frequent, but not so rare that we could argue that in deliberating by trying to tell our story coherently, we always only favor stories that conserve most fully the bulk of the story we have already told.

Orientational narratives serve the purposes of deliberation by reflecting upon the past as a way of continuing the story into the future. They answer the question "What is to be done?" They orient us to that question by telling us a retrospective story, which tells us where we are, as a way of helping us to decide where to go next. These narratives may be called into play not only when what to do next is a question of which action is next, but also when we ask what project is next. The college graduate is not just deliberating about whether to mail the application off to law school. She is deliberating about her next project. Often when one makes such decisions, one attempts to maximize the coherence between one's story so far and the next chapter. Perhaps our college student has a talent and a relish for argumentation and that inclines her toward starting a career in law. Law to her feels like a good way of continuing the story coherently.

However, it may also be the case that when one takes the measure of one's past projects, one discovers that they have been pursued as far as possible and that it is time to look for a new beginning. Thus, an aging athlete tells the story of his days of glory and, realizing that that story is ending, becomes convinced that he needs to search for a new story. Should he put his well-earned reputation, his backstory, in the service of a company that advertises alcoholic beverages in a way that is seductive to minors by becoming its spokesperson? Is that how he wants the narrative to continue? In this way, narrative reflection is not only useful for moral deliberation; it is a natural and effective way of conducting it.

The gauge, so to speak, of the stories told to oneself for the purposes of deliberation come in different scales. As we have seen, they can be told in relation to actions or to projects. But they can also take as their unit of interrogation an entire life. In this way narrative can contribute to the question that most interested ancient ethicists, namely what makes a life worthy or excellent or good, or, as the question is often posed today, what makes a life meaningful?[27]

Though the question of the meaning of life is often neglected in contemporary moral theory, it is traditionally an ethical question of the highest order and one that almost inevitably perplexes every thoughtful person. But it is also fraught with at least two daunting challenges. Though the question seems unavoidable, there is the problem of whether it makes sense: are lives, in contrast to linguistic utterances, the sorts of things that can have meaning? And even if they can, how is one to go about organizing the messy, transitory details of a life in a way that would render them cognitively accessible – that is, legible enough for scrutiny? Narrative, I contend, answers both of these questions.[28]

Though linguistic utterances are paradigmatic examples of what has meaning, narratives also can be said to be meaningful or not. A meaningful narrative, as we have seen, is one in which later stages in the story are intelligible as realizations of possibilities called forth by earlier stages. In a perfectly ordinary sense of the phrase, a meaningful story is a story that can be followed – a story that is not so cluttered that it is impossible to determine what possibilities are at stake and that does not end without realizing some of the possibilities that it has put in motion. Whether the narrative of a life is meaningful depends on whether it can be followed intelligibly.

In order to be in a position to tell whether a life is worthwhile, first we need to be in a position to produce a meaningful narrative of that life. Have the questions posed by that life narrative been answered? Have the possibilities (or, at least, some of them) that were opened been realized? Is the story coherent in its continuation of its past into its future, and, if not, were there good reasons for changing the story? Does the story make sense? Presuming that the life narrative is an honest one, if it makes sense, then it indicates that the life in question has a degree of unity – as much unity as can be captured by a sincere and intelligible life narrative. Thus, the narrative, if meaningful and sincere, gives us a holistic, though selective, configuration that is open to scrutiny. That configuration, in turn, is something that can be evaluated in terms of whether or not it is worthwhile – in terms of whether the possibilities elected, given where one finds oneself, as Heidegger says, "thrown into the world," were worthy ones pursued well and whether those possibilities figure in a coherent evolution of past concerns and actions into the projects and activities of the later stages of life.

The notion of a meaningful life, then, is parasitic on the notion of a meaningful narrative, a narrative that coherently connects past segments of the story to their future as projected possibilities realized. This is not to say that lives are stories, but that the ability to produce a meaningful narrative is a test for the coherence of a life. Moreover, structurally speaking, narratives, as we noted earlier, are necessarily selective. A life narrative is one that is told retrospectively, using later stages of a life story to focus narrowly on the earlier events and recurring themes that have brought the agent to the relevant juncture in her life. By retelling one's life in this way, one begins to organize it, filtering out a mass of ephemeral details and hierarchically ordering those that remain. In this way, narratives prepare the apparently inchoate confusion of a life for close examination and then evaluation.

Once one has configured one's life narratively into a manageable unity, one is in a position to ask whether the story told represents something worthwhile. In this way, narrative is probably the only tool at the disposal of most for organizing the data pertinent to assaying whether a life as a whole is worthwhile.[29] Of course, finding that a life can be configured as a meaningful narrative does not entail that it is a worthwhile life; coherence is not enough. Whoever is telling the story, whether the agent herself or some outside party, must also weigh the worthiness of the coherent themes isolated by and exhibited in the life narrative. However, constructing that coherence, finding that life story, is a necessary condition for this next stage of deliberation.

And, of course, one reflective test that the agent of the life story has at her disposal to estimate the worthiness it implies is whether or not it is a story that she finds satisfying to tell and then to tell again. Perhaps, that is what Nietzsche had in mind with his notion of the Eternal Return.

Life stories are indispensable to deciding about the worthiness of one's life when one is entering the home stretch. But they also have a purpose to serve at earlier stages. One can construct retrospective life stories long before the end is in view as an orientational narrative designed to plot where one has been in order to find a way forward.[30] A life story assembled before most of one's life is over can function as an opportunity to locate the best possibilities to pursue in the near and/or distant future and as an instrument to reflect on what sorts of activities and commitments need to be either abandoned or emphasized for the story to continue in accordance with one's deepest themes. And life stories may also serve deliberation as thought experiments about how one might change one's life by imagining setting off on a different branch of possibilities other than those one has been pursuing thus far. Imagining alternative life stories, in short, is also a means of conducting in the mind what John Stuart Mill called life experiments. The narrative of such an experiment, in turn, can then serve as a map for planning and plotting the rest of one's life.

4   Conclusion

In this chapter, I have explored the ways in which narrative can be related to ethical life. As we have seen, there is no single way, but several, and, in addition, I do not claim that I have exhausted the connections in this cursory tour of the landscape. To sum up, I hope to have shown that, due to their structural features, typical narratives can clarify our understanding of situations that call for moral judgments, especially in cases that involve the recognizing and comprehension of virtue. But narratives do not only play a role in evaluating and morally understanding actions and events that we observe from the outside. Narrative also contributes to the kinds of facility with projecting possibilities that we need to deliberate on how we shall act; and, in fact, telling ourselves narratives that link our past, present, and future together coherently provides an important instrument for reaching the pertinent decisions. Philosophers like to reduce the relation of practices like narrative and ethics to a single dimension; they prefer economy and elegance. That the relation between narrative and ethical life is so multifarious may be one of the reasons it has eluded philosophical attention for so long. But insofar as a *prima facie* case for the relevance of narrative can be made, as I have attempted to do in this chapter, then the time is ripe to begin to articulate, in greater depth than achieved here, the many and diverse ways that narrative plays an intimate role in moral understanding and deliberation.

Notes

1   For example, Adam Zachary Newton, *Narrative Ethics* (Cambridge, MA: Harvard University Press, 1995).
2   Philip Hallie, *Tales of Good and Evil, Help and Harm* (New York: Harper Collins, 1997), p. 6.
3   Hallie and I were colleagues at Wesleyan University in the 1980s.
4   Hallie, *Tales of Good and Evil*, p. 7.
5   That is, selectivity is a necessary condition of narrative. No narrative can tell the "whole story" (if it even makes sense to speak of such a thing).
6   Peter Munz, "Introduction," *The Shapes of Time* (Middletown, CT: Wesleyan University Press, 1977); Nina Rosenstand, *The Moral of the Story* (Mountain View, CA: Mayfield Publishing Co., 1994), p. 28; and G. W. F. Hegel, *Introductory Lectures on Aesthetics* (London: Penguin, 1993).
7   In order to avoid cumbersome verbiage, throughout I speak of typical narratives and their potential contributions to ethics. But obviously I am not speaking of *every* typical narrative since some may have little or nothing to do with ethical matters and others that intend to contribute to ethics may fail to do so. So the reader should understand that in this chapter I am only talking about *some* typical narratives, namely those that are concerned with ethical issues and which deliver on that interest successfully. This chapter is an attempt to say something about the structures of such narratives which make their success possible. I do not mean to be claiming that all typical narratives are successful in these matters or that all concern ethical issues, but only that some are and that part of their success – in ways to be spelt out above – is due to the structures discussed herein.
8   Gerald Prince, "A Point of View on Point of View or Refocusing Focalization," in Willie Van Peer and Seymour Chatman, eds., *New Perspectives on Narrative Perspective* (Albany, NY: SUNY Press, 2001).
9   See Noël Carroll, "Art, Narrative, and Emotion," in *Beyond Aesthetics* (Cambridge: Cambridge University Press, 2001).
10 Some readers may feel that what I am referring to as the emotive address of the typical narrative would be better labeled the aesthetic address. I have no objection, so long as the aesthetic address is understood as including the emotive address. Baumgarten introduced the concept of the aesthetic as his name for sensitive knowledge – knowledge acquired through feeling. If this is what is meant by "the aesthetic" and if the emotions are counted as feelings in the broad non-technical sense, then I see no problem in saying that

typical narratives succeed where moral principles may falter because of their aesthetic address. If aesthetics refers to the mode of presentation of whatever a representation is about – its mode of sensuous embodiment as Hegelians might say – then criterial pre-focusing is an aesthetical strategy that yields a feeling response. My point is only that this can be even further specified as, more precisely, an emotional response. Furthermore, if Hegelians want to refer to narrative artworks as sensuous universals, I am happy to accommodate their lingo by means of the de-mythologizing notion that the works in question are representations of (sensuous) particulars presented under general emotion concepts.

11   James L. McGaugh, *Memory and Emotion: The Making of Lasting Memories* (New York: Columbia University Press, 2003).

12   Throughout this section I have been influenced by the writing of Robert C. Roberts, including: "Virtues and Rules," *Philosophy and Phenomenological Research* 51 (1991): 325–43; "The Philosopher as Sage," *Journal of Religious Ethics* 22 (1994): 409–31; "Kierkegaard, Wittgenstein, and a Method of 'Virtue Ethics'," in M. Matustic and M. Westphal, eds., *Kierkegaard Post-Modernity* (Bloomington, IN: Indiana University Press, 1995); "Narrative Ethics," in Philip Quinn and Charles Taliaferro, eds., *A Companion to Philosophy of Religion* (Oxford: Blackwell, 1999); and *Emotions* (New York: Cambridge University Press, 2003).

13   Here exemplars function as a subclass of what psychologists call "personae." See Robert Nisbett and Lee Ross, *Human Inference: Strategies and Shortcomings of Social Judgment* (Englewood Cliffs, NJ: Prentice-Hall, 1980), p. 35.

14   Ludwig Wittgenstein, *Philosophical Investigations*, trans. G. E. M. Anscombe (New York: Macmillan, 1953), p. 116.

15   Philip Hallie, "Scepticism, Narrative, and Holocaust Ethics," *Philosophical Forum* 16/1–2 (Fall–Winter, 1984–5): 46.

16   Richard Smith, "Teaching Literature," in Randall Curren, ed., *A Companion to the Philosophy of Education* (Oxford: Blackwell, 2003), p. 387; Duke Maskell, "Education, Education, Education, or, What has Jane Austen to Teach David Blunkett?" *Journal of the Philosophy of Education* 33/2 (1999): 157–74.

17   See Noël Carroll, "Art and Friendship," *Philosophy and Literature* 26/1 (April, 2002): 199–206.

18   Robert C. Roberts, "Narrative Ethics," p. 473.

19   This theme is also explored in Noël Carroll, "Art, Narrative, and Moral Understanding," *Beyond Aesthetics* (Cambridge: Cambridge University Press, 2001).

20   Noël Carroll, "The Wheel of Virtue: Art, Literature, and Moral Knowledge," *Journal of Aesthetics and Art Criticism* 60/1 (Winter, 2002): 2–26.

21   Noël Carroll, "On the Narrative Connection," in *Beyond Aesthetics* (Cambridge: Cambridge University Press, 2001).

22   Steven Pinker, *How the Mind Works* (New York: Norton, 1997), pp. 538–43.

23   R. C. Shank and R. Abelson, *Scripts, Plans, Goals, and Understanding* (Hillsdale, NJ: Lawrence Erlbaum, 1977).

24   It is sometimes argued that exposure to narratives can be of little use for actual deliberation, since the stories agents have at their disposal are unlikely to match the situations in which they find themselves. However, if it is the case that what is practiced and expanded by exposure to narratives is a skill for projecting future possibilities, then the problem of mismatches falls by the wayside. At the deepest level, the importance of exposure to narratives is that they increase one's facility for projecting future possibilities, not that the stories we hear can be mapped onto to the circumstances and predicaments in which we are engulfed on a one-to-one basis. Instead the value of exposure to narratives is that it can extend our ability to process new situations because we have already become adept at following all different kinds of stories.

25   Though undoubtedly reading narratives and watching narrative motion pictures also helps people develop their narrating skills. Part of this has to do with appreciating professional narrators and modeling our own attempts on them. But these products also shape our own narrating practices when, as is so often the case, we re-tell the plots of such fictions to friends and family.

26   For parallel observations see Hilde Lindeman Nelson, *Damaged Identities, Narrative Repair* (Ithaca, NY: Cornell University Press, 2001), especially chapter 3.

27   That is, whereas the primary focus of contemporary ethics is said to be "what makes an action good?" it is often observed that the ancients, including Aristotle and the Stoics, were concerned with the question of what makes a human life worthwhile.

28   The connection of narrative to the meaning of life is a theme of Continental philosophers such as Paul Ricoeur and Hannah Arendt, and of analytic philosophers who have studied that tradition deeply, including Alasdair MacIntyre, Charles Taylor, and Richard Rorty. Perhaps the idea originates in Nietzsche's notion that meaningful lives are works of art – a view also endorsed by Michel Foucault late in life. Sartre then in *Nausea* specifies the kind of artwork in question as a narrative. And, of course, the hero of that novel goes on to discover the meaning of his life by writing a book, presumably the book we are reading, which is a fictional narrative. Though some of these philosophers appear to claim that meaningful lives *are* narratives, one need not enter that ontological quagmire in order to benefit from their speculation. One need only maintain that the construction of a meaningful narrative is the best means at our disposal for approaching the question of whether our lives, as unified wholes, are worthwhile.

29   One might argue that there is no need to speak of narratives here; one can determine the worth of a life in terms of the roles lived. However, roles

themselves come with subtending narratives, so the appearance of a zero-sum rivalry here is misleading. And, in any event, one will have to consider how well the agent played her roles and this, of course, will send us in the direction of narrative.

30   One important source for learning to tell life stories is literature, especially certain genres, like the *Bildungsroman*.

3

A NATION OF MADAME BOVARYS: ON THE POSSIBILITY AND DESIRABILITY OF MORAL IMPROVEMENT THROUGH FICTION

Joshua Landy

1 Prudence or Oneiromancy?

> *. . . men shal nat maken ernest of game.*
> – Chaucer, *The Miller's Tale*

Imagine you are a professor teaching Chaucer's *Canterbury Tales* to a group of undergraduate students, and that today's class is on the *Nun's Priest's Tale*. You summarize the plot for them, to remind those who have bothered to do the reading what the gist of it was, and to give the rest a graceful opportunity to escape with their dignity intact. There is a rooster, you say, named Chauntecleer, who dreams he is carried off by a fox. When he wakes up, he tells his wife, Dame Pertelote, that he is in grave danger, since dreams are – as is well known – portents of things to come. She, however, will have none of it: far from predicting the future, she retorts, dreams merely testify to the digestive system of their maker, so that what Chauntecleer needs to take is not preventative action against predators but only (she does not mince words) "som laxatyf" (l. 177).[1]

Pertelote fails to persuade her husband, but a vigorous bout of love-making drives his dream clear from his mind, and he wanders out into the yard, where, sure enough, he finds a suitably hungry fox lying in wait for him. Being as cunning as any self-respecting fox should be, Daun Russell asks Chauntecleer to sing for him with that beautiful voice of his, and to close his eyes in order to concentrate better; being as susceptible to flattery as one might expect from a puffed-up rooster, Chauntecleer readily acquiesces, allowing the fox to snatch him up in his mouth and start bringing him home for dinner. Chauntecleer is only saved, you remind the students, by his own native wit: turning the fox's trick against him, he convinces Daun Russell to crow (no pun intended) triumphantly – at which point, the fox's mouth being open, Chauntecleer makes good his escape.

Now imagine that you go on, feeling generous with your wisdom, to point the moral of the story – so generous, indeed, that you offer two separate morals, in two different speeches. "Chaucer's story is highly instructive," Speech A begins. "It warns us against being like that silly rooster, who closes his eyes and begins to sing, seduced by the fox's flattery, indifferent to the danger of his situation. We learn from the story to be more prudent in our own lives. Chaucer is writing not just for fun but to help his audience become better and happier people." Speech B starts and ends similarly, but runs somewhat differently in between: "Chaucer's story is highly instructive. It warns us against being like that silly rooster, who ignores the prophetic significance of his dream, and thus rushes headlong into the yard where the fox is waiting for him. We learn from the story to accept oneiromancy in our own lives. Chaucer is writing not just for fun but to help his audience become better and happier people."

My suspicion is that you could quite easily convince your students of proposition A (the prudence moral), but that you would have a much harder time convincing them of proposition B (the prophecy moral). They furiously scribble notes at first, then quietly put their pens down. Why? What is the difference between the two claims? Is it that the story adequately proves we should be more circumspect, but somehow does not adduce enough evidence to show that we should be more credulous? Surely not. If anything, it is the other way around: the one and only piece of "support" for the prudence moral is a ludicrously fictional scenario in which a talking fox captures a talking rooster by convincing him to sing with his eyes closed (can this story really "prove" anything other than the claim that if you happen to be a talking rooster, you should beware of talking foxes, talking foxes tending to be particularly seductive?), whereas the argument for dream interpretation, which draws its strength from ancient precedent, is so extensive that it occupies more than a quarter of the tale. In the course of a scene occupying 173 lines out of the story's 626, in fact, Chauntecleer cites no fewer than eight authoritative stories, at least some of which – those that come from the Bible – Chaucer's listeners, and indeed many of your students, could reasonably be expected to believe. Here are five of those exempla, concerning Scipio, Daniel, Joseph, Croesus, and Andromache respectively:

> Macrobeus, that writ the avisioun [vision]
> In Affrike of the worthy Cipioun [Scipio],
> Affermeth dremes, and seith that they been
> Warninge of thinges that men after [later] seen.
>
> And forthermore, I pray yow loketh wel
> In the Olde Testament, of Daniel,
> If he held dremes any vanitee.
>
> Reed eek of Ioseph, and ther shul ye see
> Wher dremes ben somtyme (I sey nat alle)
> Warninge of thinges that shul after falle.
> Loke of Egipte the king, daun Pharao,
> His bakere and his boteler also,
> Wher [whether] they ne felte noon effect [significance] in dremes.
> Whose [whoso] wol seken actes [histories] of sondry remes [realms]
> May rede of dremes many a wonder thing.
>
> Lo Cresus, which that was of Lyde king,
> Mette [dreamt] he nat that he sat upon a tree,
> Which signified he sholde anhanged be?
>
> Lo heer Andromacha, Ectores wyf,
> That day that Ector sholde lese his lyf,
> She dremed on the same night biforn,
> How that the lyf of Ector sholde be lorn [lost]
> If thilke day he wente into bataille;
> She warned him, but it might nat availle;
> He wente for to fighte nathelees,
> But he was slayn anoon [immediately] of Achilles.
> (ll. 357–82; line breaks added)

It might, of course, be argued that it is quality, rather than quantity, that counts. Chauntecleer could produce 18 or 80 or 800 classical sources without advancing the cause of the prophecy moral an iota; one simple fable of a fox, by contrast, suffices to show how important it is to be cautious. The dream narratives prove nothing, however copious their number, because they are all invented. Whereas the farmyard narrative . . . But is the farmyard narrative not every bit as invented as the

Homeric account of Hector's last night on earth? Why do we ascribe to it any greater corroborative power?

Perhaps we should talk in terms of the *vraisemblable* rather than the *vrai*. Perhaps, that is, we are swayed by the fable because it, or at least its translation into the human realm, seems plausible to us – people behave this way in real life (even if roosters do not) – whereas the dream narratives, having no basis in real-world events, leave us utterly cold. Yet there is a serious problem with the antithesis thus phrased, and that is that *we have already assumed the very thing we set out to prove*. We say that the story fails to convince us that dreams are prophetic because it offers, as its only evidence, a series of tales which do not seem likely; but the reason such stories do not seem likely is that dreams are not prophetic. In circular fashion, the *Nun's Priest's Tale* convinces us only of what we already believed before we began to read it. Which means, strictly speaking, that it convinces us of nothing at all.[2]

2   A Parody of Didacticism

> *The [Nun's Priest's] Tale could only have been written for a medieval audience which looked at life seriously . . . If we turn to the poetry, we can see that it is of a kind which could only proceed from a fine moral concern.*
> – Holbrook, "The Nonne Presstes Tale"

The bell rings (or rather, since such bells only ring in movies, the end of class is announced by a tumultuous relocation of papers from desk to backpack), and you move on to your graduate seminar, where you explain what has just happened. You have, you note, failed to convert any of your students to oneiromancy. They have learnt three things at most: (1) that *you* believe dreams to be prophetic; (2) that *you* believe you can use a tale by Chaucer as evidence (just as, within the tale, Chauntecleer thinks he can draw on stories from Homer); and (3) that Chaucer may possibly have thought so too. They have *not* learnt (4) that they have any reason to accept the view themselves. You have, in other words, only succeeded in convincing your students of your own insanity. They have responded to your second harangue in the same way that a non-believer would respond to the claim that Genesis, with its injunction from God to be fruitful and multiply, constitutes a cast-iron argument against birth control: few people wish to rule their lives on the basis of a work they take to be pure fantasy.

You do, of course, have a number of rather vulpine graduate students in the seminar, and one of the very shrewdest (let us call him Daun Bertrand

Russell) raises an ingenious objection. "The prudence moral," he argues, "is borne out by the story, whereas the prognostication moral is not. It just so *happened*, on this occasion, that a dream matched up to reality; rash behavior, on the other hand, *necessarily* proved costly, such being the way of the world. Chaucer probably meant moral A, but was surely too sensible to stand behind moral B." Has Bertrand bested you? Not necessarily. You do not even have to play devil's advocate and claim, on behalf of the oneiromancers' union, that dreams match up to reality more often than not. You merely have to remind Bertrand that rashness is not always a bad thing. Sometimes, to be sure, it is good to look before one leaps; but he who hesitates is also, at other times, lost.[3] As Picasso put it, surprisingly aptly for your purposes, "to draw, you must close your eyes and sing."

Bertrand now falling silent, Dame Erica Auerbach, a graduate student who knows her literary history, directs us to the story's postscript:

> But ye that holden this tale a folye,
> As of a fox, or of a cok and hen,
> Taketh the moralitee, goode men.
> For Seint Paul seith that al that writen is,
> To oui doctryne it is y-write, y-wis.
> (ll. 672–6)

"As a good medieval Christian," opines Erica, "Chaucer could not possibly have told stories unless he thought they could be in some way edifying."[4] You feel tempted to ask her for the moral of *The Miller's Tale*, but content yourself with making two points. First, St Paul is, as Chaucer and his readers know perfectly well, referring to holy scripture, not writing in general.[5] And this is only reasonable, since if "*al* that writen is," from litanies to laundry lists, yielded equally valuable lessons, the value in question would be pitifully small. Secondly, when the nun's priest exhorts us to take the "moralitee," we are placed in something of a quandary: *which one* does he mean? Is he referring to the prognostication moral? the prudence moral? the fatalist moral that "destine . . . ma[y] nat been eschewed" (l. 572)? the downbeat moral that "ever the latter ende of joye is wo" (l. 439)? the upbeat moral that, thanks to God's justice, "mordre wol out" (l. 286)? or, finally, the charming moral that the advice of women should not be heeded (ll. 490–94), since "*mulier est hominis confusio*" (l. 398)?[6]

All of these morals can surely not be true at once. The confident claim of divine justice stands in tension with the more pagan, pessimistic wheel-of-fortune discourse;[7] more importantly, neither of the first two can square with the instigation to forethought. We cannot possibly take the nun's priest seriously, and indeed he himself is perhaps not speaking seriously, when he blames not only Chauntecleer (for his lack of prudence) but also Pertelote (for her failure to believe in dreams) and even destiny (for its relentlessness) –

> O destinee, that mayst nat been eschewed!
> Allas, that Chauntecleer fleigh [flew] fro the bemes!
> Allas, his wyf ne roghte nat of [paid no heed to] dremes!
> (ll. 572–4)

– as though any room for belief and prudence could be left over once destiny has extracted its due.

Dame Erica is right about one thing: medieval audiences expected the stories they heard to have easily detachable, easily assimilable morals. And the nun's priest obliges his (and by extension Chaucer's) audience. He just obliges a little too much. Like the hawker of panaceas, he oversells his product, claiming for it every virtue imaginable – with the result that we trust it less than if he had only promised to cure a single ill. The *Nun's Priest's Tale* is, in fact, a *parody* of didacticism, a story that reminds us of how extraordinarily easy it is to draw edifying lessons from any narrative. As long as our listeners already subscribe to a particular piety, they will happily consider a story to illustrate it, indeed consider it to emerge automatically from the story, as the only possible inference; they will, under certain circumstances, go so far as to consider the story all the evidence it needs.

3   Preaching to the Converted

> *This was a murie tale of Chauntecleer.*
> *But by my trouthe, if thou were seculer [layman],*
> *Thou woldest ben a trede-foul [rooster] aright.*
> *For if thou has corage as thou hast myght,*
> *Thee were nede of hennes, as I wene [think],*
> *Ya, moo than seven tymes seventene.*
> — Chaucer, *The Nun's Priest's Tale*

Fictions, you are forced to conclude, preach to the converted alone. Since they offer no substantiation for their implicit claims,[8] they are powerless to shake our deeply held convictions. It is always open to us to

dismiss them as fantastical.[9] The fact that an author is capable of portraying roosters, say, as able to talk does not even mean that *one* rooster
is able to talk, let alone that the *typical* rooster is able to talk; while a
real-life example is at least proof of possibility (if not prevalence), a fictional
example is proof of absolutely nothing. If we happen to have already seen
talking roosters, we will accept the accuracy of the depiction. If we have
not, we will reject it, and (if we choose) everything that follows from it.
In neither case will our minds have been changed.[10]

The nun's priest must know this, for otherwise he would not pretend
that his story is a true one, and worthy *on those very grounds* (as the punc-
tuation indicates) of careful moral attention:

> Now every wys man, lat him herkne me:
> This storie is also [as] trewe, I undertake,
> As is the book of Lancelot de Lake,
> That wommen holde in ful gret reverence.
> (ll. 444–7)

Someone is, of course, joking here – since we know what the nun's priest's
feelings are with regard to women,[11] we can infer what kind of reverence
he has, or at least should have, toward "the book of Lancelot de Lake;"
either he is trying to trick his employer, the nun, into taking the fable as
fact and, equally foolishly, into "tak[ing] the moralitee," or Chaucer is
mocking his inconsequence – but what is clear is that everyone takes true
stories to be more convincing than fictions. The nun's priest knows it,
and Chaucer must know it too, however medieval he may be. Far from
depicting cases of conversion-by-exemplum, Chaucer has a way of
presenting us with characters who do *not* learn from stories – characters
like Chauntecleer himself. After reciting his endless catalogue of ancient
anecdotes, designed to impress upon Pertelote the seriousness of his plight,
what does Chauntecleer do? He saunters out into the yard, and starts
singing with his eyes closed.[12]

No one learns anything from *The Nun's Priest's Tale*. Those who agree
that we should be prudent already thought so before they read it; those
who disagree are likely to be as little affected as the Wife of Bath by her
husband's harangues.[13] It is not even the case that we learn *this* from
the *Nun's Priest's Tale*[14] – not even the case, that is, that we learn how
ineffectual fictions are as a tool for conversion. The *Nun's Priest's Tale* is
a parody of didacticism, but true to its own implicit principles, it fails to
teach even the impotence of literary instruction. Had it done so, then
there would surely not exist today the voluminous and intensely earnest

bibliography of devout interpretations, reading the *Tale* as an allegory of the Fall,[15] an allegory of the Church,[16] a positive exemplum (via the frugal widow who opens and closes the tale),[17] or a negative exemplum (via the rooster).[18] *The Nun's Priest's Tale* is a story which fails to prove even its own futility – and which, in so doing, vindicates itself.

4   The Asymmetry of "Imaginative Resistance"

> CHARLES: *You can't expect much sympathy from me, you know. I am perfectly aware that your highest hope was to murder me.*
> ELVIRA: *Don't put it like that, it sounds so beastly.*
> – Noel Coward, *Blithe Spirit*

Human nature is a strange thing. We know how blissfully immune we are to influence from artworks whose underlying worldview departs from our own (am I really likely to become a con-man after watching *The Sting*? an advocate of whaling after reading *Moby Dick*?), and yet we carry on assigning films and novels and plays and poems to friends we consider in dire need of inner change. "Read this," we say, "it will make you see things differently" (by which of course we mean "it will make you see things my way"). Perhaps we give a copy of *Candide* to one who is laboring under the delusion that God works in the world. Perhaps she returns the favor by forcing us to read some C. S. Lewis. The two of us end up, like the positivist and the priest in *Madame Bovary*, as firmly entrenched in our positions as we ever were before. We should all just come out and admit it: *"morally improving" is merely a compliment we pay to works whose values agree with ours.*

Such a view is not likely to be widely shared in the age of the "ethical turn." Quite the contrary, substantial quantities of time and journal space have recently been dedicated to assessing the precise ways in which literature contributes to a better society. Some (like Richard Rorty) have argued that literary texts foster empathy with an ever-widening circle of human types, gradually bringing more and more of "them" under the designation "us."[19] Others (like Gregory Currie) have suggested that literary texts serve as spaces for "simulation," in which we imaginatively apprehend the likely consequences of certain decisions, indeed of certain overall value systems, and as a result learn what it is that we want to do – which, by a magic that betrays a certain residual Socratism, turns out to be what is objectively *good* to do.[20] Or, finally, the simulation is said to fine-tune our moral decision-making faculty, so that we are better equipped to notice and respond to subtle claims on our moral attention (this is Martha Nussbaum's view).[21]

In almost all cases, the salutary effect on readers is presented as automatic, inevitable, "inescapable" (to use a term as beloved of Wayne Booth as, in related contexts, of Charles Taylor) – as though novels were so many bricks with which to hit recalcitrant unbelievers over the head, in hopes of shaking their skepticism loose. Thus for Booth, "all of our aesthetic judgments are inescapably tied to ethics;"[22] when we read, we are "inescapably caught up in ethical activity."[23] For Noël Carroll, similarly, "the narrative artwork *unavoidably* engages, exercises, and sometimes clarifies and deepens moral understanding."[24] And for Nussbaum, "the [novelistic] genre itself, on account of some general features of its structure, constructs empathy and compassion in ways highly relevant to citizenship."[25] In particular, works like Dickens's *Hard Times* positively oblige us, whether we like it or not, to become better people. "It is impossible to care about the characters and their fate in the way the text invites," according to Nussbaum, "without having some very definite political and moral interests awakened in oneself."[26]

Good literature, in short, simply leaves us no choice but to be improved by it. Bad literature, on the other hand – and this is a striking asymmetry in the moralist position – *has no effect on us whatsoever.*[27] We are all blessed with what has been dubbed "imaginative resistance:" when presented with a fictional world in which, say, murder is good, we find ourselves unable (Hume) or at least unwilling (Gendler) to imagine it; by consequence, the work will fail to move us as it wishes, and thus come up short not only ideologically but also aesthetically (Walton).[28] As Tamar Gendler puts it, "I have a much easier time following an author's invitation to imagine that the earth is flat than I do following her invitation to imagine that murder is right."[29] Is this correct? First of all, we might object that to use such a beastly word (as Noel Coward might put it) is already to stack the deck, since "murder," unlike "killing," is a moral term. What if we called it, say, "taking care of"? What, in other words, if we consider the case of mafia fiction, in which the very worst thing one can do is to report crimes to the police, and the very best thing one can do is, at times, to "take care of" an unarmed human being, someone whose only blemish is, perhaps, to have reported crimes to the police?[30]

It is a fascinating fact about certain mafia movies, and virtually all outlaw movies,[31] that they perform an imaginative "re-evaluation of values" *without us resisting in the slightest.*[32] (Mummy movies, incidentally, have a related effect: when the ultra-rationalist – the one who insists loudly that there is no such thing as mummies – is the first to be strangled to

Plate 3.1: The skeptic, before.
The Mummy (produced by Michael Carreras, 1959)
Source: Clip & Still Licensing, Warner Bros. Entertainment Inc.

death, we feel no sorrow, since obviously he should have known better. For the duration of the movie, we are people who would rather spend time with believers in the paranormal than with seekers of fact; we are people whose firm conviction it is that to base one's judgments on logic and empirical evidence is to merit extermination.[33]) And perhaps this attitude, which we could term "imaginative inertia," is the standard case. Far from resisting the different, sometimes opposite, values of the fictional world, we positively delight in trying them on for an hour or two, like a carnival costume. Even works like *Hamlet*, which do not depart quite so radically from our everyday worldview, nonetheless require us to imagine not only that ghosts exist but also that it is proper to avenge murder with murder, indeed that it is a positive moral failing to leave a murderer alive.

Those who follow Kendall Walton's lead in understanding mimetic fictions as games of make-believe are surely in the right; what they often overlook, however, is the fact that players of such games take on *roles* in order to play them. (The four-year-old who pretends that her doll is

Plate 3.2: The skeptic, after.
The Mummy (produced by Michael Carreras, 1959)
Source: Clip & Still Licensing, Warner Bros. Entertainment Inc.

a baby, for example, also pretends that she herself is a parent.) We do not enter the fictional world as tourists, anthropologists, passive spectators of the strange goings-on; instead we are granted temporary citizenship.[34] We share its values, operate within its rules, define heroism and villainy by the standards that apply here – not, or at least not exclusively, by those that hold on our home-world.[35]

At all events, any honest account of the aesthetic experience must be symmetrical. If I am virtuous, then I will certainly resist the promptings of Sade to rape and torture; but if I am vicious, then I will just as strongly resist the urgings of Dickens to do unto others what I would have done to myself, or to be kind to escaped convicts, or to embrace (heaven forfend) the Christmas spirit. Perhaps I will resist Dickens *even if I am good*, which is to say even if I share the values his texts appear to be endorsing. After all, there is something about sanctimonious fictions which makes one either burst out laughing – "one must have a heart of stone," Oscar Wilde famously remarked of *The Old Curiosity Shop*, "to read the death of Little Nell without laughing" – or respond with indignation.[36] In my more Dostoevskian moments, I do not consider it impossible for previously well-meaning readers to become just a little bit immoral, out of spite.

Conversely, while absorption in Martin Scorsese's film *Goodfellas* does not make me into a mafioso, since the persona I send into the fictional world is disconnected from my everyday self, it must be added that absorption in the novel *Clarissa*, by Samuel Richardson, does not make me into a paragon of patience, and for analogous reasons.[37] Indeed, one of the most seductive pleasures such wholesome fictions offer us is the satisfaction of being, for an hour or two, supremely equitable, unbendingly thoughtful, unadulteratedly righteous. "How good I was! How just I was! How satisfied I was with myself!" writes Diderot about the experience of reading *Clarissa*, and one wonders if there might be a modicum of wry Diderotian irony in the third exclamation.[38] The version of ourself that we send into Richardson's world is indeed unerringly noble, uncompromisingly idealistic. The pleasure we derive is that of being on the side of the angels, making (for once) categorical judgments, unqualified by the nuances and objections required in the everyday world; like the pleasure of hissing the villain at the pantomime, it is a fantasy of moral clarity, a form of escapism for the morally obsessed. It may even be a profoundly narcissistic sentiment – the sentiment of utter moral perfection – brilliantly disguised as altruism. We convince ourselves that we are doing the world a favor by reading *Clarissa*, while the only person to whom any favors are done is ourself. For when we put *Clarissa* back on the shelf, we return to being the very same earthbound, pragmatic, exception-making individual we were before.[39] (Perhaps we are even *less* likely to make a positive contribution to society, having purged ourselves of all benevolent emotions in our favorite armchair.[40]) If we cannot be harmed by fictions, then we cannot be improved. Fictions, to repeat, preach only to the converted.

5   Virtue Ethics and Gossip

> *SOCRATES: And a just man does just things, I take it?*
> *GORGIAS: Yes.*
> — Plato, *Gorgias*

It is, perhaps, for this reason that theorists of moral improvement tend inadvertently to argue against their own position. Thus when Richard Posner reports having enjoyed Dickens's *Hard Times* for entirely non-moral reasons – a feat utterly inconceivable, as we saw above, in the eyes of

Martha Nussbaum – the latter responds, curiously enough, by summoning Dickens from beyond the grave to castigate the obdurate judge. "Well, Judge Posner," the resurrected Dickens scolds, "you are not a very valuable member of society."[41] Deep down, Posner's resistance to ethical criticism is really "an assault on political egalitarianism;" deep down, "insisting on taking his stand with works that keep him at a distance from the demand of the poor and the weak" is just a way to evade "the claim of a painful reality."[42] Now leaving aside the question of whether someone who has devoured all those improving novels by Dickens and James could be expected to rise above such *ad hominem* attacks,[43] Nussbaum's rejoinder stands at least as an acknowledgment that Posner *has not been affected by his reading.* And if Dickens does not succeed in converting those who, like Posner, ostensibly *require* moral improvement, what good does he actually do? Those who, like Nussbaum, are already benevolent egalitarians will remain so; those who, like Posner, enter as self-indulgent aesthetes will depart unchanged.[44] Tacitly, Nussbaum is admitting Posner's point.

The moralists have, after all, only shaky empirical evidence at hand to suggest that well-intentioned art actually makes any difference in people's behavior. Even proponents of ethical criticism, like Noël Carroll, concede that "we still understand virtually *nothing* about the behavioral consequences of consuming art."[45] Such theorists, who wish nonetheless to find moral value in the experience of reading, are reduced to positing some kind of effect on the inner structure of the mind, one which (conveniently and mysteriously enough) fails to translate into measurable everyday praxis. Thus Nussbaum, under pressure, says that she is only talking about "the interaction between novel and mind during the time of reading."[46] Since, on her view, the mere fact of recognizing subtleties in the moral world constitutes "moral conduct" all on its own, we can score virtue points *merely by (correctly) reading a Henry James novel,*[47] even if we return the next day to our job at the plantation.

There is something pleasantly Greek-flavored about the approach, implying as it does that goodness refers to a state or shape of the soul, rather than the decisions to which it gives rise. Still, even the Greeks insisted on proof through action: in Plato's *Gorgias,* for example, Socrates and Gorgias clearly agree that a man behaving badly is a man who lacks virtue, even if they disagree about whose fault it is. With such doubts nagging at her, perhaps, Nussbaum quickly seeks to take back what she conceded to Posner, writing – a mere two pages after having localized our increase in virtue to the period we spend with a book in our hand – that "the activities of imagination and emotion that the involved reader performs during the time of reading . . . strengthen the propensity so to conduct oneself in other instances."[48]

Yet the fact is that there is nothing whatsoever to prevent us from taking an intensive, vigorous, sustained, detailed, painstaking interest in the moral entanglements of other lives while remaining entirely remote from the moral fray. This intensive, vigorous, sustained, detailed, painstaking yet detached interest even has a name: it is called gossip. And as irony would have it, the very work Nussbaum considers the archetype of morally improving fiction – Henry James's *The Golden Bowl* – features a gossip of world-class caliber. If, as Nussbaum claims, "the activities of imagination and emotion that the involved reader performs during the time of reading are not just instrumental to moral conduct, they are also examples of moral conduct,"[49] then Fanny Assingham, who spends all day every day picking apart in thought and conversation the predicament of her friends, has surely clocked up enough instances of moral conduct to earn herself a niche on the portal of Notre-Dame.

A clear *reductio ad absurdum* of Nussbaum's position, the Fanny Assingham case shows, if it shows anything, that a fascination with (or even a fine awareness of) interpersonal niceties need not fuel any concern for our fellow human being. Fine awareness is, to phrase it in Jamesian terms, no guarantee of rich responsibility. We do not have to be a vicious anti-egalitarian in order to read *Hard Times* for non-moral reasons. On the contrary, that is probably the way *most* of us read it. Like Fanny Assingham, we are infinitely curious (even pruriently so) about the lives of others, whether fictional or actual; if, as Nussbaum correctly states, Fanny stands as a model for the reader,[50] this is because her interest is just as amoral as ours, not because ours is just as moral as hers.[51]

6   Qualifications

> *Oh! children, see! the tailor's come*
> *And caught our little Suck-a-Thumb.*
> – Heinrich Hoffmann, *Struwwelpeter*

What, however, about the very chapter you are now reading? Did it not begin precisely with a fiction, a made-up scenario (two classrooms) with made-up characters (Daun Bertrand Russell, Dame Erica Auerbach)? And did I not intend to affect your views on the basis of it? It has some-times been argued[52] that the examples used in philosophical arguments are miniature fictions and so, conversely, fictions are nothing but

extended philosophical examples, perfectly serviceable as tools for secur-
ing conviction. The comparison is misleading, however: one only needs
to imagine trying to have my little classroom fantasy published in the *New
Yorker* in order to register the vast distance between literary fictions and
philosophical examples. The latter tend, first of all, to be as general as
possible, dispensing with details (if I told you about Erica's interests, it
was just for fun; and you know nothing about what she looks like, where
she comes from, or what her ambitions are). Secondly, they hew with
obsessive tenacity to the way in which events (are taken to) unfold in the
real world.[53] Philosophical examples must begin in self-evidence – in
situations, that is, on whose plausibility almost all readers will readily agree
– in order to elicit intuitions supporting controversial hypotheses.
Literary fictions, by contrast, add in such elements as drama and surprise.[54]
Their endings tend to have an appropriateness (consider the dénouement
of *The Nun's Priest's Tale*, a traditional case of the trickster tricked) rarely
to be met with in real life.

Let us say, then, that philosophical examples (like mine) are types
of fiction – but non-literary fiction – which can be used to summon
intuitions. Let us also add that it is entirely possible for a philosophical
author to compose a serious treatise, full of claims and arguments, and
then encompass it in a fictional frame (by attributing it, say, to a
character, perhaps with an exotic name like Zarathustra). Parmenides' poetic
treatise on truth and opinion is a similar case, beginning as it does
with an account of a mythical journey before launching into its intricate
metaphysical disquisitions.[55] There are even (and this would be a third
concession) borderline cases, hybrid works which combine the imaginative world-building of literature with the argumentation of philosophy.
(Proust's *Recherche* is one example, and Sartre's *La Nausée* might be
another, but James's *Golden Bowl* would most definitely not constitute
a third.[56]) In such cases, I would suggest that we do indeed learn from
novels, *but only insofar as they are philosophical*, which is to say only
insofar as they deploy convincing chains of reasoning (as for instance
does Roquentin, in *La Nausée*, when he proves that "adventure" is a
structure we impose on the sequence of events).

Finally, we should acknowledge that even canonically literary fictions
can be used as tools of education, *as long as they are backed up by the
sanction of an external authority*. I said above that your putative students
may have derived from your lecture the idea that you and Chaucer share
a belief in the prophetic power of dreams. Now if, in addition to believ-
ing this, your students are also sufficiently misguided to take you
(and/or Chaucer) for an *expert* on such matters, they may change their

minds on that very basis. The story may then serve them as a vivid reminder, a mental image helping them to remember how important dreams are. It seems to me that edifying children's literature works in just this way. What children learn is that it is good *according to their parents* to share their toys, keep their thumbs out of their mouth, or resist eating the gingerbread walls of rustic houses in the woods, and that *according to their parents* unpleasant consequences will necessarily follow.[57] The children respond by adjusting their behavior in the direction of the parents' implicit agenda (or indeed, if they are old enough and self-willed enough, in exactly the opposite direction).

Without such sanction, mind you, the outcome is completely unpredictable. You might think that La Fontaine's fable *Le Corbeau et le Renard*, the tale of a crafty fox who tricks a vain crow out of his cheese by persuading him to sing, inevitably encourages its young readers to be a little less vain; you would, however, be mistaken. Jean-Jacques Rousseau was shocked to discover that eighteenth-century pupils (who were so well acquainted with the poem that they could recite it from memory) spontaneously identified with the *fox*, taking the poem as a handy reminder that if you wish to steal, it helps to use fake praise.[58] And I daresay the same would have been true if the story had featured a vain rooster, named Chauntecleer perhaps, instead of a vain crow. Even your students might – who knows? – have read it as advocating flattery and deception, were it not for the fact that, fortunately enough, they have you there to reveal the deep oneiromantic truth to them.

Now your students may, given a list of recommended readings, start concluding on their own – that is, without specific confirmation from you each time – that it is good to help the poor (*Hard Times*), or to avenge murder with murder (*Hamlet*), or to throw strangers out of railway carriages (*Les Caves du Vatican*). Indeed, numerous literature courses at universities assemble sequences of novels, penned by representatives of unquestionably deserving groups, with a view to conditioning the students into taking each successive novel as an object-lesson in empathy for the group concerned.

Notice that those who run such courses are not merely training their students to be better moral agents but also training them *in how to be trained*, teaching them how to learn. (We could call this higher-order instruction "meta-training.") Just as I tell my child not only that Beijing is the capital of China but also that such facts can be found in the encyclopedia, so I tell her not only that she should share her toys but also that answers to other ethical dilemmas are to be found in fables. Now telling our children, our students, and our citizens to go to the movies for moral instruction is a serious mistake. For anyone who can be converted to a view by a fiction can be converted *out* of it by a fiction. If *Gandhi* is enough to turn me into a pacifist on Thursday night, then *Malcolm X*, which I watch the following evening, is enough to make me believe in the necessity of violence. If *The Nun's Priest's Tale* makes your students prudent during week one of your survey course, then *The Open Road* will make them reckless by week ten. (Just so, rhetoric was sufficient to convince the Athenians to slaughter all the men on Mytilene, and rhetoric was sufficient – mere hours later – to make them change their minds.[59]) Our culture is full of competing values, and of stories to "prove" any one of them;[60] conversions through fiction are simply not reliable. We are breeding a generation of what Harry Frankfurt would call "wantons," easily swayed from one well-meaning but un-nuanced value judgment to the next.[61] We are on our way to producing a nation of Madame Bovarys.[62]

7   Positive Views

> *Why, some people may lose their faith by looking at that picture!*
> – Dostoevsky, *The Idiot*

It will be tempting for some on both sides to conclude, in horror or delight, that literature, if it has no edifying function, has no function at all. Indeed, part of what is so troubling about the moralist line is that it so frequently sets up a stark "with us or against us" opposition. If novels are not morally improving, then they are morally depraving, or at best frivolous – which, as it turns out, still means pernicious. "Some works," writes Nussbaum, "promote a cheap cynicism about human beings, and lead us to see our fellow citizens with disdain. Some lead us to cultivate cheap sensational-istic forms of pleasure and excitement that debase human dignity. Others, by contrast, show what might be called respect before humanity."[63] In other words, there are only three choices: improve, corrupt, or distract (and by distracting, "debase human dignity"). Pleasure, on this view, is not something humans can justifiably seek in between helping little old ladies across the road. It is, instead, a *diversion* from a little-old-lady-helping that should, by rights, constitute our full-time occupation. Aesthetic pleasure – which, like all pleasure, is inherently sinful, not just amoral but immoral – can just about become acceptable if it subserves the end of edification;[64] otherwise, whether sought by readers or offered by authors,[65] it is a positive shirking of our responsibilities to humankind.

We would probably do well to preserve a space for reading without ulterior motives. (Perhaps it could even be argued, for benefit of the irretrievably utilitarian, that society *requires* such amoral pleasures, as a "pressure valve" for pent-up self-directed or indeed antisocial energies.[66]) But there is also a third way, in between hedonism and moralism, a way in which fiction can aid our emotional growth without turning us all into social workers. For while novels only tell us what we already knew, and only convince us of what we already believed, *that very process may be indispensable.* As Posner puts it, "If you don't already sense that love is the most important thing in the world, you're not likely to be persuaded that it is by reading Donne's love poems, or Stendhal, or Galsworthy. But reading them may make you realize that this *is* what you think, and so may serve to clarify yourself to yourself."[67] Literature, in short, helps us to find our *own* values, which *may* turn out to be moral values such as rich responsibility, but which may just as well turn out to be, say, an individualist (and other-sacrificing) perfectionism. Literature cannot edify, but it can clarify.[68] Wayne Booth is right that literary works can stand to us in the same relation as friends. But few of us today ask our friends to treat us in accordance with Aristotle's concept of "philia," or as Job's so-called "friends" (is this a rare case of irony in the Old Testament?) treat him: far from expecting them to repeat indefinitely how irremediably mired in sin we are, and enjoining us to meet an abstract, universal standard, we rather prefer them to invite us to be who we are.

A work of narrative art can be a true friend of ours when, first, its background scheme of facts and values is close enough to our own, so that it makes sense to speak of a simulation shedding light on the intuitions of our real-world self.[69] A second, and absolutely vital, precondition is that it be axiologically *complex*. If it is to spur us to serious reflection on our attitudes, then it must challenge us by placing at least two of our values into conflict, allowing each to assert its claim on us, rather than simply reinforcing one of them (in imagination) and making us feel, like Diderot, how astonishingly good and just we are. The most useful texts are the *Antigones*, not the *Clarissas*.[70] However tempted we are to use purportedly "improving" novels as electrodes with which to jolt the misfiring neurons of the benighted, we should remember that those works which try hardest to change us are those which succeed the least.[71] It is, perhaps, no coincidence that certain segments of the population place a premium on artworks that spur lengthy discussion, rather than those which proceed from incontestably noble moral principles.[72]

We might even – my last, and most important, compromise proposal – be able to use certain axiologically complex works in order to improve ourselves morally. Nussbaum is surely right that fully moral behavior requires not only an adherence to general precepts but also an attention to nuances which tend to escape the latter's grasp. (This is why her contribution to moral philosophy has been so important.) And she is surely also right that a certain kind of engagement with a certain kind of text can fine-tune our capacity for such attention, acting as a moral obstacle-course, training us to navigate the treacherous road conditions and sudden swerves of real life. Her suggestion, finally, that the most important type of knowledge I gain from my reading is know-how, not propositional (or even experiential) knowledge, is equally welcome. *I must, however, be good already in order to use texts in the way she prescribes.* I must be predisposed to moral improvement, and indeed must come to the text *for* that, at least among other goals.

Literary texts, in other words, *can* make us more finely aware and more richly responsible. But they will only do so if we want them to.[73] If we are not already virtuous, they may leave us unaffected, or even enable us to render ourselves still more grossly obtuse and still more richly irresponsible than we were to begin with. (Any theory with pretensions to adequacy must, to repeat, be symmetrical.) If we come in with murderous desires, then literary texts may offer us new and exciting ways of killing people; while fictions do not, I think, turn good people into criminals, there is nothing to stop them inspiring *specific* crimes in nefarious appreciators. Simulation, by helping us to plan, may assist us in implementing any altruistic schemes we happen to have, but simulation may also assist us in implementing a successful bank heist, a successful kidnapping, or a successful cull of spotted owls.

Back in your classroom a week later, you address the crowd of sleepy undergraduates, retracting what you said last time about dreams. Literary texts do not teach us anything, you say, unless it is who we are as individuals. Literary texts can, however, *train* us – or rather, they can offer us the *opportunity* to train ourselves in certain skills. We can hone, in reading, the talents necessary to intricately fine-grained concern. Maybe, if we try really hard, we can even take some "moralitee" from *The Nun's Priest's Tale*. As the nun's priest's hilarious antics remind us, one can, if one wants to, find a moral in just about anything.

Notes

I am deeply grateful to Alexander Nehamas, Thomas Pavel, and Lanier Anderson for their detailed comments on this paper. I would also like to mention the very helpful exchanges I have had with Stanley Corngold, Caryl Emerson, Stacie Friend, Sean Greenberg, Françoise Meltzer, Robert Morrissey, Gary Saul Morson, Elena Russo, Angela Sebastiana, Susan Stewart, Blakey Vermeule, Michael Wood, and the wonderful students of Phil. 81.

1   Geoffrey Chaucer, *The Canterbury Tales* (New York: Norton, 1989).

2   Cf. Paisley Livingston, *Literature and Rationality: Ideas of Agency in Theory and Fiction* (Cambridge: Cambridge University Press, 1991), p. 82. Lewis's *The Monk*, he points out, offers no confirmation of demonology; why then do we take it, and other novels, as evidence for psychological theories of various types?

Compare also Noël Carroll, "Art, Narrative, and Moral Understanding," in Jerrold Levinson, ed., *Aesthetics and Ethics: Essays at the Intersection* (Cambridge: Cambridge University Press, 1998), pp. 126–60, at p. 130: "where artworks . . . express general moral precepts, or are underwritten by them, those principles or precepts are typically so obvious and thin that it strains credulity to think that we learn them from artworks. Instead, very often, it seems more likely that a thoughtful preteenager will have mastered them already. Yes, there is an argument against murder in *Crime and Punishment*, but surely it is implausible to think that it requires a novel as elaborate as Dostoyevsky's to teach it, and even if Dostoyevsky designed the novel as a teaching aid, did anyone really learn that murder is wrong from it? . . . In fact, it is probably a precondition of actually comprehending *Crime and Punishment* that the readers already grasp the moral precepts that motivate the narrative."

3   Cf. Jerome Stolnitz, "On the Cognitive Triviality of Art," *British Journal of Aesthetics* 32/3 (1992): 191–200, at p. 196.

4   Erica speaks in accordance with the view of any number of Chaucer scholars. Thus, for example, the epigraph to this section – David Holbrook, "The Nonne Presstes Tale," in Boris Ford, ed., *The Age of Chaucer* (London: Penguin, 1969), pp. 118–28, at p. 119: "The *Tale* could only have been written for a medieval audience which looked at life seriously . . . The poetry . . . is of a kind which could only proceed from a fine moral concern."

5   See Stephen Manning, "The Nun's Priest's Morality and the Medieval Attitude toward Fables," *Journal of English and Germanic Philology* 59 (1960): 403–16, at p. 414. Here is what Paul actually says: "For everything that was written in the past was written to teach us, so that through endurance *and the encouragement of the Scriptures* we might have hope." (*Romans* 15:4, my emphasis).

6   Walter Scheps counts 10 morals in all, in his "Chaucer's Anti-Fable: *Reductio ad absurdum* in the Nun's Priest's Tale," *Leeds Studies in English* 4 (1970): 1–10, at p. 5. There could be more: intriguingly, the nun's priest refuses to reuse the *original* moral tag for the fable – "the wicked are caught in their own nets" (*Proverbs* 11:6) – from John Bromyard's *Summa*

Praedicantum. See D. E. Myers, "Focus and 'Moralite' in the Nun's Priest's Tale." *The Chaucer Review* 7 (1973): 210–20, at p. 212.

7   Cf. "Lo, how Fortune turneth sodeinly / The hope and pryde eek [also] of hir [her] enemy!"(Chaucer, ll. 637–8).

8   Cf. Stolnitz, "On the Cognitive Triviality of Art," p. 196; Richard A. Posner, "Against Ethical Criticism: Part Two," *Philosophy and Literature* 22 (1998): 394–412, at p. 405; Daniel Jacobson, "Sir Philip Sidney's Dilemma," *Journal of Aesthetics and Art Criticism* 54 (1996): 327–36, at p. 330. David Lewis cannot quite seem to make up his mind on this point: fictions, he writes, can prove "modal truths," such as whether there could be such a thing as a dignified beggar; but fictions can also persuade us to believe in impossibilities ("Truth in Fiction," *Philosophical Papers*, vol. 1, Oxford: Oxford University Press, 1983, pp. 261–79, at p. 278). If the second statement is true, then surely the "proof" of the first statement is no proof at all.

9   Cf. Richard A. Posner, "Against Ethical Criticism," *Philosophy and Literature* 21 (1997): 1–27, at p. 14. Carroll recognizes this as a limit on the effectiveness of simulation – "I am also not convinced that simulations à la Currie play much of a role in our moral deliberations, since we are aware that the pertinent scenarios are made up" (Carroll, "Art, Narrative, and Moral Understanding," p. 160 n. 28) – but not, for some reason, as a limit on the effectiveness of novels.

10   Carroll ("Art, Narrative, and Moral Understanding," p. 146) points out that we do not need *fictional* examples to persuade us that, for example, power corrupts, or no one should be called happy until he is dead: the real world offers us quite enough case studies.

11   "Wommenes counseils been ful ofte colde [fatal]; / Wommenes counseil broghte us first to wo, / And made Adam fro Paradys to go" (ll. 490–92). Admittedly, the nun's priest goes on to disclaim the allegation, hiding behind his character: "Thise been the cokkes wordes, and nat mine; / I can noon [no] harm of no womman divyne" (ll. 499–500). But this is presumably only for the benefit of his patron, the prioress. Nothing in the context suggests that it was Chauntecleer speaking.

12   Cf. Edward Wheatley, *Mastering Aesop: Medieval Education, Chaucer, and His Followers* (Gainesville, FL: University Press of Florida, 2000), pp. 112–13.

13   But al for noght; I sette noght an hawe [I don't give a fig]
Of his proverbes n'of his olde sawe,
Ne I wolde nat of him corrected be.
I hate him that my vices telleth me,
And so do mo, God woot, of us than I.

(*Wife of Bath*, ll. 659–63)

14   As Susan Gallick claims ("Styles of Usage in the *Nun's Priest's Tale*," *Chaucer Review* 11 (1977): 232–47, at p. 244).

15   For two variants, see Holbrook, "The Nonne Presstes Tale," pp. 122–3, and A. Paul Shallers, "The 'Nun's Priest's Tale': An Ironic Exemplum," *ELH* 42 (1975): 319–37, at p. 327.

16   Myers describes (but does not endorse) this reading. See Myers, "Focus and 'Moralite'," pp. 210–11.

17   Peter W. Travis lays out and also critiques this interpretation in his "Reading Chaucer *Ab Ovo*: Mock-*Exemplum* in the *Nun's Priest's Tale*," in Lawrence M. Clopper et al., eds., *The Performance of Middle English Culture: Essays on Chaucer and the Drama in Honor of Martin Stevens* (Cambridge: D. S. Brewer, 1998), pp. 170–73.

18   For the rooster as negative exemplum, see (among others) Holbrook, "The Nonne Presstes Tale;" and Lenaghan, "The Nun's Priest's Fable," *PMLA* 78 (1963): 300–307. Some critics (Lenaghan again, and Myers, "Focus and 'Moralite'," pp. 219–20) view the nun's priest himself as the key negative example – but they are still arguing for the moral effectiveness of fictions (in this case, Chaucer's, as opposed to the fiction-within-a-fiction of the nun's priest). Chaucer appears to head off even this higher-level exemplarity when he has the host, Harry Bailly, respond in the basest physical terms to the nun's priest's story (see the epigraph to this section). Those most in need of improvement, Chaucer seems to feel, are also those most indifferent to moral tales.

19   Richard Rorty describes his brand of Pragmatism as "urging that we try to extend our sense of 'we' to people whom we have previously thought of as 'they'" (*Contingency, Irony, and Solidarity*, Cambridge: Cambridge University Press, 1989, p. 192). "That is why," he continues, "detailed descriptions of particular varieties of pain and humiliation (in, e.g., novels or ethnographies), rather than philosophical or religious treatises, [are] the modern intellectual's principal contributions to moral progress." (See also pp. 94–5.)

20   See Gregory Currie, "Realism of Character and the Value of Fiction," in Jerrold Levinson, ed., *Aesthetics and Ethics: Essays at the Intersection* (Cambridge: Cambridge University Press, 1998), pp. 163, 166, 173; "The Moral Psychology of Fiction," *Australasian Journal of Philosophy* 73/2 (1995): 250–59, pp. 251, 257. Kendall Walton has also been tempted by this view: see "Morals in Fiction and Fictional Morality," *Proceedings of Mind Supplementary* 68 (1994): 26–50, p. 34 (and for the general simulation view see Walton, "Spelunking, Simulation, and Slime: On Being Moved by Fiction," in Mette Hjort and Sue Laver, eds., *Emotion and the Arts*, Oxford: Oxford University Press, pp. 37–49). For Socratism in Nussbaum, cf. Posner, "Against Ethical Criticism," p. 10.

21   Nussbaum sometimes takes a more Rortyan line, writing that "works of art can cut through our tendencies to deny humanity to our fellow human beings" ("Invisibility and Recognition: Sophocles' Philoctetes and Ellison's Invisible Man," *Philosophy and Literature* 23 (1999): 257–83, p. 265.) Cf. Nussbaum, "Exactly and Responsibly: A Defense of Ethical Criticism,"

Philosophy and Literature 22 (1998): 343–65, pp. 350, 356; and *Poetic Justice: The Literary Imagination and Public Life* (Boston, MA: Beacon Press, 1995), p. 39. Her reading of Ralph Ellison's *Invisible Man* is a Rortyan one. It is an open question to what extent the two outlooks are compatible, given that, as Eileen John points out, there is no need for subtlety – subtlety can, indeed, be a positive *obstacle* – when it comes to addressing problems like racism (John, "Subtlety and Moral Vision in Fiction," *Philosophy and Literature* 19 (1995): 308–19, pp. 314, 318). For another critique of Nussbaum, see Peter Lamarque and Stein Haugom Olsen, *Truth, Fiction, and Literature* (Oxford: Oxford University Press, 1996), pp. 386–97.

22 Wayne C. Booth, "Why Banning Ethical Criticism is a Serious Mistake," *Philosophy and Literature* 222 (1998): 366–93, pp. 378–9.

23 Ibid., p. 374. It is true that Booth's definition of "ethics" is so broad as to encompass, apparently, all of human activity ("*Vision? Powerful?* Again ethical language," p. 392); under such a description, ethics does indeed appear "inescapable." On the other hand, the examples Booth gives of ethical improvement through fiction – such as recognizing the humanity of other racial groups (p. 337) – tend to be standardly (and narrowly) moral.

24 Carroll, "Art, Narrative, and Moral Understanding," pp. 154–5. My emphasis.

25 Martha Nussbaum, *Poetic Justice: The Literary Imagination and Public Life* (Boston, MA: Beacon Press, 1995), p. 10. Cf. "the novel . . . is a morally controversial form, expressing in its very shape and style, in its modes of interaction with its readers, a normative sense of life" (p. 2). Mind you, Nussbaum does claim, later in the article, that "[her] argument is confined to a narrow group of pre-selected works" ("Exactly and Responsibly," p. 346) – by which she presumably means Anglo-American realist novels dealing with "social and political themes" (*Poetic Justice*, p. 10).

26 Nusssbaum, "Invisibility and Recognition," p. 278.

27 Thus Nussbaum believes that novels will only affect us when their influence is beneficial: "Reading can lead us to alter some of our standing judgments, but it is also the case that these judgments can cause us to reject some experiences of reading as deforming or pernicious" (*Poetic Justice*, p. 10). If, however, our standing judgments are sufficiently well formed as to be up to the task of rejecting pernicious reading material, why do they need to be altered? And if they need altering, how do they manage to ward off Sade and Riefenstahl?

Relatedly, Gregory Currie argues that simulation through fiction can have two effects on our moral outlook:

> projecting myself into the life of another has, potentially, the double function of telling me about his mental life and about my own possible future course of action; whatever I do, I had better make sure that things don't turn out *that* way for me. These are two potential functions of imaginative projection. Both of them have a moral significance. In empathizing with others I come to share their mental states, which powerfully reinforces my tendency to take their interests into account . . . And the same process makes the actions and

outcomes of others guides to my own planning. ("Realism of Character and the Value of Fiction," p. 169)

Again, there is an asymmetry. If the empathy and aversion (Aristotle might call them "fear" and "pity," but Currie does not) are to serve *moral* purposes, then surely our empathy must be directed towards deserving individuals, our aversion towards suspect characters. But how, if we are not already properly disposed, do we make the distinction? What is to stop us empathizing with villains, and thus reinforcing our tendency to take the interests of mafiosi (*Goodfellas*) and child abusers (*Lolita*) into account? Conversely, what if I watch a dramatization of the life of Christ and decide that I had better make sure that things don't turn out that way for me?

Currie's optimism here is all the more surprising when one considers what he wrote on the subject of empathy three years earlier: "In order to defeat my enemy I may need to simulate his mental operations, so as to know what he will do. That need not make me like him any better" ("The Moral Psychology of Fiction," p. 257). There are clearly two Curries, one who believes that simulation evolved because it helped us to become "better social creatures" ("The Paradox of Caring," in Hjort and Laver, eds., *Emotion and the Arts*, pp. 63–77, at p. 72), and another – red in tooth and claw – who knows that simulation also makes us more effective *fighters*.

28   "If the work's obnoxious message does not destroy its aesthetic value, it nevertheless renders it morally inaccessible. That must count as an aesthetic as well as a moral defect." (Walton, "Morals in Fiction and Fictional Morality," p. 30) Notice that only the beauty of "obnoxious" works is inaccessible, not that of (say) sanctimonious works.

29   Tamar Gendler, "The Puzzle of Imaginative Resistance," *Journal of Philosophy* 97 (2000): 55–81, at p. 58.

30   Gendler's version of imaginative resistance is, to be fair, the most convincing, precisely because she rules such cases out of court: as long as it does not look like I am being invited to "export" the deviant value system to the real world, she writes, I do not feel it necessary to resist (ibid., p. 73–4). Still, one wonders how many works are left once we apply this restriction. How many Sade-like cases are there, in which an author tries to force real-world depravity upon us by fictional means? And even here, is it really moral squeamishness that makes us resist? As I will argue below, it is just as easy for me to resist excessively *pious* fictions – even those with whose values my real-world self agrees.

31   Perhaps we do not always imaginatively endorse murder while watching, say, *Goodfellas*. But I believe we do imaginatively endorse theft, larceny, bank robbery, fraud, and so on while watching *The Sting*, *Butch Cassidy and the Sundance Kid*, and so on for any number of outlaw films. And the conclusion of *Silence of the Lambs* leaves us, quite curiously, feeling glad for Hannibal Lecter that he has secured himself a meal (of human flesh).

32 Conversely, I am not convinced that our imaginative resistance drops so dramatically when it comes to facts. When philosophers discuss this question, they naturally tend to think in terms of impossible propositions ("six times two is not twelve") which we are, they say, perfectly happy to imagine. But these are not the interesting cases. Instead, we should be thinking in terms of *internal* infringement: events, that is, which break the laws of the fictional world (or genre) itself, rather than (or in addition to) natural laws. Thus when a dozen machine guns are all firing continuously, from different angles, upon a hero whom we admire for his ingenuity, and he escapes death because somehow every single bullet misses its target, we may very well cease (temporarily) to make-believe the world presented.

33 Gendler ("The Puzzle of Imaginative Resistance," p. 77) suggests that cowboy films reduce our moral outrage by making the victims appear (objectively) to deserve their fate. The mummy-denying rationalist, however, only deserves his fate by the standards of the topsy-turvy worldview internal to the fiction. Objectively speaking, the rationalist is an innocent, and we should, on the Humean account, be resisting with all our might. I would suggest that much of what goes on in outlaw films (think, for example, of the Mexican police massacred, to our great satisfaction, by Butch Cassidy and the Sundance Kid) follows a similar pattern.

Compare Currie: "The lovers in *The Postman Always Rings Twice* are not very appealing examples of humankind, but most of us manage some sort of identification with their murderous project" ("The Paradox of Caring," p. 74). Nor is such misplaced empathy limited to such extreme cases, according to Currie. "We frequently take the part of people in fiction whom we could not like or take the part of in real life," he writes, citing the example of a novel about Oxbridge dons competing for the position of master. "The way I care," he continues, "seems at odds with the kind of person I am" (p. 65). Currie, however, takes this empathetic engagement to have positive moral effects (pp. 72–3). One wonders quite how this is supposed to work in the two cases just mentioned, and countless more like them.

34 Cf. Thomas G. Pavel, *Fictional Worlds* (Cambridge, MA: Harvard University Press, 1986), pp. 85, 90, 92.

35 Cf. Posner, "Against Ethical Criticism: Part Two," p. 404. And Eileen John: "Works of fiction do not provide 'normal' perceptual fields, and readers do not approach them with 'normal' perceptual habits" ("Subtlety and Moral Vision in Fiction," p. 309).

36 Daniel Jacobson points out that a tear-jerker may (inadvertently) *preclude* the kind of empathy I might very well feel in a real-life situation (Daniel Jacobson, "In Praise of Immoral Art," *Philosophical Topics* 25 (1997): 155–99, p. 186). Richard Moran also acknowledges that moralizing fictions are a prime source of imaginative resistance ("The Expression of Feeling in Imagination," *Philosophical Review* 103 (1994): 75–106, p. 99). Still, Moran sees such fictions as inspiring resistance by precluding

autonomous judgment on the part of their consumers, not by proposing standards to which the latter do not aspire. When it comes to this second type of resistance (p. 105) – resistance, that is, to specific implied norms, rather than to a general sense of coercion – Moran clearly thinks in terms of norms that are deficiently rather than excessively moral. Thus the prime example he gives is the difficulty we would experience if faced with a variant of *Macbeth* in which Duncan's murder "was unfortunate only for having interfered with Macbeth's sleep" (p. 95). He thus rejoins Walton, it seems to me, on this point.

37   Of course, there are plenty who believe that *Clarissa* is improving and *Goodfellas* harmful. But this view leaves me skeptical. If my mental capacities are so ill-formed as to leave me at the mercy of *Goodfellas*, so that I am easily led to conclude that it is excellent to kill and dreadful to report crimes, then why should I be trusted to draw the appropriate lessons from *Clarissa?*

38   Diderot, "Eloge de Richardson," *Oeuvres Complètes*, vol. 5 (Paris: Le Club Français du Livre), pp. 127–46, at p. 128. The hypothesis of lurking irony may gain some support from Diderot's remark, in the *Paradoxe sur le Comédien* (Paris: Flammarion, 1981) about the citizen who leaves his vices at the door only to "take them up again on the way out. There he is just, impartial, a good father, a good friend, a friend of virtue; and I have often seen wicked men next to me taking deep umbrage at actions which they would not have failed to commit if they had found themselves in the same circumstances" (p. 167, my translation). Although the speaker is officially "the first interlocutor," he is clearly identified as Diderot at p. 147.

39   Cf. an odd, possibly inadvertent, admission from Booth: "Thus in our moments of actual reading we are led to become quite different from who we are *when we put down the book*." ("Why Banning Ethical Criticism is a Serious Mistake," p. 378, my emphasis). And Posner, more deliberately: "one of the pleasures that literature does engender in its readers . . . is the pleasure of imagining utopian resolutions of the conflicts that beset the human condition. I just don't think this pleasure translates into action" ("Against Ethical Criticism: Part Two," p. 411 n. 14).

40   Thus Rousseau writes, in his *Lettre à d'Alembert* – d'Alembert being famous for asking, after a performance of Racine's *Bérénice*, "qu'est-ce que cela *prouve?*" – that the best tragedies "reduce all the duties of man to some passing and sterile emotions that have no consequences, to make us applaud . . . our humanity in pitying the ills that we could have cured" (quoted in Jacobson, "In Praise of Immoral Art," p. 156). And

Tom Stoppard once said that if you see an injustice taking place outside your window, the least useful thing you can do is to write a play about it. I would go further, suggesting that there is something wrong in writing plays about that sort of injustice in which we have an obligation to intervene, since it puts the audience at just the sort of distance the concept of psychic distance means to describe." (Arthur Danto, *The Transfiguration of the Commonplace*, Cambridge, MA: Harvard University Press, 1981, p. 22)

41 Nussbaum, "Exactly and Responsibly," p. 360.

42 Ibid., pp. 344, 361.

43 It is, in general, a curious fact that those who spend their time reading great literature appear to be no more moral than anyone else (Posner, "Against Ethical Criticism," p. 5). Nussbaum's response – that "professors of litera-ture are often jaded and detached," and "don't read with the freshness and responsiveness of ordinary readers" ("Exactly and Responsibly," p. 353) – presumably does not apply to Nussbaum herself, whose passion for James remains palpably undiminished.

44 Cf. Posner, "Against Ethical Criticism," p. 18.

45 Carroll, "Art, Narrative, and Moral Understanding," p. 133. Suzanne Keen's recent work confirms this. After performing an exhaustive survey of empirical studies on reading, empathy, and altruism, she concludes that "the link between narrative empathy and altruism is . . . tenuous" ("A Theory of Narrative Empathy," *Narrative* 14 (2006): 207–36, at p. 212).

46 "Exactly and Responsibly," p. 353.

47 "The artist can assist us by cutting through the blur of habit and the self-deceptions habit abets . . . When we follow him as attentive readers, we our-selves engage in ethical conduct, and our readings themselves are accessible ethical acts" ("Exactly and Responsibly," p. 344); "our own attention to his characters will itself, if we read well, be a high case of moral attention" (" 'Finely Aware and Richly Responsible': Literature and the Moral Imagination," in Anthony J. Cascardi, ed., *Literature and the Question of Philosophy*, Baltimore, MD: Johns Hopkins University Press, 1987, pp. 167–91, at p. 186). Indeed "the *highest* task is to be people 'on whom nothing is lost' " (p. 169, my emphasis). Cf. Noël Carroll, who agrees, perhaps for com-parable reasons, that "Reading a novel . . . is itself generally a moral activity" ("Art, narrative, and moral understanding," p. 145).

48 "Exactly and Responsibly," p. 355.

49 Ibid.

50 Bob and Fanny Assingham, writes Nussbaum, "perform the function, more or less, of a Greek tragic chorus. 'Participants by fond attention' just as we are . . . , they perform, together, an activity of attending and judging and interpreting that is parallel to ours, if even more deeply immersed and implicated" (" 'Finely Aware and Richly Responsible'," p. 181) One has to wonder: if Fanny Assingham is "even more deeply immersed and implicated" than we are, and yet even she takes an "aestheticizing" attitude (ibid.) towards Maggie and company, then what chance do we readers have?

To be fair, Nussbaum does acknowledge that Fanny "takes fine-tuned perception to a dangerously rootless extreme" and "delights in the complexity of these particulars for its own sake, without sufficiently feeling the pull of a moral obligation to any" (" 'Finely Aware and Richly Responsible'," pp. 181–2). Yet this moral obligation is precisely what Nussbaum claims, over and over again, is "constructed" (*Poetic Justice*, p. 10), "awakened" ("Invisibility and Recognition," p. 278), "shaped" ("Exactly and

Responsibly," p. 353) by novels like *The Golden Bowl*. I shall return at the end of this essay to how the core of Nussbaum's view can be saved, with important modifications.

51 On this point, see Eileen John, "Henry James: Making Moral Life Interesting," *Henry James Review* 18 (1997): 234–42, at pp. 236–8.

52 See e.g., Eileen John "Reading Fiction and Conceptual Knowledge: Philosophical Thought in Literary Context," *Journal of Aesthetics and Art Criticism* 56/4 (1998): 331–48, at p. 343. For a position closer to mine, see Onora O'Neill, "The Power of Example," *Philosophy* 61 (1986): 5–29 (especially pp. 9, 18).

53 Some might argue that Derek Parfit's examples constitute an exception. Others (myself included) would counter that many of his science fiction cases are so far-fetched as to be unreliable even as a guide to our own intuitions.

54 On this point, see Daniel Jacobson, "Sir Philip Sidney's Dilemma," *Journal of Aesthetics and Art Criticism* 54 (1996): 327–36, at p. 331.

55 This, I think, is the one lacuna in Jerome Stolnitz's argument: he overlooks the fact that philosophical ideas can come packaged in literary forms (Parmenides, Berkeley, Nietzsche). Ironically, he cites Plato as having complained that artists do not have first-hand knowledge of their topic ("On the Cognitive Triviality of Art," p. 198) – forgetting that this complaint is uttered, in the *Ion*, by a *fictional character* ("Socrates").

56 Nussbaum considers *The Golden Bowl* a "persuasive argument that these features hold of human life in general" ("Flawed Crystals: James's *The Golden Bowl* and Literature as Moral Philosophy," *New Literary History* 15 (1983): 25–50, at p. 41). It is an argument *a fortiori*: if even the virtuous Maggie sees that the bowl is broken, then it must be broken for everyone. But its force depends on seeing a literary character's journey from birth to death as a "human life" (ibid.), and fiction as a straightforward extension of reality (" 'Finely Aware and Richly Responsible'," p. 180).

57 For the unpleasant consequences of sucking one's thumb, see Heinrich Hoffmann, "The Story of Little Suck-a-Thumb," *Struwwelpeter* (1845).

58 In Rousseau's words, "they are taught less to let [the cheese] fall from their beaks than to make it fall from the beak of another." (Rousseau, *Emile, or, On Education*, trans. Allan Bloom, New York: Basic Books, 1979, p. 115) Rousseau also cites *La Cigale et la Fourmi*, in which an industrious ant refuses assistance to an indolent cricket. Children, says Rousseau, take it to be recommending not that they be less indolent (like the cricket) but rather that they refuse assistance (like the ant). Nor does this situation always come to an end with childhood: consider the fact that the film *All Quiet on the Western Front* was actually used as propaganda by the military in the 1940s (Bill Broyles, Jr., "Flix For Warniks," *On the Media*, NPR, November 4, 2005); consider also the strange situation in 1943 Paris, when Anouilh staged *Antigone* as a protest against occupation, and the Germans allowed it because they read it as a paean to Creon (Bernard Knox, "Introduction," *Sophocles: The Three Theban Plays*, trans. Robert Fagles. New York: Viking Press, 1982, p. 22).

In this last case, both sides were wrong, guilty of a deep misunderstanding about Sophocles' play (on which more below).

59   See Thucydides, *History of the Peloponnesian War*, trans. Rex Warner (London: Penguin, 2003), 3:37–48.

60   Cf. Michael Tanner, "Morals in Fiction and Fictional Morality," *Proceedings of Mind Supplementary* 68 (1994): 51–66, at p. 62.

61   Of course, the concomitant danger is that of censorship: if we rely on fictions for the moral education of our youth, then we will be forced to regulate its content.

62   It is often (and correctly) noted of Emma Bovary that she makes the mistake of deriving her opinions on love from novels. What is less often seen is that her interests, during her convent years, keep *changing*. She, too, is easily swayed from one value to another, from adventure to history to mysticism:

> Couriers were killed at every relay, horses ridden to death on every page; there were gloomy forests, broken hearts, vows, sobs, tears and kisses, skiffs in the moonlight, nightingales in thickets; the noblemen were all brave as lions, gentle as lambs, incredibly virtuous, always beautifully dressed, and wept copiously on every occasion. *For six months*, when she was fifteen, Emma begrimed her hands with this dust from old lending libraries. *Later*, reading Walter Scott, she became infatuated with everything historical and dreamed about oaken chests and guardrooms and troubadours . . . *When her mother died* . . . she let herself meander along Lamartinian paths, listening to the throbbing of harps on lakes, to all the songs of the dying swans, to the falling of every leaf, to the flight of pure virgins ascending to heaven, and to the voice of the Eternal speaking in the valleys. *Gradually these things began to bore her* . . . (Gustave Flaubert, *Madame Bovary*, trans. Francis Steegmuller, New York: Random House, 1992, pp. 43, 45; my emphasis)

I am, of course, aware of the irony involved in citing *Madame Bovary* in the context of the present argument, and hope I will not be taken as implying that Flaubert's novel has the power to change the minds of its readers, neatly converting them from Bovarysts to anti-Bovarysts. The fact that today's advocates of a fiction-rich diet are themselves almost certain to have read *Madame Bovary* at some point in their lives speaks, in my opinion, for itself.

63   "Invisibility and Recognition," p. 274.

64   Thus Nussbaum claims not only that Ralph Ellison helps us to understand "how a history of racial stereotyping can affect self-esteem, achievement, and love" but also that "Ellison's work conveys this understanding through in the pleasure that it imparts" ("Invisibility and Recognition," p. 267). Any dangerous pleasure we risk deriving from the narrative is thus mercifully redeemed by being put to an honorable end.

65   "In a genre such as the novel, a turning away from traditional political concerns to private concerns and formal experimentation is awfully likely to express a wish to avoid some unpleasant social reality," Nussbaum writes ("Invisibility and Recognition," p. 280), echoing her earlier claim that Posner selects

his reading material so as to shelter himself from "the claim of a painful reality" ("Exactly and Responsibly," p. 361). As always, a healthy moral concern – indeed an obsessive and exclusive moral concern, ruling every aspect of our life – is presumed to be where we *start*; amoral areas of our life are carved out *later*, by willed acts of irresponsibility. The novel is, by default, about "traditional political concerns," and only subsequently perverted to private matters. Nussbaum may perhaps have a point when it comes to Virginia Woolf (as long as we overlook the feminist overtones of, say, *Mrs Dalloway*, and references to the War in *Jacob's Room*), but one does wonder what she would say about (say) Samuel Beckett, a formalist who served in the Resistance.

66   Cf. M. M. Bakhtin, *Rabelais and his World*, trans. Hélène Iswolsky (Bloomington, IN: Indiana University Press, 1988).

67   Posner, "Against Ethical Criticism," p. 20.

68   On this point, see also Harold Bloom, *How to Read and Why* (New York: Scribner, 2000) p. 22. See also Carroll: "the successful narrative becomes the occasion for exercising knowledge, concepts, and emotions that we have already, in one sense, learned;" "in mobilizing what we already know and what we can already feel, the narrative artwork can become an occasion for us to deepen our understanding of what we know and what we feel." ("Art, Narrative, and Moral Understanding," pp. 141, 142) Carroll, however, believes that clarification can easily lead to "re-gestalting," and thus profound "moral reform" (pp. 143, 149). In my view this is a little too optimistic. Even if re-gestalting does result directly from engagement with literary texts (which I doubt), there is certainly no guarantee that it will operate in the direction of increased altruism. As in almost all writings on ethical criticism, the assumption is that engagement with high art can only improve us if it changes us at all. Dostoevsky knows better.

69   Cf. Currie, "Realism of Character and the Value of Fiction," pp. 163, 174. Walton writes that we judge characters by our everyday moral standards, no matter what the genre ("Morals in Fiction and Fictional Morality," p. 37); this claim seems unwarranted to me, for reasons I have already articulated.

70   "Of all the masterpieces of the classical and the modern world," Hegel famously writes, "the *Antigone* seems to me to be the most magnificent and satisfying work of art of this kind" (G. W. F. Hegel, *Aesthetics*, vol. 2, trans. T. M. Knox, Oxford: Oxford University Press, 1975, p. 1218); "the heroes of Greek classical tragedy are confronted by circumstances in which, after firmly identifying themselves with the one ethical 'pathos' which alone corresponds to their own already established nature, they necessarily come into conflict with the opposite but equally justified ethical power." (p. 1226) (On Robert Pippin's interpretation, perhaps even *The Golden Bowl* fits this Hegelian model. See Robert B. Pippin, *Henry James and Modern Moral Life*, Cambridge: Cambridge University Press, 2000.)

It would be hard to see the *Antigone* as seeking to equip us with "fine awareness:" surely we already understand the duties we have to our family and to the larger community, and even the fact that they cannot all be satisfied at once. What the play does, instead, is make us think hard about the relative *strength* of their claims on us, and how we wish to adjudicate between them in cases of conflict. In the end, a *hierarchy of values* may well be of more use to us than the most finely tuned intuitions.

71   In some general sense, it might be true that prejudice rests on stereotypes and a certain distance from the reality of particular lives, and that gripping literary accounts of such individuals might begin to make one uneasy about one's prejudices, but if the novel is not very good (like, in my view at least, Dickens's saccharine *Hard Times*, and like other novels out to make such a point) it is just as likely that 'the individual' presented will instantiate just another Christian cliché, the good-hearted worker uncorrupted by power and money, or that the villains will be stereotypes, and one's moral reaction . . . itself will be stereotypical, will amount to a self-satisfied feeling that because one has rejected Grandgrind, one has a good heart, that one's sympathies are all in the right place. (Robert B. Pippin, " 'The Felt Necessities of the Time': Literature, Ethical Knowledge, and Law," *Ars Interpretandi* 7 (2002): 71–90, at p. 83)

72   Misguided readers, writes Milan Kundera, "seek at the novel's core not an inquiry but a moral position" (*The Art of the Novel*, trans. Linda Asher, New York: Grove Press, 1988, p. 7). For in reality, "the novel's spirit is the spirit of complexity. Every novel says to the reader: 'Things are not as simple as you think.' That is the novel's eternal truth, but it grows steadily harder to hear amid the din of easy, quick answers" (p. 18). Compare Bakhtin, who privileges "heteroglot" novels (M. M. Bakhtin, *The Dialogic Imagination*, trans. Caryl Emerson and Michael Holquist, Austin, TX, and London: University of Texas Press, 1981, p. 278); Putnam, in whose view literature serves not to "depict solutions" but rather to "aid us in the imaginative re-creation of moral perplexities" (Hilary Putnam, "Literature, Science, and Reflection," *New Literary History* 7 (1976): 483–91, p. 485); and Harrison, whose narrator writes that "le mouvement affirmatif m'a toujours déçu, et m'a toujours fait revenir en courant à la littérature, comme en quête de perplexité. Avec la littérature, on ne peut chasser les incertitudes, puisqu'elles constituent la trame même du texte" (Robert Pogue Harrison, *Rome, la Pluie: A quoi Bon la Littérature?* Paris: Flammarion, 1994, p. 77).

73   Booth admits that "no story will produce changes in readers unless they are already in some respect susceptible to a given kind of influence" ("Why Banning Ethical Criticism is a Serious Mistake," p. 368); Currie writes that fictions, like electron microscopes, are best used by "those well able to benefit from them" ("Realism of Character and the Value of Fiction," p. 178); and Nussbaum recognizes the objection that "a person who is obtuse in life will also be an obtuse reader of James's text. How can literature show us or train

us in anything, when . . . the very moral qualities that make for good reading are the ones that are allegedly in need of development?" (" 'Finely Aware and Richly Responsible'," p. 187.)

Still, this does not stop Currie from claiming that fiction can take control over our minds ("Imagination and Simulation: Aesthetics Meets Cognitive Science," in Martin Davies and Tony Stone, eds., *Mental Simulation: Evaluations and Applications,* Oxford: Blackwell, 1995, pp. 151–69, at p. 163). Neither does it stop Nussbaum from insisting – as we saw above – that "it is impossible to care about the characters and their fate in the way the text invites, without having some very definite political and moral interests awakened in oneself" ("Invisibility and Recognition," p. 278).

4

EMPATHY, EXPRESSION, AND WHAT ARTWORKS HAVE TO TEACH

Mitchell Green

1   Introduction

A work of art such as a novel or movie can convey propositional knowledge, such as that pride comes before a fall, war is hell, or nice guys finish
last. On some theories, works of art such as photographs convey perceptual
knowledge: one view, for instance, has it that a photograph enables us
literally to see the object of which it is a photo. I take these cases as comparatively familiar, and while they remain a source of controversy, I will
only be glancing at those disputes here. Rather, I wish to argue that in
addition to their capacity to convey propositional and perceptual knowledge, some works of art can also convey phenomenal knowledge and/or
affective knowledge: these forms of knowledge are, respectively, knowledge of how some object or state of affairs looks, sounds, smells, etc; and
knowledge of how an emotion or mood feels. I don't claim that only
works of art do this; nor do I claim that the works of art that convey
phenomenal or affective knowledge only do this. I do contend that their
ability to convey phenomenal or affective knowledge is an important dimension of what works of art do, and it is a dimension that has not been
adequately appreciated either in aesthetics or the philosophy of mind. In
particular, I shall argue that an adequate appreciation of these two
aspects of the epistemic value of works of art sheds light on (1) artistic
expression, and (2) empathy.

2   Three Forms of Showing

I will elucidate the notion of expression, or those aspects of this notion
that will be pertinent to our purposes, in terms of the commonsense notion

of showing. This latter comes, so far as I can tell, in three forms. First of all, I might show my courage by acting bravely. My brave behavior is good evidence of my courage. Or I might, by means of extensive calculations, show *that* there is a black hole in the center of the Milky Way. In these cases I don't make what I show perceptible; I certainly couldn't make the black hole perceptible, and it is not clear what it could mean to perceive courage. Rather, in these cases I provide compelling evidence for a conclusion that could be grasped even by someone with no capacity for vision or other sensation. A grammatical tag for this category is *showing-that*. Because my brave behavior (calculations, etc.) is good evidence of my courage (the existence of the black hole, etc.), an appropriately situated thinker aware of that evidence is in a position to know of my courage (of the black hole, etc.). Showing-that thus enables propositional knowledge.

Secondly, I might show something in such a way as to make it perceptible. I show my bruise, and thereby enable others to see that bruise. Although it is most natural to speak of showing in visual terms, showing is not limited to vision: one can show someone a rough texture (you would need to feel the texture) or a coyote's howl (you would have to hear it). What I show you in this sense depends on your perceptual capacities and your position in the environment. If you had electroreception like a hammerhead shark, I could show you the electrical activity in the body of a fish hiding under the sand. In that case you would not only perceive the fish, you would "electroreceive" it. Likewise, even if there are a few mice in the field, and some light bounces from them onto your retina, I don't show you them from an airplane passing 200 yards above the field. On the other hand, if you have the visual acuity of a hawk I might well do so. Let us put this perceptual-knowledge enabling form of showing under the rubric of *showing-α*, where "α" is a singular term referring to a perceptible object or affair.[1]

Finally, I might also *show how* something looks, feels, sounds, etc. Apply friction to a scratch-and-sniff picture of a skunk. You won't thereby smell any skunk, but if your nose is functioning properly, you will learn how skunks smell. By accurately painting Mary's profile you will show how Mary looks in profile – what she looks like from that angle – thereby enabling me to know how Mary's profile looks. I can then manifest this knowledge by reliably discriminating the Mary-like profiles from the rest. Similarly – and in a way to be explored more fully below – the trepidation in my voice might enable you to know how my anxiety feels if you are sufficiently empathetic. If you are sufficiently empathetic, then hearing my voice may enable you to imagine feeling my anxiety. If you can reliably do that, then you know how I feel. Showing-how can provide qualitative knowledge for those with appropriate sensory capacities. It can also enable empathy for those with the capacity for empathy.

Again, someone might show me how to imagine a chocolate mountain by describing what it would look like, and if I follow that description I might then be able to imagine it. If I do that, then I will know how a chocolate mountain would look even if I have never seen one. In a similar way the old bluegrass song about the Big Rock Candy Mountain both invites and enables us to imagine such a thing, and by means of its descriptions enables us to know what such a thing would look like, how it would feel to the touch, etc.[2] Oenological description of a merlot that you've never tasted can still enable you to imagine that taste, and can enable you to know how that wine would taste were you to have a mouthful of the stuff. Again, a novelist might enable me to imagine being ostracized within a small rural community. Jane Hamilton does this in her *A Map of the World*.[3] In its skillful depictions of various conversations, tones of voice, facial expressions, etc., of characters, Hamilton shows us what a sense of social isolation feels like. She does this by enabling me to imagine being in that situation, and thereby enables me to know how I would feel if I were in that situation. Even if I have never felt ostracized, the excellence of the novel consists at least in part in its ability to show me how ostracism would feel. We'll return to this point later in our discussion of empathy.

One thread that unites the above cases is justification: evidence, either from the senses or from other forms of knowledge, enables those who are shown the things mentioned above, and who are in the right circumstances (being empathetic, being in the right perceptual location, possessed of the right background knowledge, etc.) to know some fact, some object of perception, or how some emotion, mood, or experience feels. This can happen whether or not any appropriate observers cotton on. I can show you my melanoma without your grasping the significance of what you see; as a result I might show it to you without your appreciating that you are seeing melanoma. Likewise I might amass evidence that taken as a whole implicates the basketball coach in the crime; the evidence might then show that the coach did it without my seeing its significance.

3   Showing How and Knowing How

So whatever shows me how to do something, or how something feels, also makes knowledge available to me. However, such knowledge is *knowledge how* rather than *knowledge that*. I urge you to join me in rejecting Ryle's form of behaviorism, both as a positive doctrine and as an attempt to dissolve the traditional problems of mind and body. Doing so does not, however, mandate rejection of his view that knowing how is a distinctive form of knowledge not reducible to propositional knowledge. Instead that view is independently plausible and marks a valuable distinction among forms of knowledge.[4]

You teach me how to do something, and if I am doing my job as a student I will come to know how to do it. You might codify that lesson in a book or in some other artifact. A geometry book will show me how to prove a theorem. If I grasp what it teaches then I will know how to prove that theorem. A recipe book will show me how to cook a soufflé. Here too if I grasp what it teaches I will know how to cook a soufflé. In both cases, reading the book might not be enough for me to learn how; I may have to practice the theorem or soufflé a few times before I get it right. Know-how is often only possible with some practice.

Consistent with our pattern thus far, a painting might show me how a certain man's hair is colored, and if I have appropriate perceptual apparatus I will thereby learn how it is colored. That is only possible if the sitter's hair is so colored, and only if the painter and other aspects of the transmission of information are reliable. If all these conditions are in place, then I can learn how that man's hair is colored. If I retain this knowledge I will be able to discriminate this color from others. That is a skill that I might retain for a while and then lose, and when I lose that skill it will no longer be true that I know the color of the man's hair except, at best, propositionally ("It's russet"). Further, if I learn what his hair looks like, then I might be able to visualize that color in the absence both of him and of his picture. However, this ability to visualize is not a necessary condition of my knowing that color. (I know what sulfur smells like without at this moment being able "olfactorily" to image that smell; the same goes for my current inability to form an image of chartreuse.) We will see below that just as empathizing is something that we do rather than something that befalls us, to empathize with another it is not enough that we have had some experience of what they are going through. In addition to knowing what they are going through, we must "feel with them." The hard work comes in knowing how to elucidate the expression with which I've just shuddered.

If a painting does not accurately and reliably portray the color of a man's hair, then it might not convey knowledge of what his hair looks like. However, even if it does not do so, it may still provide me with qualitative knowledge, and thereby a skill, because it exemplifies the qualitative information that it also represents. It enables me to know what russet looks like because in looking at it I perceive that color, and because, in general, that perceptual experience will in turn enable me later on to discriminate that color from others. As a result, if I've never seen russet before, I learn something new. Further, even if I know what russet looks like, this painting can activate that knowledge in such a way as to provide me with the ability to visualize that color in its absence. So a painting can both provide knowledge-how and enable me to bring what I know into consciousness.

Can a work of literature, in spite of being fictional, convey know-how? I shall argue that it can, but let us first take a moment to note how literary works can convey propositional knowledge. Compare them with the case of bumper stickers: a Jesus-fish-eating-a-Darwin-lizard is not going to convince anyone not already converted to creationism. It conveys opinion, not knowledge. The same is true of the biblical story of Lot and his wife. If you are not already convinced that gloating over someone else's downfall will turn you either literally or metaphorically into a pillar of salt, then that story is not going to give you a reason for thinking that such behavior will do so. By contrast, consider a Zen koan, a very short story, that goes like this:

> Tanzan and Ekido were once traveling together down a muddy road. A heavy rain was still falling. Coming around a bend, they met a lovely girl in a silk kimono and sash, unable to cross the intersection. "Come on, girl," said Tanzan at once. Lifting her in his arms, he carried her over the mud. Ekido did not speak again until that night when they reached a lodging temple. Then he no longer could restrain himself. "We monks don't go near females," he told Tanzan, "especially not young and lovely ones. It is dangerous. Why did you do that?" "I left the girl there," said Tanzan. "Are you still carrying her?"[5]

This koan, known as Muddy Road, not only contains an implicit claim (roughly: sometimes it's better to break a rule and get on with it than it is to get hung up on a strict adherence to that rule), but also gives some basis for that claim. One sees the obvious reasonableness of the monk who carried the woman in contrast to that of the monk who challenges him. That is not to say that the story conveys an *a priori* truth. You have to have some background practical rationality, and some basic world knowledge (of things like puddles, and the human tendency to get hung up on the letter rather than the spirit of a rule). But if you have that rationality and that knowledge then the koan can teach you something new in the sense of drawing out a consequence that is implicit in that capacity and that knowledge.

The setting of a literary work is thus like a supposition entered in a Fitch-style natural deduction system.[6] We could, in fact, reconstrue Muddy Road, with little loss of content, in the form, "Suppose two monks were walking down a muddy path after a heavy rain . . ." Within the scope of that supposition the narrator argues down to the conclusion that the monk who carries the woman across the puddle better respects the spirit of the monastic prohibition against touching women than the monk who does not touch her. On that basis we may infer a conclusion no longer within the scope of the supposition, namely that there can be situations in which breaking a rule is a better way of adhering to its spirit than is adhering to the rule's letter. At this point, of course, we are not far removed from the structure of some counterexamples to certain species of rule-utilitarianism.

One might indeed be tempted to puzzle over how it is possible to get knowledge out of fiction. It may, after all, seem mysterious how an epistemic rabbit can be pulled from a make-believe hat. But supposing something for argument's sake is, in relevant respects, a form of fiction, too. Hence if one is puzzled how knowledge can be got out of fiction, one ought to be no less puzzled how knowledge can be got out of supposition for the sake of argument. Obviously, though, we know perfectly well how the latter is possible; if there is a problem about how knowledge can be got out of fiction, it does not arise merely from the *fictionality* of the work in question.

This is not to suggest that suppositions of the sort we use with formal systems are exactly the same as the suppositions I am suggesting we entertain in engagement with fiction. Any proposition already established can be reiterated into a subproof in a natural deduction system. By contrast, how much background knowledge we are expected to leave at the door of the fictional work is often signaled by the genre, and often by basic elements of the narrative structure. New Journalist fiction invites us to reiterate pretty much any of our background knowledge into the fiction; Magical Realism, by contrast, asks us to leave most of human psychology fixed but leaves us unsure how much physics we can presuppose. Perhaps most Western fiction of the last two centuries falls somewhere in between these two extremes.

A work of literature can show that something is the case beyond the fictional world it creates. Can a literary work also show how in a way that enables us to acquire a skill? Consider this series of examples.

1   Because of my sheltered life I might never have felt disgust toward anything. A movie might portray things that are disgusting to normal human

observers and thereby invoke disgust in me if I am normal. Disgust has a pretty well-established autonomic pattern of response that can be elicited in the absence of any belief that the disgusting object is real. (Just imagine an animated close-up of an open, deep, and infected wound, where the animation is not so realistic as to cause us to believe that we are seeing a real wound.) So the movie might be a fictional film and yet show me how disgust feels simply by eliciting that emotion in me. Simply by looking at the disgusting film I can acquire a skill, even if the film is overtly a work of fiction.

2   Most people who see gross movies have known disgust before. However, a further consequence of our example is that even if I am acquainted with disgust, the movie will activate that knowledge in me by reminding me of how it feels. By reminding me how disgust feels the movie enables me to image that feeling, for at least a little while after the filmic experience. (Presumably I'll have some inclination to suppress that knowledge as well.) It thereby reawakens a skill that had been dormant. As we'll see presently, that will in turn make me better able to "feel with" someone else who is going through the same thing.

3   When we read literature we are to imagine the scenes portrayed, a claim made plausible by J. O. Urmson.[7] To do this we are to visualize the things described, imagine hearing them, imagine touching them, and so on. Now suppose the novel we are reading incites us to imagine something quite disgusting. So long as our imaginative powers are sufficiently acute we can come to know disgust for the first time, or have that knowledge activated when it was merely dormant before.

By the time we have reached Case 3 above we have, I contend, found a case in which a literary work gives us knowledge of how disgust feels. More complex emotions are elicited by more sophisticated fictions. If I were that Zen monk who challenged the other for carrying the woman over the puddle, I would feel *embarrassed* by the answer given in the story. Further, if I identify with that monk in the following sense, then I might feel embarrassed as well: the sense in which I might identify with him is simply finding his question reasonable under those circumstances.[8] If I do that, then I will feel genuinely embarrassed by the other monk's answer so long as I am acute enough to discern the propriety of that answer. At one point I feel it reasonable to ask the other why he touched this woman, given a monastic proscription against doing so. After hearing his reply, I see the error in my adherence to rules in situations in which adherence does not serve the ends those rules were constructed to serve. Not only that, but I will feel embarrassed for not having realized that before. This is not quasi- or make-believe embarrassment. I, the student of the koan, will feel true embarrassment for having not foreseen the second monk's answer. That of course will show me how embarrassment feels. Not only that, but it activates my knowledge of how embarrassment feels so that even if I have been embarrassed in the past, my knowledge of that feeling is now brought to consciousness. As a result, if the first monk, the one who challenged the other, is embarrassed by his question (the koan does not say), I am in a position to identify with him.

In the film *The Rapture* (1991) the main character Sharon's husband is murdered by a disgruntled employee, and she sacrifices her own daughter after waiting in the desert for what she was sure would be a sign from God. Now the Apocalypse really does come and she ends up with the option of entering Heaven if only she will say, either aloud or in her heart, that she loves God. Sharon refuses to do so, however, and will remain in Purgatory for an unspecified amount of time. After witnessing what she has been through, some viewers feel they can understand why she feels the way she does. How could God have allowed these things to happen? This is to say that one can imagine being in Sharon's situation and feeling justified in refusing to accept God's love. This is in turn to say that on the basis of this fictional work one can identify with her. In this case, and in contrast to the case of the embarrassed monk, one need not feel resentment toward God in order to feel with the character. One can understand how she feels while feeling no resentment toward God, either because one is not a theist or because one takes a different attitude toward the problem of evil from hers.

Some forms of engagement with works of art, then, either convey or activate a skill, which itself has two dimensions. The first is simply a discriminatory capacity, such as the ability to identify russet or disgust or embarrassment when one sees or feels it. The second is the capacity to image that experience or feeling. This second ability can then, as we shall now see, be used to help feel with others. Showing how, then, enables the acquisition of cognitive, experiential, and affective skills, where the last of these consists in the ability to imagine having an emotion or mood of a certain kind. Showing how thus puts us in a position to know how, and, in the area of emotions and moods, thereby enables us to know how an emotion or mood feels.

4   Perceiving Aspects and Affects

We mentioned above that a painting or drawing shows some aspect of what it represents. It does not thereby enable us to perceive the thing represented, even when the thing represented is a perceptible object. Nevertheless a painting or drawing shows us, and thereby enables us to perceive, aspects of what it represents – the color of the sitter's hair, the pattern of his tie, the slope of his forehead, the strain in his face. So, too, when we look at a painting we can learn how certain things look – the color, the pattern, the slope, the strain.

This ability of works of art to teach us things no doubt depends upon there being a reliable causal connection between the thing represented and the pictorial representation itself. Again, if the painting or drawing is not of anything that is real, it is not clear that we learn from it any fact about what a particular thing looks like. The most that can be said is that from such a picture we can learn what a *kind* of thing looks like – a winged horse, an underwater city. Likewise, to the extent that the artist's depiction is influenced by her imaginative construction, the depiction does not convey knowledge of its subject matter (as opposed to knowledge about the artist). Thus if the painting is a conjectural reconstruction of the emperor Justinian being felled by a barbarian's arrow, then insofar as it is imaginative it will not convey knowledge of, for instance, how Justinian looked when he got hit, and in what way he fell.

Research in aesthetics often explains the expressive qualities of artifacts in terms of expressive behavior among human beings. The latter is then frequently left as an unexplained explainer; yet the notion of literal human expression hides some subtleties of its own. Consider the difference between my scowling and my coolly saying, "I'm angry." The scowl, at least if it is caused in the right way by a felt anger, shows my anger. It also expresses that anger. By contrast, the cool assertion, "I'm angry," reports my anger, but it is not plausible to describe it as either showing or expressing anger. Showing and expressing can be jointly instantiated, and some speech acts might exemplify neither. However, I wish here to argue for a stronger claim, namely that all cases of expression are also cases of showing.

As the example of scowling suggests, expression differs from representation at least in that the former involves making a state of the self palpable. This is reinforced by the term's origin in the Latin *exprimere*, meaning "to press out."[9] It is also reinforced by some paradigm usages. Consider a remark by Frederick Douglass as he recalls the songs he and his fellow slaves would sing while not working for their masters: "The mere recurrence to those songs, even now, afflicts me; and while I am writing these lines, an expression of feeling has already found its way down my cheek. To those songs I trace my first glimmering conception of the dehumanizing character of slavery."[10] The tear to which Douglass refers is an expression of feeling at least in part because it is a direct manifestation thereof. Likewise, in his *The Expression of Emotions in Man and Animals*, Charles Darwin speaks of expressive movements as revealing our thoughts and impressions more reliably and directly than do our words.[11] This comports with the fact that an expression of emotion or thought is more than an indication of that thought or emotion. Assuming indication is an evidential relation such that if A indicates B, A's presence increases the probability of B's occurrence, a construal of expression as indication would not be accurate. When I am angry my respiration increases, as a result of which I emit more CO_2 than is usual. An increase in CO_2 around my body is thus evidence – an indication in the present sense – of my anger. It is not, however, an expression of anger because its presence is compatible, even under normal circumstances, with many other etiologies. By contrast, in the absence of reasons to think that onions were being sliced near where Douglass was writing his memoirs, etc., the tear running down his cheek provides a good deal more evidence than mere indication.[12]

Again, to express my love I need to put the strength and depth of my feelings on the table – if at all possible in the form of a self-sacrificing act or pricey artifact. This, however, is just to say that to express a psychological state I must make that state knowable to an appropriate observer. Although the relation between expression and what is expressed is not always so straightforward as the relation between tears and grief, I suggest that one theme binding together different forms of expression is the ability of the expressive behavior or artifact to enable in an appropriate observer knowledge of what it expresses. We have seen that this is in contrast to indication. It is also in contrast to representation. Although some representations are produced by sufficiently reliable causal chains to enable knowledge of what they represent, a representation of a state of affairs is not, *per se*, enough to enable knowledge of that state of affairs. An expression is.

Expression makes something knowable to appropriate observers; making something knowable to appropriate observers is, in turn, to show it; hence expression is a species of showing. As we saw in Section 2, showing can occur whether or not anyone cottons on. Since expression is a species of showing, the same goes for it: although I express my love, trepidation, regret, you might be too distracted, obtuse, or self-absorbed to get my drift.

Our discussion of showing in Section 2 and our current account of expression tie together in another way. The reason is that our emotional expressions sometimes take the showing-α form, that is, sometimes make those emotions quite literally perceptible. To see why, consider that at least the so-called basic emotions (anger, fear, surprise, disgust, sadness, happiness) are syndromes, in that they tend to manifest themselves, in relatively consistent pan-cultural ways in (1) a neurophysiological pattern, (2) a pattern of facial behavior, (3) a range of action, (4) a distinctive phenomenological dimension. Consistent with these pan-cultural patterns is the existence of optional "display rules" that can affect the ways in which those emotions are displayed in one society or another, and relative to one social situation rather than another. Further, some emotions may constitutively require that the subject judge true or at least accept as true certain contents. Thus for instance it seems impossible to be proud in the absence of certain beliefs about oneself. On the other hand, fear is possible in the absence of any judgment or acceptance of a proposition that, say, a certain stimulus is dangerous.

At the same time, we often, perhaps even usually, perceive objects by perceiving certain characteristic components thereof. I see the apple without seeing all of its parts, but only by seeing its facing surface. (I have to see a substantial part of that facing surface to count as seeing the apple; seeing a square micron of that facing surface under a microscope does not suffice to make it the case that I see either the apple or the facing surface, for a square micron is not a characteristic component for a perceiver like me in my normal ecological environment.) Similarly I see your anger by seeing the scowl in your face, and I hear your exuberance by hearing your exuberant voice. I might also feel your anxiety by feeling your hand as you shake mine. In these cases we perceive the emotions of others because we perceive characteristic components of those emotions. That is not to say that we perceive all of the parts of the emotion by virtue of perceiving the emotion. We see the apple without seeing its core, and we see Paris from above without seeing each newspaper stand in that city. So it is with emotions.[13]

We can, then, perceive emotions. Further, I shall assume that Kendall Walton is correct in his view that a photograph enables us to see what it is a photograph of.[14] We quite literally see Abe Lincoln in a photo of Lincoln, in spite of the fact that Lincoln does not now exist. Accepting this assumption, together with my earlier claim that we can perceive emotions, we may infer that a photograph can enable us literally to perceive someone's emotion. So if we had a photo of Lincoln looking enraged, that photo would not only enable us to see Lincoln, it would also enable us to see his rage.

What of a drawing or painting of that same man that also shows his anger? I contend that just as a drawing or painting can show us how a man's hair looks, it can also show us how his anger looks. Further, just as the drawing or painting of his hair might not enable us to perceive that hair, so too a drawing or painting of his angry face might not enable us to perceive his anger. The reason is that we can learn what something looks like without seeing that thing. Moreover, if the drawing or painting is not accurate, or the chain of transmission from man to representation is not reliable, then it will not show us how the man's anger looks, but might nevertheless show us how *anger* looks. A drawing of an enraged face, such as one finds for didactic purposes in Gary Faigin's *The Artist's Complete Guide to Facial Expression*,[15] shows what human anger looks like; a drawing of a disgusted face shows what human disgust looks like. This is so even if there is no actual person whom the drawing is a drawing of; and it is so even if, if there be such a person, she never made a face quite like that.

We can learn from works of art other than photographs how emotions look, at least for the basic emotions. In addition, aside from these basic emotions which have pan-cultural facial signatures, people often have idiosyncratic ways of manifesting their emotions that can nevertheless form characteristic patterns. Those patterns can become conventionalized but need not do so. Whether or not a given pattern becomes thus conventionalized, a given manifestation of emotion might still be a characteristic component of that emotion for a certain group, or even for an individual. If that happens it might still be possible for a manifestation of emotion to enable others to perceive that emotion. Rosie Vincy in *Middlemarch* has a characteristic way of displaying her determination: she twists her neck. Eliot describes her thus in at least four places in that novel, and it seems plausible that one who sees that neck-twist while aware of this regularity has also seen a characteristic component of that determination. This is so in spite of its not being the case that a neck-twist is a pan-cultural manifestation of determination.

While our dominant sense is vision, which for this reason is our best means of detecting characteristic components of emotions, nothing in principle prevents the perception of emotions through other sensory modalities. Fear has a characteristic sound in the human voice; that is why we can literally hear someone's fear. Fear sometimes also has a tactile manifestation in clammy hands, and is thus something that others can perceive tactually. One also hears talk of the "smell" of fear, but it's an open question whether this piece of common parlance has any objective basis.

5   Expressiveness and Showing How

No doubt this ability of art to show how emotions manifest themselves is one way in which art is expressive. Music that shows how fear sounds will also sound fearful; a picture that shows how anger looks will also look angry, at least in one place. (Whether the entire picture is also angry is a further question, and depends on what else is in the picture.) The question is whether showing an emotion's appearance (visual, aural, or otherwise) is the heart of expressiveness.

One influential theory of musical expressiveness, the "contour and convention" theory of Peter Kivy,[16] offers an affirmative answer in contending that music's expressive qualities are due to its bearing a perceptible resemblance to expressive human behavior. Kivy's "contour theory," holds that music's "sonic 'shape', bears a structural analogy to the heard and seen manifestations of human emotional expression."[17] Kivy does not require that the discernment of resemblance between the structural features of the music and the structural features of human emotional expression be a conscious process. For this reason he can account for the fact that our discernment of an object's expressiveness can be instantaneous rather than the result of a conscious calculation. In addition, Kivy is aware of the fact that a piece of music can bear a structural analogy to many other things besides expressive behavior (exploding geysers, cascading waterfalls, stampeding bison) and while on occasion program music might represent such things, music does not express them. Kivy proposes an evolutionary hypothesis to the effect that human beings are simply prone to see analogies with expressive behavior in favor of the many other analogies that they might discern, just as we are prone to see a face in an electrical plug in a wall instead of the many other things that we could see there.[18]

According to this "contour and convention theory," then, music might have a sad sound by virtue of containing structural features isomorphic to the heard or seen structural features of a person's behavior when she is displaying her sadness. However, the sadness of a bit of music might also be due its ability to show how sadness *feels*. As Kivy acknowledges, the sadness of music might be due either to structural features of the music, such as the development of a melody over a few measures, or because of the peculiarly melancholy sound of a chord. Kivy's account applies in a fairly straightforward way to the former sort of case, but not to the latter. He is candid about this, writing,

> we have yet to work one further element into the contour theory: that is the expressive chords, major, minor and diminished. These chords are generally

perceived as cheerful, melancholy, and anguished, respectively . . . The problem is that these individual chords, not having a contour, being experienced
as simple qualities, do not seem to bear any analogy at all to human behavior
– hence must be expressive of cheerfulness, melancholy and anguish in
some other way than that allowed by the contour theory of musical
expressiveness.[19]

Kivy goes on to observe that there is no generally accepted explanation
for the expressive features of these chords, and infers that the contour
theory is no worse off than any other theory in this regard.[20] He also
essays an account of the expressive qualities of chords, observing that the
major triad C–E–G sounds stable; for instance a movement could easily
end on it. By contrast it would not sound at all natural to end a movement on the diminished triad C–E-flat-G-flat. The same is true, if to a
lesser extent, of the minor triad C–E-flat–G. Kivy suggests that this may
be why the major triad sounds cheerful, the minor triad melancholy, and
the diminished triad anguished.

These remarks are suggestive but cannot stand on their own as a solution to the problem that Kivy has raised for himself. Kivy does not tell
us why cheerfulness, melancholy, and anguish should be considered in
increasing order of instability. Nor is it clear why, if that were established,
it would fall under the "contour" theory: in what way is instability an
aspect of the contour of anguish, and is that way anything like the way
in which sad behavior tends to have a drooping character that can be
mapped onto a temporal progression of sounds?

I shall try to answer such questions while explaining the extent to
which Kivy's and related theories approach the truth. When I express an
emotion or experience I either show it objectually or show how it feels;
that way of showing must also be the product of design. One way to
show my emotion or experience objectually is to make that emotion or
experience perceptible rather than merely representing it. I don't express
pain by saying coolly, "I'm in pain." I need to yell, recoil, cringe,
grimace, or something of the kind.[21] Another way to express my pain is
to show how it feels. From our discussion thus far, we know that this
means: I make available to others knowledge of what my pain feels like.

This suggests a larger pattern. An artifact or bit of behavior expresses
emotion or experience either by objectually showing that emotion or experience, or by showing how that emotion or experience feels. Similarly,
an artifact or bit of behavior is expressive of emotion or experience (instead
of expressing emotion or experience) either by showing how that emotion or experience appears (visually, aurally, etc.), or by showing how it

feels. If Kivy's account at least gives us a sufficient condition for the expressiveness of music, then that is because in his showcase examples the music shows how an emotion either *sounds* or *looks*. It shows how an emotion sounds if it perceptibly resembles the sound of the human voice manifesting that emotion. It shows how an emotion looks if it perceptibly resembles the look of a human being manifesting that emotion. (In this latter case structural features of the music bear an isomorphism to structural features of human action.) This point in turn suggests the following generalization: where α is a perceptible object, φ is an emotion or experience, and γ a sensory modality or feeling:

α is expressive of φ just in case α shows how φ γ's.

This generalization would also predict that a painting has an expressive dimension when it shows how an emotion looks – that is, how its visual features are displayed on the human face and elsewhere on the body. Likewise for other artifacts and affective qualities. However, emotions have more than looks and sounds; many of them have characteristic ways that they feel. So, of course, do experiences. In addition, many of our richer emotions lack characteristic ways of exhibiting themselves in behavior. I doubt that there is a characteristic way people act, sound, or look when they are experiencing a sense of crisis, isolation, loneliness, or regret. Yet surely it is possible for an artifact to be expressive of a sense of crisis, isolation, loneliness, or regret, and the above pattern enables us to see how that can be.

Take the example of a sense of crisis. An artifact might show us what a sense of crisis *feels like*. Flo Liebowitz suggests that this is precisely what happens in the final scene of *Bonnie and Clyde*.[22] The two protagonists are finally caught in a trap and the Feds open fire on them with an overwhelming amount of artillery. The entire scene occurs in slow motion, giving us a sense of time stopping while we take in the carnage. In so doing, that scene not only shows us what the demise of Bonnie and Clyde might have looked like; it also shows us what a sense of crisis feels like. Again, here is a passage from Peter Taylor's story "Rain in the Heart." In it a sergeant returns to his new wife for a brief leave from his army duties.

> The sergeant stood up. The room was very still and close. There was not even the sound of a clock. A light was still burning on her dressing table, and through the open doorway he could see the table lamp that was still burning in the living room. The table there was a regular part of the

furnishings of the apartment. But it was a piece of furniture they might
have chosen themselves. He went to the door and stood a moment study-
ing the effect she had achieved in her arrangement of the objects on the
table. On the dark octagonal top was the white lamp with the urn-shaped
base. The light the lamp shed contrasted the sharp of the urn with the global
shape of a crystal vase from which sprigs of ivy mixed with periwinkle sprang
in their individual wildness. And a square, crystal ashtray reflecting its exotic
lights was placed at an angle to a small round silver dish.

   He went to the living room to put out the light. Yet with his hand on
the switch he hesitated because it was such a pleasing isolated arrangement
of objects.[23]

This passage conveys a sense of isolation, and indeed dislocation. The
husband is seeing his new wife for the first time in a while and yet he is
preoccupied with an arrangement of objects on a table. His fascination
with their individual separateness seems to reflect his feeling of dislocation, of being out of synch with his environment. In this way it
exemplifies T. S. Eliot's notion of an "objective correlative" of emotion.[24]
I suggest also that by representing the arrangement of objects on the
table as he does, Peter Taylor enables us to know what isolation
feels like.

6   Congruence of Sensation and Affect

Representation of a state of affairs is not the only way to show how an
emotion or experience feels. We can also do this by exploiting what we
might call congruence between experiences of one sensory modality
and another, and between experiences of one sensory modality and an
emotion. Experimental psychology has established a large body of data
showing robust interpersonal consistency in judgments across sensory modalities: some sounds, like that of the piccolo, are bright, while others, like
that of the oboe, are dim. This is so in spite of the fact that brightness
and dimness are strictly speaking only properties of light sources rather
than sounds.[25] Again, some smells, like vanilla, are smooth, while others,
for instance musk, are rough. Not only can we find congruence between
elements of one set of experiences for a given sensory modality and another
set for another modality; we can also find congruence between elements
of a given set of experiences for one sensory modality and various
emotions. Yellow is a happy color. That, however, is not because it looks
the way happiness looks; happy people are not in the habit of turning
yellow, and there is no obvious affinity between this color and the way

happy people are wont to behave. Rather, yellow is happy because it *shows how happiness feels.* Brown on the other hand shows how sadness feels.

Let me now clarify these claims. For each sensory modality we can construct the set of possible experiences available through that sense modality. For vision there is a class of possible visual experiences, for sound a set of possible sonic experiences, and so on. In addition, for any of these classes one can map its members onto multiple dimensions such as

pleasantness/unpleasantness
intensity/mildness
agitation/calm.

Let us suppose that there are three dimensions of assessment, and that they are these.[26] Then we have an experiential 3-space onto which experiences of each sensory modality may be mapped. Further, elements of the set of emotions and moods can be mapped onto this space as well. In some cases, two emotions will be mapped onto the same point in this 3-space, just as there will likely be cases in which two experiential elements from a single sensory modality, or two experiential elements from distinct sensory modalities, that will be mapped onto the same point in this 3-space.

Suppose now that an experience E1 and emotion E2 map onto the same co-ordinate, (x, y, z), in that three-space. In that case, E1 may be used to show how E2 feels. E1 might be pleasant, intense, and agitated, say as a result of being a visual expanse of yellow with lines arranged in such a way that it appears to be scintillating; as a result it shows how exuberance feels. Or E1 might be unpleasant, intense, and calm; as a result it shows how sadness feels. (Were it more agitated it would become closer to grief.) This is not at all to say that we are consciously aware of these congruences when we discern the happiness of E1. We might well become conscious of these congruences but need not do so.[27]

The foregoing also does not imply that if E1 and E2 are mapped onto the same point in the 3-space, E1 will show every aspect of E2. For instance, if E2 is anger, then it will probably have a content component, that is, what its owner is angry about. However, knowing how an emotion feels does not normally require sharing the content of that emotion, if only because content is not in general part of the phenomenology of emotion. Again, any tokening of an emotion will carry with it a distinctive phenomenology: my exuberance will often be suffused with a variety of visual, auditory, and other experiences. These experiences are not, however, part of what it is to feel exuberant, so if those features are not captured by congruences with other sensations, that will not upset the approach being mooted here. Finally, many of our emotions lack a distinctive phenomenology, so that if we are to express them it won't be by showing how they feel. If we are to express them, it will instead have to be by showing how they appear (if there be any such way), or portraying a situation apt to evoke such an emotion in me.

I have argued that a work's expressiveness is due either to its showing how an emotion, mood, or experience appears, or to its showing how an emotion, mood, or experience feels. The former is the natural home of a "contour" theory of expressiveness such as that of Kivy; I would say the same of Stephen Davies.[28] Yet that is not the only way in which expressiveness is achieved. Indeed, Kivy, as we have seen, worries whether he can account for the expressiveness of elements of music that bear no clear isomorphism to aspects of expressive behavior, either visually or sonically. I have suggested that the expressive quality of these elements is due to their being "congruent" with the emotion of which they are expressive in the way I have outlined above.

7   Empathy and Epistemology

Expressiveness is a matter of either showing an emotion, mood, or experience, or showing how an emotion, mood, or experience feels. The latter is particularly important for explaining how we can learn from things that are expressive and why that species of learning is important. In particular, one would expect that knowing how an emotion or experience feels enables me to "feel with" someone who is actually in the grip of that emotion or experience. This is to say that artworks that are expressive by virtue of showing how an emotion or experience feels enable me to empathize with others. However, to get a handle on this thought we will peer deeper into empathy.

Many writers both in aesthetics and the philosophy of mind distinguish between sympathy and empathy. Sympathy seems to involve taking a concern for the well being of another (not necessarily another person), and taking steps to provide them succor. It does not involve sharing any of what they are feeling. Thus I can sympathize with your grief by providing a shoulder on which to cry, and in other ways taking an active interest in aiding you. To sympathize with you, however, I need not share your grief. By contrast, many writers hold, for A to empathize with B, or more precisely for A to empathize with B's φ, where φ is an emotion, experience, or perhaps even a thought, A must feel φ.[29] On this view, to empathize with your terror I must feel terror myself, and to empathize with your resentment of God I must resent God too. Of course this is not a sufficient condition; I don't empathize with your aching just-stubbed toe by stubbing mine. In addition to sharing your emotion (or experience), on this account I must use my own replication of your situation to imagine my way into what you are feeling.

This view of empathy is, however, intuitively implausible. It is of course *not* enough for me to empathize with your feeling of being ostracized that I have been ostracized in the past. Nor is it enough that I have been ostracized in the past and am now capable of calling up that memory into consciousness. One is not empathetic simply by virtue of having dormant skills. Instead I have to do something that makes me count as feeling with you. But it is a mistake to infer that feeling with others requires actually duplicating their feelings in myself. After all, to get myself to feel ostracized I'd have to induce certain beliefs in myself, such as that I am being excluded from a group on the basis of inappropriate considerations.[30] But suppose I don't happen to feel that way at this point; as it happens, I feel more or less accepted by the groups I care about. Writers like Berys Gaut, Alex Neill, and Ute Frith would infer that I am incapable of empathizing with your feeling of ostracism, but surely that is untrue. It would be awfully nice of me to follow a Pascal-style routine to get myself to believe that I am being excluded, but by the time I carry this off it will probably be too late for my empathy to be worth anything to you anyway. Instead, I could save a lot of time and effort simply by calling up into conscious awareness my *memory* of how I felt when I was ostracized in the past. On the basis of that conscious awareness, I now know how you feel, not dispositionally but occurrently. If I then go on to use this conscious awareness as a prop in which I imagine that you are feeling *this*, then I have empathized with you.

Gaut didn't claim that for me to empathize with your anguish it is sufficient that I feel anguish. He takes this as a necessary but not sufficient condition. Following Neill,[31] Gaut also holds that, "empathy requires one imaginatively to enter into a character's mind and feel with him because of one's imagining of his situation".[32] So on this view, to empathize with another's feeling of φ, I not only have to feel φ, I must also use that feeling of φ as a kind of prop on the basis of which to imagine being in your situation. This further condition of imaginative identification seems eminently plausible. What it does not do is mandate any requirement that I actually feel what I imagine you to be feeling.

Rather, it is enough that I be able to call into consciousness my experience of that feeling without actually reliving it, and then on that basis to imagine my way into your situation. That seems to be sufficient to enable me to feel with you.

Again, I've had some bad ankle sprains in my time, and I can still vividly recall how it felt when I went off that curb in Pittsburgh one beautiful spring day while running. Now I watch you sprain an ankle and there you are writhing on the pavement. I don't need to injure myself to empathize with you. Rather I need only recall feeling what you are suffering right now, and use that recalled feeling as a prop in which I imagine myself feeling as you do.

For a less experiential and more cognitive case, note that I can understand Sharon's position in *The Rapture* when she decides not to say she loves God. After all, look at what God has allowed happen to her. I can grasp the reasonableness of her position: Sharon resents God, and I can understand why. I used to feel the way she does at that point in the movie. As it happens, after thinking about some aspects of the problem of evil, I don't feel that way any more. Even if I were a theist, I'd now be inclined to reject the commonly held assumption that God is obliged to create the best possible world that it is in His power to create. Because of that I don't resent God. But for all that I can empathize with the character's feeling of resentment.

We can, then, empathize with the emotions, thoughts and experiences of others without duplicating those things in ourselves. Instead, it is enough that we be consciously aware of those feelings, thoughts, or experiences, if only by virtue of our memory of having gone through those things ourselves.

Is memory of an earlier experience or emotion the only alternative to actually feeling that experience or emotion for the purpose of empathy? I will now argue that it is not, and more precisely that imaginative engagement with various works of art is another way of achieving empathetic competence.

8   Art and Skill

It is not controversial that empathy involves exercise of a skill. Those suffering from some forms of autism have great difficulty empathizing with others, quite possibly for reasons having to do with dysfunction of the so-called Mirror Neuron System.[33] Others of us are simply too boorish to empathize with others, at least with regard to particular issues. Bob might simply never have taken the time to put himself in the shoes of an unwed teenage mother; that's why he has no patience with her inability to find work elsewhere than on lower rungs of the service economy. Yet others might have too narrow a range of experience to draw on to empathize with others: much as I'd like to, I simply don't know how to empathize with a woman living under the Taliban because my own experience is too removed from hers.

Imagination is often distinguished from other mental acts and processes on the dimension of direction of fit. While belief purports to fit the world (and thus has mind-to-world direction of fit), and desire purports to mold the world (and thus has world-to-mind direction of fit), imagination falls naturally into neither of these categories. When I imagine a neutron bomb going off in Denver, I am not beholden to represent how things are, nor (one hopes) am I trying to get the world to be one way or another. Yet even here I am beholden to some norm of accuracy. If I visualize a daffodil swaying in the breeze, I'm simply not imagining a neutron bomb going off in Denver.

Imagination of the sort required for empathy is also beholden to a norm of accuracy. I'm not empathizing with your sense of isolation by imagining any old thing. I need to put myself in your shoes in the correct way, or else my imagination misses its target. If I call up to consciousness a feeling of *amae* (the Japanese emotion of satisfaction in the knowledge of having submerged one's identity in a group), I'm simply not imagining your sense of isolation. From what we have said thus far, we know that to empathize with your sense of isolation I need to do two things correctly: (1) activate my possibly latent or dormant knowledge of how that sense of isolation feels; and (2) use that as a prop to imagine how I would feel were I in your situation. Each of (1) and (2) might be done better or worse, and a failure of either one might cause me to be under the illusion of having empathized with you when I have not in fact done so. Further, we now know that one can achieve condition (1) not just by having experienced the emotion in question before; one can also achieve this condition by having learned how it feels from exposure to a novel, painting, sonata, or other work of art. The artwork might show how that emotion feels by exploiting congruences between sensation and affect.

Such an artwork can show how an emotion feels without being representational. A non-representational painting might be congruent, in ways discussed in Section 6 above, with central aspects of exuberance. By possessing this congruence, the painting might show me how exuberance feels without representing anyone or anything being exuberant, and without making me exuberant. Likewise for many other sensory modalities, and many other emotions and moods. A work of art might also exploit the power of representation to show how an emotion feels. I'll close with an illustration of this possibility.

We tend to think of ourselves as being called upon to empathize with those suffering rather than those experiencing some pleasant or enjoyable emotion. That is presumably because sufferers tend to solicit our empathy more often than do others. Nevertheless it makes perfectly good sense to empathize with someone feeling a "positive" emotion or mood. So consider a photograph from Rodchenko entitled *Pioneer Girl* (see Plate 4.1). Notice the point of light in each of her eyes; that from her hair and the bit of her clothes you see, she's not overdressed for plowing a field or hammering railroad ties. Too, you're looking at her from below, and so it is natural to see her as large and strong. Yet the classical cut of her nose and upper lip suggest nobility. I can't but *admire* the Pioneer Girl. Correlatively, I can now empathize with the admiration that Rodchenko felt for her, or at least the admiration felt by the persona that his work embodies.

This photo shows me a lot of things, then. It shows me the girl, her scarf, and tousled hair. It also shows me *what admiration feels like*. Of course it has a polemical dimension as well, since it aims to convince me that the girl's face is representative of the coming workers' revolution. I can remain neutral on that issue, though, while still admiring the girl's combination of earthy strength and nobility. I would, furthermore, still admire these characteristics if I were gazing at what I know to be a painting, even a hyper-realist painting in the style of Chuck Close, of the same subject. Here it is doubtful that I would feel any admiration of the painting's subject, since to do that I would have to believe that subject to exemplify properties of a certain kind – and I am not likely to do that with an entity I don't believe to exist. Nevertheless, such a painting might show me how admiration feels by enabling me to imagine admiring its sitter.

A work of art can show me how an emotion or mood feels, then, without that being its primary aim. Also, a work of art can show me how an emotion or mood feels even if I am no stranger to that emotion or mood. I might be acquainted with a certain emotion or mood although I am not able to access it consciously, through disuse, as it were. A work of art can reacquaint me with an emotion or mood by bringing it to consciousness. Further, a work of art can show me how an emotion or

Plate 4.1: *Pioneer Girl* (Alexander Rodchenko, 1930)
Source: Copyright Estate of Alexander Rodchenko/RAO, Moscow/VAGA, New York.

mood feels without causing me to feel that emotion. It might do that either by engaging the imagination, or by exploiting our sensitivity to congruences between experiences, on the one hand, and emotions and moods on the other.

Expressiveness and empathy are, then, closely linked. Something that is expressive of an emotion, mood, or experience shows how that emotion, mood, or experience appears or feels. In so doing, that thing makes know-how available to appropriately constituted and situated observers. When what has been made available is how an emotion or mood feels, such observers are then in a position to employ their imagination in such a way as to empathize with others. While expressiveness in the service of empathy is not the exclusive domain of art, and while a great deal of art aims at nothing of the kind, it nevertheless appears that *one* central function of art forms as disparate as painting, music, literature, film, and photography is that they show how emotions and moods feel in such a way as to equip us to achieve a greater rapport with others.

Notes

Research for this paper was supported in part by a grant from the Office of the Provost at the University of Virginia. Earlier versions were presented at the Central Division Meeting of the American Philosophical Association, Chicago, April 2005, at the American University of Beirut, May 2005, and at Virginia Commonwealth University, October 2005. I thank audiences on all three of those occasions for their comments and suggestions for improvements. Jenefer Robinson and Cynthia Freeland commented at the Chicago session, and Hans Muller commented at the Beirut session; I am grateful for their insightful remarks.

1   This usage is to be distinguished from that in A. Miklósi et al., "Intentional Behaviour in Dog-Human Communication," *Animal Cognition* 3 (2000): 159–66. The authors define showing as a communicative action comprising both a directional component related to an external target and an attention-getting component directing the attention of the perceiver to the informer or sender. Although I make no use of this notion here, we might call it overt showing to distinguish it from that used in the text. Also, this paper shares with Tim Wharton ("Natural Pragmatics and Natural Codes," *Mind and Language* 18 (2003): 447–77) a conviction of the importance of the notion of showing for certain aspects of communication; insofar, it shares with that work the conviction that much of so-called natural meaning deserves the attention of students of communication.

2   Here is one verse:

> In the Big Rock Candy Mountain
> You never change your socks
> And little streams of alkyhol
> Come trickling down the rocks
> O the shacks all have to tip their hats
> And the railway bulls are blind
> There's a lake of stew
> And ginger ale too
> And you can paddle
> All around it in a big canoe
> In the Big Rock Candy Mountain.

3   Jane Hamilton, *A Map of the World* (New York: Doubleday, 1994).
4   Jason Stanley and Timothy Williamson argue that all alleged cases of knowledge-how are analyzable as cases of knowledge-that, while the converse relation of analyzability does not hold (Jason Stanley and Timothy Williamson, "Knowing How," *Journal of Philosophy* 98 (2001): 411–44). However, their "analysis" appeals to what they call "practical modes of presentation," and as Tobias Rosefeldt points out, in the absence of an elucidation of this notion we cannot tell whether the putative analysis succeeds without remainder (Tobias Rosefeldt, "Is Knowing-How Simply a Case of Knowing-That?" *Philosophical Investigations* 27 (2004): 370–79).
5   This and other famous koans may be found at www.ashidakim.com.
6   A fuller account of supposition and its norms is given in Mitchell Green, "The Status of Supposition," *Nous* 34 (2000): 376–99.
7   J. O. Urmson, "Literature as a Performing Art," in George Dickie and Richard Sclafani, eds., *Aesthetics: A Critical Anthology* (New York: St Martin's, 1977), pp. 334–41.
8   Berys Gaut argues persuasively that in spite of skeptical challenges by some aestheticians, the everyday notion of identification at play in cases such as this is innocuous (Berys Gaut, "Identification and Emotion in Narrative Film," in Carl Plantinga and Greg M. Smith, eds., *Passionate Views: Film, Cognition and Emotion* (Baltimore, MD: Johns Hopkins University Press, 1999): 200–16).
9   Oxford Compact English Dictionary, p. 934.
10 Frederick Douglass, *Narrative of the Life of Frederick Douglass, an American Slave* (1845), p. 14.
11 Charles Darwin, *The Expression of the Emotions in Man and Animals*, 3rd edn., ed. Paul Ekman (Oxford: Oxford University Press, 1998), p. 359.
12 I offer more detailed arguments against a conception of expression as indication in Mitchell Green, "Expression, Indication, and Showing What's Within," *Philosophical Studies*, forthcoming. David Owens also highlights the inadequacies of such a conception (David Owens, "Testimony and Assertion," *Philosophical Studies* 130/1 (July 2006): 105–29).
13 Paul Griffiths develops the case for the pan-cultural nature of the so-called basic emotions (Paul Griffiths, *What Emotions Really Are*, Chicago, IL: University of Chicago Press, 1997). Mitchell Green, *Self-Expression* (Oxford: Oxford University Press, forthcoming), chapters 4–5, defends in further detail the claim that some emotions can be perceived.
14 Kendall Walton, "On Pictures and Photographs: Objections Answered," in Richard Allen and Murray Smith, eds., *Film Theory and Philosophy* (Oxford: Oxford University Press, 1997), pp. 60–75.
15 Gary Faigin, *The Artist's Complete Guide to Facial Expression* (New York: Watson-Guptill, 1990).
16 This theory is updated and defended in Peter Kivy, *Introduction to a Philosophy of Music* (Oxford: Oxford University Press, 2002).
17 Ibid., p. 40.

18   Ibid., p. 41. Jerrold Levinson offers a general objection to all views of musical expression (and perhaps artistic expression generally) that depend upon a perceived resemblance between the work and an agent who is literally expressing her emotion (Jerrold Levinson, "Musical Expressiveness as Hearability-as-Expression," in Matthew Kieran, ed., *Contemporary Debates in Aesthetics and Philosophy of Art*, Oxford: Blackwell, 2006). Levinson holds that seeing or otherwise perceiving a resemblance between A and B is never on its own a sufficient condition for seeing (hearing, etc.) A as B. He gives the example of seeing the resemblance of a leafy tree and a bushy head. In seeing such a resemblance, Levinson contends, we do not thereby see the tree as a bushy head. Perceiving a resemblance is thus not a sufficient condition for seeing- (hearing-, etc.) as.

    Levinson is right to point out that perceiving a resemblance is not a sufficient condition for seeing- (or otherwise perceiving-) as. The point does not, however, undermine resemblance-based views of musical (or other forms of non-sentient) expression, for it is not clear that in order to perceive the expressiveness of an object one must see it as anything other than what it is. I see the Newfoundland's face, and I see the sadness in that face, for I perceive that the face has a sad look. In order to do this, must I also see it as sad? That evidently depends upon how we construe the truth conditions of this locution. Does seeing α as Φ require that I imagine α to be Φ, or to be the vehicle of some agent's expression of Φ? In that case the seeing-as requirement is too strong: surely I can perceive the sad look in the Newfoundland's face, or the contemptuous look in the face of a man whose face has been disfigured by an accident, without imagining anything at all? On the other hand if the seeing-as condition does not require use of the imagination, then for all Levinson has said, perception of a resemblance will be enough to satisfy it.

19   Kivy, *Introduction to a Philosophy of Music*, p. 43.

20   Kivy infers that the fact that the contour theory cannot provide an explanation here is, as he says, "no great deficit." This is of course a fallacy. If no theory in a class C can account for a datum that is in the domain of C-type theories, it is equally possible that all theories in that class are incorrect, not that any one of them is off the hook.

21   If I only coolly say, "I'm in pain," I express my belief that I'm in pain but not my pain, for this cool utterance does not show my pain.

22   Flo Leibowitz, "Personal Agency Theories of Expressiveness and the Movies," in Allen and Smith, eds., *Film Theory and Philosophy*, pp. 329–42.

23   Peter Taylor, "Rain in the Heart," in *The Old Forest and Other Stories* (New York: Doubleday, 1941).

24   Eliot writes,

    The only way of expressing emotion in the form of art is by finding an "object-ive correlative;" in other words, a set of objects, a situation, a chain of events which shall be the formula of that particular emotion; such that when the external facts, which must terminate in sensory experience, are given, the emotion is immediately evoked. If you examine any of Shakespeare's more successful tragedies, you will find this exact equivalence; you will find that the state of mind of Lady Macbeth walking in her sleep has been communicated to you by a skilful accumulation of imagined sensory impressions; the words of Macbeth on hearing of his wife's death strike us as if, given the sequence of events, these words were automatically released by the last event in the series. The artistic "inevitability" lies in this complete adequacy of the external to the emotion; and this is precisely what is deficient in Hamlet. (T. S. Eliot, "Hamlet and His Problems," in *The Sacred Wood: Essays on Poetry and Criticism*, London: Methuen, 1921)

25 See Lawrence E. Marks, *The Unity of the Senses* (New York: Academic Press, 1979); and "Intermodal Similarity and Cross-Modality Matching: Coding Perceptual Dimensions," in R. Duncan Luce et al., eds., *Geometrical Representations of Perceptual Phenomena* (Mahwah, NJ: Lawrence Erlbaum, 1995), pp. 207–33.

26 We don't have to be certain of either of these suppositions for the following elucidation to help clarify the thesis I am suggesting.

27 If some version of the present hypothesis is correct, it would provide another case of unconscious cognitive processes along with others currently being collected together under the rubric of the *adaptive unconscious* as characterized and elucidated in Timothy Wilson, *Strangers to Ourselves: Discovering the Adaptive Unconscious* (Cambridge, MA: Harvard University Press, 2003).

28 See Stephen Davies, "Philosophical Perspectives on Music's Expressiveness," in *Themes in the Philosophy of Music* (Oxford University Press: Oxford, 2003).

29 See for instance Gaut, "Identification and Emotion in Narrative Film;" and Carl Plantinga, "The Scene of Empathy and the Human Face on Film," in Plantinga and Smith, eds., *Passionate Views*. Ute Frith also takes empathy to require an actual sharing of emotions, writing, "Empathy presupposes, amongst other things, a recognition of different mental states. It also presupposes that one goes beyond the recognition of difference to adopt the other person's frame of mind with all the consequences of emotional reactions" (Ute Frith, *Autism: Explaining the Enigma*, Oxford: Blackwell, 1989), pp. 144–5.

30 I am not presupposing that emotions are a species of judgment; I am assuming something much weaker, namely that certain emotions require judgments or beliefs as necessary conditions.

31 Alex Neill, "Empathy and (Film) Fiction," in David Bordwell and Noël Carroll, eds., *Post-Theory: Reconstructing Film Studies* (Madison, WI: University of Wisconsin Press, 1996), pp. 175–94.

32 Gaut, "Identification and Emotion in Narrative Film," p. 206.

33   Jeanette Kennett, "Autism, Empathy and Moral Agency," *Philosophical Quarterly* 52 (2002): 340–57, reviews some of the basic studies of autism. Dapretto and colleagues report striking neurological evidence in support of the relation between autism and dysfunction in the Mirror Neuron System (Mirella Dapretto et al., "Understanding Emotions in Others: Mirror Neuron Dysfunction in Children with Autism Spectrum Disorders," *Nature Neuroscience* 9/1 (2006): 28–30).

Part III
Literature and Moral Responsibility

5

"SOLID OBJECTS," SOLID OBJECTIONS: ON VIRGINIA WOOLF AND PHILOSOPHY

Paisley Livingston

Virginia Woolf explicitly criticized the idea that a novel should be the source of a detachable philosophical content:

> When philosophy is not consumed in a novel, when we can underline this phrase with a pencil, and cut out that exhortation with a pair of scissors and paste the whole into a system, it is safe to say that there is something wrong with the philosophy or with the novel or both.[1]

Woolf's main point here seems to be that the philosophical significance of a novel ought not to be reducible to a character's (or narrator's) quotable generalizations serving to illustrate the tenets of a philosophical system. She also expresses reservations about the soundness of any system articulated in this manner. Yet it does not follow that there is no other way in which a novel could contribute to philosophical insight, and many of Woolf's own literary fictions indeed engage critically with the philosophical problems and positions with which she was familiar.[2] In what follows I shall develop this thought with reference to Woolf's 1920 short story, "Solid Objects."[3] Many commentators have interpreted this story as a kind of allegorical critique of apolitical artists and aesthetes. I shall argue that the story functions instead as a *reductio ad absurdum* of some faulty philosophical generalizations. I have in mind, more specifically, ideas about aesthetic experience and value that Woolf was likely to have associated with the aesthetic theory that Clive Bell had rather tenuously based on G. E. Moore's *Principia Ethica*.[4]

Section 1 provides a brief description of the story and identifies some interpretative claims that have been made about it. Section 2 challenges these claims and begins to set forth an alternative interpretation. In Section 3 I identify the story's implicit *reductio* argument. Although I present evidence in support of the idea that Woolf had Bell's views in mind, my claims about the philosophical significance of the story do not hinge entirely on this conjecture about the writer's intentions. If Woolf had a more charitable or sympathetic understanding of Bell's theory of art than I conjecture, she may instead have been satirizing other, more popular, notions of aesthetic contemplation. Section 4 summarizes my claims and draws a connection with a passage from *To the Lighthouse*.

1   "Solid Objects" and Its Interpretations

The narrator of "Solid Objects" relates a deceptively simple anecdote: two young men, John and Charles, have been engaged in a lively political discussion while walking on the beach. When they sit down for a rest, John digs his fingers into the sand, uncovers a lump of green-tinted glass, and marvels over its qualities. In the days that follow, he finds himself eager to discover similarly fascinating objects, and soon devotes himself entirely to this unusual pursuit. His career in politics founders, and "no longer young," he leads a solitary existence. When Charles visits him, John cannot understand his friend's failure to appreciate the remarkable pieces of iron, glass, and porcelain arranged on the mantel-piece. "Horribly depressed" by the disorder in John's rooms and by his friend's "fixed and distant" expression, Charles is indeed oblivious to these cherished objects. He concludes that it is no use trying to revive John's political career, and leaves John's rooms "for ever." Critics writing about "Solid Objects" tend to agree that the story has a theoretical point. Bill Brown refers to a "small critical consensus" around the idea that the story is a "cautionary tale warning against aesthetic absorption at the expense of the practical, the ethical, the political."[5] Panthea Reid, for example, states that "The intention of this story is to ridicule all who privilege the merely aesthetic over the ethical, the artistic over the practical."[6] Several other critics can be cited in this vein.[7] Douglas Mao plots John's collecting of objects as a futile attempt to overcome the limitations of Walter Pater's aestheticism, with its excessive emphasis on contemplative experience as opposed to useful, productive action. Woolf's story, he suggests, expresses her anxiety about the uselessness or "nonproductivity" of an aesthete's life, to which an artist's production of intrinsically valuable solid objects was contrasted.[8]

If these interpreters are to be believed, Woolf's tale has a very clear moral, which is that ethical values must take priority over aesthetic ones. Yet some interpreters, while agreeing with this general idea, have been less eager than others to criticize John's eccentric pursuits, or to attribute such criticisms to Woolf or to her narrator. Brown, for example, proposes that Woolf's story is "underwritten by the sense that the economic reason of the West has been exhausted."[9] John's interest in detritus is "an alternative mode of experiencing scarcity,"[10] which Brown relates to wartime rationing and Marcel Duchamp's readymade. Natania Rosenfeld reckons that John's "objects represent society's border cases." John is engaged in an effort to revise "the entire historical plot of exploitation and enslavement, of rapacity and division, upon which the social system of England in 1920 (or '23) was built."[11]

Although I agree with these interpreters that Woolf's tale has a theoretical point, I am not persuaded that any of their readings successfully identify its nature. As the citations suggest, most of the critics writing about the story assume that John is a credible representative of artistic or aesthetic values and experience. In many versions of this story, John stands for the artist or the aesthete, to be set in clear opposition to Charles, who represents "the practical" or "the political." Yet such an assumption is far from obvious, and features of Woolf's text constitute serious problems for any such reading. In the next section, I describe these aspects of the story in order to set the stage for an alternative interpretation of this fiction's philosophical significance. As Woolf's thinking here remains "consumed" in the story, we must pay careful attention to the details of her narrative.

2   Towards an Alternative Interpretation

"Politics be damned!" exclaims John in conclusion to his discussion with Charles. This is for John the conclusion, not merely to this particular dispute with Charles, but to an entire way of life, as is vividly symbolized by the nearby presence on the beach of a stranded pilchard boat, twice mentioned in an otherwise sparse description of the setting. John is at the time "standing for Parliament upon the brink of a brilliant career,"[12] but his stated disgust with politics indicates that as far as his deeper motives are concerned, this career is already a wreck. As he relaxes on the beach, John's bodily posture expresses "in the looseness of its attitude a readiness to take up with something new – whatever it may be that comes next to hand."[13] When John begins to burrow his fingers playfully into the sand, he regains a childish attitude of wonder and fancy, and imagines that the hole he is digging could be a moat, a well, a spring, or a secret channel to the sea. John's eyes have already lost the "background of thought and experience which gives an inscrutable depth to the eyes of grown people."[14] Before his fingers contact the lump of glass, John has, then, somehow already undergone a striking and unusual transformation. The goals and motives around which one life was organized have dissolved, and are to be replaced by a new set of aims.

The narrator offers elaborate reports on the contents of John's pleasurable perceptions of the object's color and shape, as well as the exalted fancies to which these perceptions give rise. Elaborate, characteristically Woolfian sentences are devoted to the description of the series of fantastical associations that make the object so apparently rewarding for John to ponder:

> Perhaps after all it was really a gem; something worn by a dark Princess trailing her finger in the water as she sat in the stern of the boat and listened to the slaves singing as they rowed her across the Bay. Or the oak sides of a sunk Elizabethan treasure-chest had split apart, and, rolled over and over, over and over, its emeralds had come at last to shore. John turned it in his hands; he held it to the light; he held it so that its irregular mass blotted out the body and extended right arm of his friend. The green thinned and thickened slightly as it was held against the sky or against the body. It pleased him; it puzzled him; it was so hard, so concentrated, so definite an object compared with the vague sea and the hazy shore.[15]

John observes and manipulates the object, feeling and looking at it, but more importantly, enlisting it in his imaginings. His next action, that of slipping the lump of glass inside his pocket to take it home, is described as a childish "impulse," the same impulse that moves a child to single out one pebble amongst thousands, glorying in the delight of an imagined "power and benignity." The child revels in the stone's imagined gratitude and gloats over the power to elect one stone and offer it a life of warmth and security.

Taken home, the lump of glass serves as an excellent paperweight on John's desk, where it attracts his attention from time to time as he tries to concentrate on his books and papers. At this point the narrator offers a brief explanation of what happens next to John:

> Looked at again and again half consciously by a mind thinking of something else, any object mixes itself so profoundly with the stuff of thought that it loses its actual form and recomposes itself a little differently in an ideal shape which haunts the brain when we least expect it. So John found

himself attracted to the windows of curiosity shops when he was out walking, merely because he saw something which reminded him of the lump of glass. Anything, so long as it was an object of some kind, more or less round, perhaps with a dying flame deep sunk in its mass, anything – china, glass, amber, rock, marble – even the smooth oval egg of a prehistoric bird would do . . . In a few months he had collected four or five specimens that took their place upon the mantelpiece.[16]

Woolf's narrator tells us, then, that it is not the real features of the object that exercise such a strange and profound influence on John's behavior, but a "haunting" ideal shape produced by an involuntary mental operation in which the object gets reworked by the "stuff of thought." And as the narration reveals, a major component of this "stuff of thought" is fantasy. A piece of broken china, for example, "seemed to be pirouetting through space, winking light like a fitful star."[17] A lump of iron "was so cold and heavy, so black and metallic, that it was evidently alien to the earth and had its origin in one of those dead stars, or was itself the cinder of a moon."[18] Clearly, it is not only the perceptible features of the objects that delight John, but what he makes of them in his imagination, and this is a process that is partly unconscious and involuntary. This imaginative process has begun well before his actual encounter with the object. And one ingredient in his childlike delight is his own power as selector, protector, and possessor of his precious objects. While in the world of politics John's task is to get others to elect him as their representative, in his pursuit of solid objects he at least momentarily seems to experience the power of the supreme elector.

One implication of the narrator's explanatory phrase ("So John found himself attracted . . .") is that John's experience of the lump of glass was so gratifying or valuable that the prospect of similar rewards, awakened by any object that happens to recall his first, wondrous discovery, is somehow compelling. The narrator says nothing more about the strange psychological process at work in such a significant personal transformation, but merely recounts the stages in its unfolding. In what is perhaps a decisive episode in John's abandonment of his political career, he happens to spot a fascinating-looking, half-hidden object on the other side of some railings when waiting for his train. His efforts to lay his hands on this treasure, which include a trip back to his rooms to improvise a special tool, cause him to miss both his train and an important meeting. Once the "freakish and fantastic" star-shaped shard of china is in his possession and on display on the mantel, he becomes "fascinated" by the contrast between it and the lump of green glass. In these and the other objects he eventually collects, he finds much "cause for wonder and speculation."[19]

The narrator's descriptions of John's imaginings have a charm quite characteristic of Woolf's more humorous and fanciful moments. An inclination for such imaginings may be what Leonard Woolf had in mind in a remark about the special nature of her genius:

> I always called it leaving the ground. She would weave not the sort of scene or conversation which one felt was what anyone else would have seen and described, but something entirely different. It was often extraordinarily amusing, but in a very peculiar way – almost like a fantasy, and sometimes it was extremely beautiful.[20]

In "Solid Objects," some of the indirect free discourse "leaves the ground" in this sense and thereby appears to participate in and sympathize with John's magical return to a state of childlike wonder. This does not, however, mean that the narrator's and authorial perspective are those of the character. As we move on into the narrative, a more sober attitude towards John's hopeful and exciting new life emerges. Having described John's initial pursuit of solid objects and his successful acquisition of a few remarkable specimens, the juxtaposition of which on his mantelpiece provides an additional source of wonder and speculation, the narration continues:

> As his eyes passed from one to another, the determination to possess objects that even surpassed these tormented the young man. He devoted himself more and more resolutely to the search. If he had not been consumed by ambition and convinced that one day some newly-discovered rubbish heap would reward him, the disappointments he had suffered, let alone the fatigue and derision, would have made him give up the pursuit . . . As his standard became higher and his taste more severe the disappointments were innumerable, but always some gleam of hope, some piece of china or glass curiously marked or broken lured him on. Day after day passed. He was no longer young. His career – that is his political career – was a thing of the past. (pp. 85–6)

As various critics have observed, this is hardly an enthusiastic account of a successful life of disinterested contemplation. But these same critics have not asked an important prior question, which is whether this is a good account of contemplative, aesthetic experience at all. John's new craft has become a teleological, ambitious, and egotistical career, a career, moreover, that is leading him to psychological ruin (whether this ruin will also be financial depends on the size and source of his income, a topic that goes unmentioned in the narrative). He is "tormented" by his failure to increase the size and value of his collection, the narrator's key phrase being "the determination to possess objects that surpassed these." What at first seemed a charming attitude of wonder and fancy has degenerated into a possessive syndrome. John's only moments of respite from his obsession are those when he experiences the rare event of successful acquisition. And what John enjoys in these moments is not primarily a contemplation of the actual qualities of the object, but delight over his own selective, acquisitive, and imaginative power. Worse still, it would seem that this collector has become engaged in a hopeless competition with his own prior experiences, as each new acquisitive reward must surpass all previous accomplishments. The prospects for success at this enterprise are slim, yet at the close of the story, John remains absurdly hopeful, still expecting to make some even more stupendous find. Such is his deluded condition when his old friend detects in him a "fixed and distant" expression.

That the story concludes by informing us that John's last friend leaves him "for ever" is no trivial detail. Even if one were to accept the proposition that Virginia Woolf, unlike her husband, might in the aftermath of the First World War have been inclined to second John's "Politics be damned!", we must add that she could hardly admire a life without friendship – one of the greatest intrinsic goods according to the Moore-inspired Bloomsbury axiology.[21] Nor is John's total loss of such a crucial intrinsic good plausibly made up for by a successful specialization in the maximization of another item on the Moorian list of intrinsic goods, the contemplation of beautiful objects (and according to Moore's definition, beauty just is that of which the contemplation is an intrinsic good). John's all-too-dogged efforts to repeat and even surpass the ecstatic, fantasy experience of his first solid object are hardly to be recommended by any lucid storyteller, for although the character may briefly enjoy isolated instances of heightened, pleasurable experience, their single-minded pursuit is no viable model of the good life, for at least two reasons. First of all, the final end he has compulsively erected over all other ends (and to their complete exclusion) ends up as a frustrating effort to maximize what turns out to be an ultimately illusory value (the solid objects or "crystals of intensity" have taken on an ersatz religious quality in his imagination). And secondly, the exclusion of other, genuinely valuable final ends, beginning with those involving caring for other people, amounts to a debilitating and severely limited monomania, and indeed to a kind of ethical bankruptcy.[22] In her implicit critique of John's vain pursuit we find an effective expression of the ethical dimension of Woolf's art, an expression that eschews the didacticism of "detachable" commentaries.

3   "Solid Objects" as a *reductio ad absurdum* of One Kind of Aesthetic Theory

What, if anything, does the characterization of John represent? Does he stand in for "the artist," or for any significant, recognizable category of artists? This is a dubious interpretative assumption because John's solitary quest for, and appreciation of, various objects hardly counts as an artistic activity on even a very broad understanding of the concept of art (both in Woolf's time and in our own). He makes nothing, undertakes no performances, and neither prepares nor presents any public displays, representations, arrangements, or events. At no point does the narrator provide the slightest indication that John's objects, his arrangements of them on the mantel, or his musings over them, are works of art. Critics' references to Marcel Duchamp and *les readymades* are not convincing here, as the differences between John's unusual hobby and Duchamp's artistic career are overwhelming. Critics who wish to support the "John as artist" theme owe us an explicit defense of the definition of art according to which some of John's doings count as good or bad works of art.

It may be retorted that what John stands for is not the artist, but the aesthete. Presumably an aesthete is someone who has aesthetic experiences and who values them above all other experiences. The absolute aesthete, perhaps, would be someone who believes that the only real value is aesthetic, where aesthetic value is understood as excluding ethical and other values. John has indeed sacrificed everything else to his single-minded pursuit of solid objects, yet it does not follow that he is an aesthete, as it is not obvious that his experiences of these objects are genuinely aesthetic experiences, or that what he appreciates in these objects is their aesthetic value. It seems highly unlikely that Woolf was a skeptic about aesthetic experience and value, and equally unlikely that she would have expected anyone to imagine that John's experiences exemplify either aesthetic experience or the apt appreciation of objects' aesthetic qualities, if only because his experiences of these objects – as described in the previous section – are so heavily conditioned by his fantasies, delusions, and subjective concerns, including his acquisitive and competitive desires. Are we to imagine that Virginia Woolf's story is based on the plainly idiotic assumption, implicit in John's behavior, that the only and truly great objects for aesthetic contemplation in London were to be found in its wastelands and sites of demolished houses, as opposed, say, to its many museums and galleries? Should we not also savor some irony in the suggestion that this avid collector's "torment" is the product of his having acquired a "higher standard" and "more severe" taste? Is this the reason why John can find no beauty worthy of appreciation outside of London's vacant lots? The point is not only that John does not represent expert, astute, or even adequate aesthetic experience or appreciation, but that his behavior as described does not even represent flawed or excessive instances of such experiences. And if it is denied that John is a case of excessive "aesthetic absorption," the characterization hardly offers a basis for a scathing indictment of "the aesthete." Whence my above-voiced skepticism about readings that describe this story as a straightforward assertion of the primacy of ethical values over aesthetic ones, the basic idea being that the latter are simply absent in the tale.

What, then, does this character represent if it is not the artist, aesthetic experience, or the wayward aesthete? Is the story just a pointless but mildly amusing case study of an eccentric character? Perhaps, but before such a conclusion is drawn, we may consider an alternative to such a deflationary reading: what Woolf draws to our attention with this fiction is not the corrupt (unethical and apolitical) personality of artists or aesthetes, but the foibles of a particular aesthetic doctrine. She takes that doctrine's tenets as her point of departure and then develops a fiction in which the characterization of John functions as a *reductio ad absurdum*, the thrust of which is that these tenets do not adequately represent the nature of aesthetic and artistic value and experience. The implicit argument of the story, then, has three main steps:

1 John's experiences, as relayed by the narrator, are not really instances of adequate aesthetic experience or of the appreciation of aesthetic value; he is not an aesthete, not even a wayward and unfortunate one;
2 Given the premises of one kind of aesthetic theory, John would have to be counted as someone engaged in adequate aesthetic experiences and in the appreciation of aesthetic value; as such value is his highest if not unique final end, he classifies as an aesthete;
3 Given that (1) and (2) are incompatible, and given that the characterization of John, or (1), is plausible, the aesthetic doctrine figuring in (2) is put in serious doubt.

The next step in the argument, a step that Woolf as storyteller does not take, would be the positive elaboration of an alternative doctrine of aesthetic experience and value, one which is in harmony with acceptable views about ethical and political value. Such a doctrine would further reinforce the claim that John's attitudes are not an example of aesthetic contemplation.

To recapitulate the bases of the first premise in Woolf's story, John's enjoyment of solid objects is essentially a matter of incommunicable emotions provoked by his projective imagining of the objects' marvelous qualities as well as by his own personal delight in finding, acquiring, and enjoying these objects. Although John's ongoing search for solid objects similar to the first lump of glass involves planning and intentional activity, his response to the solid objects is largely involuntary and not a matter of the application of any knowledge or skill. John's desire to repeat his pleasurable experiences by finding and acquiring rare solid objects turns out to be a frustrating, competitive endeavor. He is seriously deluded about the actual value of the objects he finds, oblivious with regard to more promising sources of aesthetic appreciation, and doomed to a solitary, frustrating existence. These are points based on what the narrative clearly indicates and on reasonable background assumptions that any broadly Woolfian author would have intended readers to employ in making out what is true in her story.[23]

The second moment in the *reductio* involves reference to an aesthetic doctrine that would erroneously classify John's relevant experiences as instances of aesthetic experience or appreciation. That doctrine consists of the proposition that an experience is aesthetic just in case it is an intrinsically good, pleasurable emotion which is a final end (or even the greatest final end). This valuable emotion is provoked by perception of the objects' formal properties, where this perception, and imaginings based on it, in no way depend on knowledge of the object's practical and historical context. John's enjoyment of his solid objects satisfies these conditions and thus counts as a genuinely aesthetic experience, given that doctrine. Yet what Woolf's narrative brings out are the delusionary and projective dimensions of these positively valued emotions, as well as features of the context which put in question their status as genuine autonomous final ends or intrinsic goods. As the doctrine in question contains no clauses that would rule such a case out, its inadequacy is revealed – provided, that is, the characterization of John is in this regard accepted as plausible, and indeed, everything the narrator recounts falls squarely within the realm of conceptual possibility.

It may be protested at this point that the target of this *reductio* is a straw dummy whose features were too patently absurd to be worth the trouble. Yet it may be responded, first of all, that such a conception of aesthetic experience is still in circulation today and is therefore hardly irrelevant. Consider, for example, how many literary scholars have been willing to take John as exemplifying the aesthetic, the artistic, or the aesthete. Secondly, one may respond that the target of Woolf's *reductio* may well have been the actual, historically influential aesthetic doctrine published by Clive Bell.

A brief review of some of Bell's salient contentions in *Art*, suitably spiced with some of his key phrases, should suffice to support the idea that Woolf may very well have had his views in mind as she devised her story.[24] Bell overtly defines aesthetic experience as the supreme intrinsic good. No state of mind can be "more excellent" than the "rapture" that is aesthetic emotion, which arises from the contemplation of pure, significant form.[25] Bell contrasts the "superb peaks of aesthetic exaltation" to the "snug foothills of warm humanity."[26] As the surest and most immediate means to the highest intrinsic good, art needs no non-aesthetic justification or value, and there is no need to look at its other consequences to assess its merit.[27] "To associate art with politics is always a mistake."[28] Yet to associate art, and the aesthetic experiences it provokes, with religion is not a mistake, as Bell repeatedly invites comparisons between religious and aesthetic value.

What Bell has to say about the conditions under which the rapturous aesthetic emotion occurs also fits into my conjecture, as he allows that the emotion is "based on subjective experience"[29] and requires "nothing but sensibility."[30] Knowledge of the work's provenance is "irrelevant."[31] We do not properly appreciate a picture or enjoy an aesthetic emotion "by dint of study."[32] Instead, genuine aesthetic emotion is more like falling in love.[33] Only those who have never really experienced true aesthetic rapture think they must go to museums to find and appreciate beauty.[34]

If it is protested that Bell's concern is with the fine arts, and primarily painting and sculpture, and that his theory thus has nothing to do with either ordinary, non-artistic artifacts or natural objects, some of his remarks in fact open the door to the idea that John's perceptions of, and musings over, the "solid objects" would have to count as aesthetic experiences given Bell's premises. Although Bell at one point distinguishes between beautiful form and significant form (where the former is natural and the latter is artistic), he allows that non-artistic objects can produce the same emotion as works of art – the aesthetic emotion.[35] Further along in his discussion,[36] he distinguishes between three different sub-species of aesthetic emotions: (1) those we experience when contemplating a work of art; (2) those felt by artists in their moments of inspiration (and which may be based on a perception of some natural or other object or scene); and (3) those that some persons feel in the rare moments when they "see objects artistically." Thus if John is neither an artist nor

an appreciator of works of art, his ecstatic perception of a striking piece
of glass, stone, or porcelain may indeed qualify as seeing these objects as
if they were works of art; or again, it may arise from his successful adop
tion of an attitude or stance akin to the artist's inspired perception, in
which the object is perceived "as an end in itself."[37] In another, even more
telling, clause that would further qualify John's pleasures as a species of
aesthetic contemplation, Bell acknowledges that there are those who arrive
at the aesthetic end (the apprehension of reality expressed in form) by
"sheer force of the imagination."[38] In this regard Bell may be echoing
Roger Fry's contrast between the "actual" and the "imaginative" life, where
both art and the child's daydreams are instances of the latter. In a
passage that Woolf was very likely to have read and may well have had
in mind in writing "Solid Objects," Fry writes: "It is only when an object
exists in our lives for no other purpose than to be seen that we really
look at it, as for instance at a China ornament or precious stone, and
towards such even the most normal person adopts to some extent the
artistic attitude of pure vision abstracted from necessity."[39]

   It may be objected that in spite of such phrases, the aesthetic doctrine
promoted by Bell and Fry does not reduce aesthetic experience to the
product of a particular axiological attitude, namely, that of valuing the
contemplation of a thing as a final end. Instead, the formalists insist on
a content-oriented condition as well. In Bell's case, this was a matter of
the doctrine of significant form. The objection would have it, then, that
John cannot be plausibly taken as satisfying Bell's conditions on aesthetic
emotion because the object of his delight is not (uniquely) the significant
form of the objects he finds and acquires. Such an objection, however,
assumes that Bell says something precise enough about significant form
to allow us to rule that John's responses fall outside the category of the
aesthetic. Bell's discussion of what the expression "significant form" is
and is not supposed to refer to is notoriously vague, so there is good
reason to doubt whether this sort of objection can be made to work.
Significant form, it would seem, is just the visual design or organization
of a picture, grasped in abstraction from what the picture depicts. The
objects of John's contemplation are not pictures or depictions, so John's
attention to their shape, design, and visual qualities would seem to count
as an experience of significant form. Woolf's narrator in fact emphasizes
John's attention to the object's perceptual and formal qualities as well
as the pleasurable imaginings to which they give rise in his mind. For
example, when John is distracted by a bit of broken porcelain, we are
told that "The colouring was mainly blue, but green stripes or spots of
some kind overlaid the blue, and lines of crimson gave it a richness and

lustre of the most attractive kind."[40] In the narrator's summary of John's new passion, we read that he was astonished "by the immense variety of shapes to be found in London alone, and there was still more cause for wonder and speculation in the differences of qualities and designs."[41] What he is looking for, we are told, is "Anything, as long as it was an object of some kind, more or less round, perhaps with a dying flame deep sunk in its mass . . ."[42] Such phrases clearly suggest that John's eye is drawn by the objects' formal qualities.

It might be complained that John's pursuit of his solid objects is too much of an active and desperate pursuit to qualify as the sort of contemplative experience Bell must have had in mind.[43] After all, John's business with these objects hardly gives him the "extraordinary exaltation and complete detachment from the concerns of life" extolled by Bell.[44] One problem here is that Bell's remarks about contemplation are so sketchy that it is hard to see how they rule out John's experiences with his solid objects. Yet there is certainly nothing in Bell's account of aesthetic experience and value to rule out John's happier moments with his objects; nor does Bell say successful contemplation of beauty forever releases anyone from all earthly concerns. What starts out for John as the sort of blissful release that Bell evokes degenerates into a hopeless pursuit for another peak experience, and Woolf's narration of this familiar pattern serves as an ethical critique of the elevation of a bad idea about aesthetic value to the supreme end. In sum, there do not seem to be any good grounds for concluding that John fails to satisfy Bell's conditions on aesthetic experience, which means the second step in the *reductio* is a sound one.

It may be objected very generally here that Woolf was not likely to have written a story designed to target the foibles of a theory promoted by her brother-in-law and friends in the Bloomsbury circle, such as Fry. Yet we have good reason to believe that Woolf read Bell's *Art* and had her doubts. Woolf's one letter to Bell on the topic is cordial and respectful, but brief and restrained. This diplomatic letter, with its explicit mention of "a great many" points of disagreement, hardly reads like what a close friend would write had she found the doctrine illuminating or convincing:

> My dear Clive,
> I ought to have thanked you before for sending me your book, considering that I read it through at once, and enjoyed it very much – I liked the chapters of theory more than the historical chapters, which seem to me too much of a generalization – and sometimes perhaps too smart, and of course

there are a great many things I dont [sic] agree with, where I understand. But its [sic] great fun, and full of ideas and I suppose will put people's backs up like cats on a roof at night – but all this you will enjoy. What do the reviews say?

yrs

V. W.[45]

Woolf did not say so in this guarded letter, but she was already aware of what at least one review of the book said, for she had earlier that month written to her husband and commented upon the review penned by Fry, remarking "poor old Roger – so humble and appreciative and eager that people should take Clive seriously."[46] That Woolf could herself be moved to make fun of Bell surfaces in a letter to Lytton Strachey written a year after the publication of *Art*. Here Woolf jokingly proposes that they and other friends contribute to buying Bell a gaudily colored parrot: "The thing is for us all to persuade him that the love of birds is the last word in Civilisation," she adds. One advantage of the plan, she jests, is that Bell "would very likely after a year or two, write another book on Birds."[47] Is it too great a stretch to conjecture here that as far as Woolf was concerned, given Bell's aesthetic theory, one must draw the laughable conclusion that there is no great difference between the appreciation of a parrot's colorful plumage and an artistic masterpiece? It is relevant, but of course not decisive, to note here that by the time Virginia Woolf wrote "Solid Objects," her assessment of Bell's criticism and character had considerably darkened, at least if the rather severe remarks in her diary are to be believed. Bell is said to "have little natural insight into literature;" his devices for appearing successful and brilliant have become "obvious;" he is "battered & dusty in the pursuit of pleasure;" "the most selfish of men;" "a buffoon;" "too appalling;" and a "pismire."[48]

4   Rapture does not Suffice

Woolf may not have had Bell's ideas in mind when she began work on "Solid Objects" in 1918, and she may have instead had a far less precise idea of her satiric target as she developed her characterization of John. She may, for example, have had in mind formalist commonplaces about aesthetic experience and value, or popular ideas that were derived from or loosely associated with Bell's, Fry's, or kindred views. Interpreters who do not think Bell was Woolf's intended target, and those who do not believe in any intentionalist strictures, may still acknowledge that the narrator's presentation of John is an excellent point of departure for exploring what is wrong with Bell's version of formalism, or at least of kindred accounts of aesthetic value and appreciation.

Woolf's story successfully underscores the weakness of any account of aesthetic appreciation, such as Bell's, that does not include sufficiently strong cognitive and content conditions along with an axiological condition. Immediate perception of the object, augmented by imagination or fancy, is insufficient to aesthetic experience, even if the result is of "intrinsic value" taken on its own or serves as a final end for the person involved.[49] Woolf's tale also targets conceptions that cannot maintain the distinction between aesthetic value and the inherently rewarding pleasures of acquisition, fantasy, and imaginative free-play. In the case of artifacts, at least, the application of contextual knowledge is a condition on adequate appreciation. As Woolf's story only represents genuine aesthetic value and experience *via negativa*, no quotable claims about the proper relation between aesthetic and other values, such as ethical ones, are on offer. It is not, however, plausible to imagine that Virginia Woolf did not believe in the aesthetic value of art or in that of aesthetic experience more generally. Yet she is likely to have had doubts about Bell's (or anyone else's) attempt to make "aesthetic rapture" – at least on his conception of that state, the highest final value, and indeed, a kind of "salvation" (as Bell put it). To his "Rapture suffices,"[50] Woolf's response seems to have been "No it does not," which is not to say she thought anything else – such as politics or a religion of art – could suffice to offer "salvation," or the end of all ends.

On this point it may be instructive to read a passage from *To the Lighthouse*:

> As summer neared, as the evening lengthened, there came to the wakeful, the hopeful, walking the beach, stirring the pool, imaginations of the strangest kind – of flesh turned to atoms which drove before the wind, of stars flashing in their hearts, of cliff, sea, cloud, and sky brought purposely together to assemble outwardly the scattered parts of vision within. In those mirrors, the minds of men, in those pools of uneasy water, in which clouds for ever turn and shadows form, dreams persisted, and it was impossible to resist the strange intimation which every gull, flower, tree, man and woman, and the white earth itself seemed to declare (but if questioned at once to withdraw) that good triumphs, happiness prevails, order rules; or to resist the extraordinary stimulus to range hither and thither in search of some absolute good, some crystal of intensity, remote from the known pleasures and familiar virtues, something alien to the processes of domestic life, single, hard, bright, like a diamond in the sand, which would render the possessor secure.[51]

Woolf's narrator here evokes an irresistible "extraordinary stimulus" to range about on the beach in search of some unusual, absolute good, some hard diamond in the sand – an object similar to the solid lump of glass found by John. The dream of discovering some "crystal of intensity" representing ultimate value and security is not presented here as the thought of artists, aesthetes, or some unusual, eccentric or childlike personality, but as the thoughts of the "wakeful" and "hopeful" observers on the beach. Yet Woolf's narrator also "comes back to earth" by going on to contrast such hopes of security and "salvation" with bracketed reports on such disastrous events as the death of Prue Ramsay in childbirth. Nature, the narrator concludes, does not supplement what the dreamy and hopeful observers had advanced: "With equal complacence she saw his misery, condoned his meanness, and acquiesced in his torture." The mirror of human hopes and desires, formed by the beauty of the scene of the seashore, "was broken."

Notes

1   Virginia Woolf, *The Common Reader, Second Series* (London: Hogarth Press, 1932), pp. 233–4. The cited phrase figures in chapter 19, "The Novels of George Meredith."

2   For an emphasis on Woolf's interest in epistemological issues, with specific reference to Bertrand Russell, see Jaakko Hintikka, "Virginia Woolf and our Knowledge of the External World," *Journal of Aesthetics and Art Criticism* 38 (1979): 5–14. Philosophers and philosophical questions about knowledge, perception, and selfhood are also central to the readings embroidered in Ann Banfield, *The Phantom Table: Woolf, Fry, Russell and the Epistemology of Modernism* (Cambridge: Cambridge University Press, 2000).

3   "Solid Objects," *Atheneum* (October 20, 1920): 543–5. Republished in *A Haunted House and Other Short Stories* (London: Hogarth Press, 1944; reprint, London: Grafton, 1982). Page numbers given in these notes refer to those of the latter edition.

4   For an overview of the Moore-Woolf connection, see Gabriel Franks, "Virginia Woolf and the Philosophy of G. E. Moore," *The Personalist* 50 (1969): 222–40. For the influence of Moore on Bloomsbury, see S. P. Rosenbaum, *Victorian Bloomsbury: The Early Literary History of the Bloomsbury Group* (Basingstoke: Palgrave Macmillan, 1987), chapter 10; and Tom Regan, *Bloomsbury's Prophet: G. E. Moore and the Development of His Moral Philosophy* (Philadelphia, PA: Temple University Press, 1986). Regan writes, of Virginia Woolf's comprehension of Moore, that "Few have understood the essential spirit of the author or his work as well" (p. 210). For an astute survey of Bell's ideas and their relation to Moore's views, see Jeffrey

T. Dean, "Clive Bell and G. E. Moore: The Good of Art," *British Journal of Aesthetics* 36 (1996): 135–45.

5 Bill Brown, "The Secret Life of Things: Virginia Woolf and the Matter of Modernism," in Pamela R. Matthews and David McWhirter, eds., *Aesthetic Subjects* (Minneapolis, MN: The University of Minnesota Press, 2003), pp. 397–430. This essay was initially published in *Modernism/Modernity* 6 (1999): 1–28; my page numbers are those of the 2003 publication.

6 Panthea Reid, *Art and Affection: A Life of Virginia Woolf* (Oxford: Oxford University Press, 1996), p. 241; cf. Panthea Reid Broughton, "The Blasphemy of Art: Fry's Aesthetics and Woolf's Non-'Literary' Stories," in Diane F. Gillespie, ed., *The Multiple Muses of Virginia Woolf* (Columbia, MO: University of Missouri Press, 1993), pp. 36–57.

7 Robert A. Watson suggests that John's idiosyncratic pursuit of objects represents the dangers of the solitary creative imagination; see his "'Solid Objects' as Allegory," *Virginia Woolf Miscellany* 16 (1981): 3–4. In his *Virginia Woolf: A Study of the Shorter Fiction* (Boston, MA: Twayne, 1989), pp. 19–20, Dean R. Baldwin describes the story as illustrating the artist's failure to communicate, and conjectures that Woolf based the character John on a suicidal artist, Mark Gertler, with whom she was acquainted. Michelle Levy reckons that one of the main points of the story is the importance of striking the right balance between "subjects" and "objects," the failure to do so being exemplified by John's solitary quest; see her "Virginia Woolf's Shorter Fictional Explorations of the External World: 'Closely United . . . Immensely Divided'," in Kathryn Benzel and Ruth Hoberman, eds., *Trespassing Boundaries: Virginia Woolf's Short Fiction* (Basingstoke: Palgrave Macmillan, 2004), pp. 139–56. With Lacanian notions in tow, Emily Dalgarno stretches the allegorical contrast even further: the two characters "mirror each other, suggesting a world divided between the visible and the intelligible, the artistic and the professional." See her *Virginia Woolf and the Visible World* (Cambridge: Cambridge University Press, 2001), p. 11.

8 Douglas Mao, *Solid Objects: Modernism and the Test of Production* (Princeton, NJ: Princeton University Press, 1998). Ruth Hoberman concurs with Mao's reading, adding that the author's emphasis on John's isolation serves to underscore the danger run by modernist artists who "overvalue the work of art itself – however hard they emphasize the labor involved – in isolation from its consumption by readers or buyers." See her "Collecting, Shopping, and Reading: Virginia Woolf's Stories about Objects," in *Trespassing Boundaries: Virginia Woolf's Short Fiction*, pp. 81–98, at p. 87. Woolf's relation to Walter Pater is explored in Perry Meisel's *The Absent Father: Virginia Woolf and Walter Pater* (New Haven, CT: Yale University Press, 1980). Meisel's claims are difficult to restate clearly, but he seems to contend that Woolf was heavily influenced by Pater but swerved anxiously away from and disavowed this model, and thereby ended up returning to

her father's moralistic condemnation of Pater's aestheticism. Meisel also appears to suggest that Pater's writings are fundamentally incoherent.

9   Brown, "The Secret Life of Things," p. 421.

10 Ibid., p. 418.

11 Natania Rosenfeld, *Outsiders Together: Virginia and Leonard Woolf* (Princeton, NJ: Princeton University Press, 2000), p. 111.

12 Woolf, "Solid Objects," p. 83.

13 Ibid., pp. 80–81.

14 Ibid., p. 81.

15 Ibid., pp. 81–2.

16 Ibid., p. 83.

17 Ibid., p. 84.

18 Ibid., p. 85.

19 Ibid., p. 84.

20 Leonard Woolf, "Virginia Woolf: Writer and Personality," *Listener* (March 4, 1965): 327–8.

21 On the (fairly tenuous) link between Woolf, Moore, and the value of friendship, see Sally A. Jacobsen, "Was Virginia Woolf an Apostle?" in Mark Hussey, ed., *Virginia Woolf: Themes and Variations* (New York: Pace University Press, 1993), pp. 329–37.

22 On monism and pluralism about final ends and "the good life," see David Schmidtz, *Rational Choice and Moral Agency* (Princeton, NJ: Princeton University Press, 1995), pp. 90–94.

23 The object of my interpretation, then, is supposed to be the story written by Virginia Woolf, not the string of sentences associated with the story and whatever meanings can be based on those sentences' basic linguistic meanings. For background on my assumptions about texts, works, interpretation, and fictional truth, see *Art and Intention: A Philosophical Study* (Oxford: Clarendon Press, 2005).

24 Clive Bell, *Art* (London: Chatto and Windus, 1912; reprint, New York: Capricorn Books, G. P. Putnam's Sons, 1958). Page numbers given in the text are those of the latter edition.

25 Ibid., p. 54.

26 Ibid., p. 31.

27 Ibid., p. 84.

28 Ibid., p. 24.

29 Ibid., p. 18.

30 Ibid., p. 73.

31 Ibid., p. 73.

32 Ibid., p. 73.

33 Ibid., p. 173.

34 Ibid., p. 173.

35 Ibid., p. 20.

36 Ibid., p. 46.

37   Ibid., p. 45.

38   Ibid., p. 48.

39   Roger Fry, *Vision and Design* (London: Chatto and Windus, 1920), p. 25. Bell and Fry had various disagreements, but in his concluding "Retrospect" of 1920, Fry tries to square his views with the doctrine of significant form.

40   Woolf, "Solid Objects," p. 83.

41   Ibid., p. 84.

42   Ibid., p. 83.

43   Thanks to Berys Gaut for raising this objection.

44   Bell, Art, p. 83.

45   Virginia Woolf, letter to Clive Bell, March 20, 1914, in Nigel Nicolson, ed., *The Question of Things Happening: The Letters of Virginia Woolf*, vol. 2 (1912–22), (London: Hogarth, 1976), p. 46.

46   Virginia Woolf, letter to Leonard Woolf, March 9, 1914, in Nicolson, *The Question of Things Happening*, p. 41.

47   Virginia Woolf, letter to Lytton Strachey, February 26, 1915, in *The Question of Things Happening*, p. 61.

48   *The Diary of Virginia Woolf*, 5 vols., ed. Anne Olivier Bell (London: Penguin, 1979), entries of January 14, 1918; May 28, 1918; July 10, 1919; October 30, 1919; September 15, 1920; March 13, 1921.

49   For a more general discussion of conditions on aesthetic experience, see my "C. I. Lewis and the Outlines of Aesthetic Experience," *British Journal of Aesthetics* 44 (2004): 378–92; and Gary Iseminger, "The Aesthetic State of Mind," in Matthew Kieran, ed., *Contemporary Debates in Aesthetics and the Philosophy of Art* (Oxford: Blackwell, 2006), pp. 98–110.

50   Bell, *Art*, p. 160.

51   Virginia Woolf, *To the Lighthouse* (London: Hogarth, 1927), p. 126.

6

DISGRACE: BERNARD WILLIAMS AND J. M. COETZEE

Catherine Wilson

1   Introduction: Williams's Critique of Moral Theory

Shame and Necessity, Bernard Williams's study of Greek ethical concepts, is regarded by many readers as his boldest and most important book. A critic of some aspects of modernity, an inheritor of the tradition of Dostoevsky and Nietzsche, Williams set himself the task of undermining the Kantianism and utilitarianism whose influence in moral and political theory was manifest in the literature of the 1960s and 1970s.

Rather than appealing to rights and principles as constraints on consequentialist projection, as John Rawls had done in his own critique of utilitarianism, Williams challenged the pretensions of eighteenth- and nineteenth-century moral theory to generality and objectivity and its assumptions concerning agency and value. He argued that moral agents could not and need not appeal to theories to manage their complex and often rationally insoluble dilemmas. Philosophy, he thought, "should not try to produce ethical theory, though this does not mean that philosophy cannot offer any critique of ethical beliefs and ideas . . . [I]n ethics, the reductive enterprise has no justification and should disappear . . . Practical thought is radically first-personal. It must ask and answer the question 'what shall *I* do?'"[1] The utilitarianism he characterized as "Government House morality," a reference to Jeremy Bentham's intellectual role in the management of the Indian subcontinent under colonial administration, was associated in his mind with a kind of interfering bureaucratic rationality that aroused nostalgia for an unmanaged, unfettered, and heroic age. Yet Williams was a subtle and well-informed critic. His views on morality and moral theory have been compared with Friedrich Nietzsche's,[2] but his urbanity and light touch distinguished him from the philosophers of alienation with whom he otherwise had much in common.[3] Unlike Nietzsche, he engaged with his subject matter not merely as a master of the cut and thrust, but as an insider competent in philosophical analysis and sensitive as Nietzsche was not to human conflicts and dependencies. As Martha Nussbaum expressed it in a remarkable obituary,

> He believed that much philosophy of the past had represented a flight from reality, a rationalistic defense against complexity, emotion, and tragedy. Utilitarianism and Kantianism, particularly, had simplified the moral life in ways that he found egregious, failing to understand, or even actively deny-ing, the heterogeneity of values, the sometimes tragic collisions between one thing we care for and another. They also underestimated the import-ance of personal attachments and projects in the ethical life and, in a related way, neglected the valuable role emotions play in good choice. Finally, they failed to come to grips with the many ways in which sheer luck affects not only happiness but the ethical life itself, shaping our very possibilities for choice.[4]

Why look at fiction? Williams asked in *Shame and Necessity*. Why not take examples from life? The question, he went on to say, is perfectly good, "and it has a short answer: what philosophers will lay before themselves and their readers as an alternative to literature will not be life, but bad literature."[5] By this he seems to have meant that the scenarios philo-sophers choose or concoct as examples are as invented as the stories of the dramatist but inferior in depth and detail. The narratives we give of our own lives may be as inflected by the fiction we have read as anything from the writer's pen and at the same time lacking in authorial distance. His aim in the book was to recover and rehabilitate certain ancient moral con-cepts that inform ancient drama and epic poetry. The "shame" of the title refers to the attitude with which the heroes of ancient literary traditions regard themselves when they become aware of some injury they have perpetrated that has brought them into a condition of disgrace. The shamed individual suddenly sees himself as others of higher status would see him, and a miasma of malign influence may already have leaked out of him and polluted his relationships. The "necessity" of the title refers in turn to a curious feature of classical tragedy, namely that the ancients possessed a somewhat less flexible view of nature, society, and the self than we moderns do. The disgraced hero does not necessarily look back on his own actions as those of an autonomous, reasoning subject, nor does he consider the multitude of chance factors that conspired to produce the tragic outcome. His shameful action was typically performed when he was beside himself with emotion, or driven by a god. Yet these circumstances are not mitigating, and wherever the hero has caused an injury, he can appreciate that he is required to atone for it and to right the cosmic balance with his own pain.

Williams wanted to refute a position he called "progresssivism" – the view that Greek notions of responsibility, blame, and reparation are primitive and inferior to post-Kantian modern notions in their superstitious reliance on notions of fate, their exaggerated conceptions of responsibility, and their appeals to the supernatural. He did not share Freud's view that literature, including classical drama, presents an imaginary world of heightened affect "sharply separated from reality" that satisfies instinctual needs by permitting the vicarious enactment of unfettered agency.[6] He went well beyond this in suggesting that modern moral philosophy would benefit from an injection of archaic notions of the inevitability of differential power into our concept of the permissible, and, by implication, that human life might be enriched by greater boldness.

The South African writer J. M. Coetzee's 1999 novel, *Disgrace*, invites a reading against Williams's analysis of tragedy and his general moral theory. The concepts of shame and necessity make multiple appearances in the novel as the author's spotlight falls on his various characters in turn, with the notions of responsibility and atonement constantly in play. Yet Coetzee's novel introduces a dimension of action and reaction that is absent in Greek tragedy, the effects on individuals, not just of winds, tides, and chance encounters, but of manmade sources of disaster – political reforms and social upheavals in which hapless subjects can be caught unprepared, as they rehearse their customary practices and go about their lives in their habitual ways. They face these events not as special heroic individuals – the usual subjects of tragedy – but as ordinary people who are at the same time representatives of types and classes. Coetzee's novel sometimes reinforces Williams's protest against moral theory, but at the same time it points to some of the limitations of the archaic framework.

"Disgrace" in Coetzee's own title refers to the particular events that stain the hero, who is publicly humiliated in a sex scandal and loses his job; his daughter, who is raped; and the family of the girl he seduced, who are troubled and dishonored by her return home. It refers as well to stains on the historical record of the human race: the subjection of Africans under colonization and then apartheid; the subjection of animals and the callousness exercised towards them when they become inconvenient, unserviceable, or simply too numerous; the careless use of women for men's pleasure and convenience. The introduction of a socio-political and historical backdrop brings Williams's individualism, his rejection of certain kinds of generalizing moral theory, and so his anti-modernism into a somewhat different focus than the concentration on ancient tragedy allows.

Equality is, after all, a notion pertaining to statistical patterns. Democratizing movements including the realignment of power relations between black and white, slave and free, female and male, seem to presuppose a utilitarian framework in which the powers and liberties of an individual, or, for that matter, a species, class, race, or sex, are limited or cancelled by powerful institutions in order to boost the welfare of a complementary group, on the grounds that, from the perspective of morals and politics, no one's interests ought to count more than anyone else's. The rationalist position Williams attacked as "Government House morality" places average or aggregate welfare, as determined by an elite class of philosophers, at the top of its list of values. The systematic association of power and virtue in archaic Greek philosophy, the tendency to regard being badly off as disgraceful in and of itself, and personal excellence or virtue as mirrored in the possession of external goods and the exercise of political powers, is foreign to such redistributive ideals. Even philosophers like Plato and the Stoics, who distinguished moral worth from worldly success, admired a kind of excellence that in principle was attainable only by a few. The notion of equality has always been something of a sticking point for Williams's moral philosophy. So it will be useful in the course of this chapter to pay attention to his views on the problems of slavery and subordination as they appear in *Shame and Necessity*, and to the problems of prestige and entitlement as they appear in his ethical writings.

2   *Disgrace* and Greek tragedy

David Lurie, the 52-year-old hero of *Disgrace*, is an ordinary academic devoid of heroic strength, cunning, or aspirations, though he harbors a secret ambition to complete an entire opera about Byron's discarded mistress Teresa Guiccioli, which he is meanwhile composing in his head. At the beginning of the story, he is living modestly and contentedly as a Communications Professor, specializing in romantic poetry. Twice-divorced, Lurie has lost confidence in marriage, but his position has enabled him to sustain himself in recent years with what he refers to as "adventures," with young women, and, as opportunities dry up, with comfortable routines with prostitutes. His abrupt discovery that his current favorite is a married housewife with young children rattles him badly, and he finds himself unable to continue with her. Soon however a lovely young girl in his literature class strikes his fancy, and a new and exciting adventure appears to be in the offing. Seduction is easy, though Melanie's reluctance is as plain to the reader, though not to the hero, as that of the sick dogs he will help to euthanize later in the story.

> She does not resist. All she does is avert herself: avert her lips, avert her eyes. She lets him lay her out on the bed and undress her: she even helps him, raising her arms and then her hips . . . not rape, not quite that, but undesired nevertheless, undesired to the core. As though she had decided to go slack, die within herself for the duration, like a rabbit when the jaws of the fox close on its neck.[7]

Her indifference and alienation provoke David's fascination with an ideal of elusive femininity. As his obsession with her grows, so does her sense of conflict and confusion. She drops out of her university course and files a complaint of sexual harassment. The complaint leads to public exposure of David's misdeeds in the local newspapers, investigation by an academic tribunal, and humiliation.

Lurie's former wife remarks later, "You've lost your job, your name is mud, your friends avoid you, you hide out in Torrance Road like a tortoise afraid to stick its neck out of its shell."[8] David's disgrace fits Williams's characterization of shame as involving the knowledge that one has been seen "inappropriately and by the wrong people in the wrong condition."[9] He flees to the cottage of his lesbian daughter, Lucy, who is homesteading in the countryside, where both become victims of a ferocious attack by thieves who rape Lucy and set fire to David. Lucy, who becomes pregnant as a result of the rape, eventually becomes the wife of her African former farmhand, Petrus, who knew her attackers and seems to have done nothing to stop them, and who is now poised and legally entitled to take over Lucy's property. David attempts to expiate his crimes with an awkward visit to Melanie's family, and he acquires a new job assisting with the disposition of the bodies of euthanized dogs at an animal welfare facility and a plain middle-aged mistress who works alongside him providing the lethal injections.

Many persons and living things in the novel have been put out of, or have left their proper places. When Melanie crosses the threshold of David's bedroom, we are aware that she shouldn't be there, and when she leaves off being a complaisant student guarding her own reputation and sues David, she leaves it again. Lucy has left her proper place as a middle-class city dweller, David is forced to resign his position in the academy and is displaced to the countryside; the gang of vicious men and Petrus are descendants of the men and women who were earlier displaced from their land but who have returned to displace the current settlers. A half-black baby is growing inside a white mother, a lesbian has become a wife in a polygamous household, and various animals, first displaced from the wild to the domestic state, are further displaced from their usual roles as companions of man to caged patients, and then euthanized and cremated victims. All these displacements are associated with confrontation and aggression. At the end of the novel, there is no restoration of things to their proper roles and locations, as the miasma of pollution is dissipated by the sacrifices of the guilty. Rather, history, morality, and politics have fashioned new and strange forms of co-operation. Despite the appearance of these new forms of getting together and getting along, *Disgrace* offers a tragic vision: David's and Lucy's lives, while still worth living, are far from the sort of lives they had envisioned for themselves.

The premise of tragedy is that human beings are capable of wrecking their own lives, of bringing upon themselves disabling conditions from which they cannot recover. As Williams says, "someone may simply have ruined his life, or if he will not let anything make such an absolute determination of it, at least he may have brought it to a state of dereliction from which large initiatives and a lot of luck would be needed to get it back to anything worth having."[10] At the same time, the unraveling of the aging seducer David's world-as-he knew-it coincides with the virginal Lucy's hopeful expectation of a child, through whom opposites will be joined, aggression forgiven, and conflict forgotten. David begins, finally, under these extreme conditions to understand and feel:

> One Sunday evening, driving home in Lucy's kombi, he actually has to stop at the roadside to recover himself. Tears flow down his face that he cannot stop; his hands shake . . . He does not understand what is happening to him. Until now, he has been more or less indifferent to animals. Although in an abstract way he disapproves of cruelty, he cannot tell whether by nature he is cruel or kind. He is simply nothing . . . Habit hardens; it must be so in most cases, but it does not seem to be so in his . . . His whole being is gripped by what happens in the theatre.[11]

As Williams points out, moral luck is such that the narratives we construct, and the descriptions and valuation agents and observers attach to beginnings, are shaped by knowledge of their endpoints. "It is an illusion to suppose that there had to be at the time of those episodes a particular kind of psychological event that occurred if things turned out in one of these ways, and not if they turned out in another."[12] An illicit affair culminating in a happy marriage becomes a story of irresistible love that brooks no obstacles; one ending in anger or dejection becomes a story of blundering stupidity and lack of self-control. Description and evaluation fluctuate depending on the observer's standpoint. David is aware on some level that he is dealing with an ordinary young woman and not a romantic heroine:

> At four o'clock the next afternoon, he is at her flat. She opens the door wearing a crumpled T-shirt, cycling shorts, slippers in the shape of comic-book gophers which he finds silly, tasteless.[13]

David nevertheless romanticizes his encounter with Melanie, insisting to himself that despite the difference in their ages, his declining attractiveness, her "blank incomprehension" of everything he says to her, and her ordinariness down to the tips of her gopher-faced slippers, they might have had a future together. "In the whole wretched business there was something generous that was doing its best to flower."[14] In his defense to the harassment tribunal, David in turn invokes the timeless and implacable demands of Eros, the force that Nietzsche described as beyond good and evil. "My case rests on the rights of desire . . . on the god who makes even the small birds quiver."

Though nothing in Melanie's behavior suggested anything was doing its best to flower, David acts from what Spinoza calls the necessity of his nature. From the first-person perspective, the emotions have extraordinary authority at the time when they are experienced, and they would not otherwise have the function they do in the animal economy. No philosopher is likely to maintain that fury and vindictiveness are beyond good and evil, but even such cool minds as Plato, Descartes, Spinoza, and Nietzsche have accorded particular respect to amorous passion. The tribunal that questions and passes sentence on him however does not. Its judges interpret David's actions from a generalized and political perspective; his interrogators insist that they exemplify an old pattern of male privilege and female submission that is now known to be a moral aberration in social life.

The first-person feeling of not being able to stop, however authoritative, one might say, occurs in a determinate and objective historical and political context, which gives it a different significance, and over time alters its intensity and manifestations. The impulse to fall on one's knees or weep no longer afflicts us with the same irresistibility, and the impression of what is appropriate emotional expression, whether it is savagery towards enemies – encouraged by the god of war; or the beating of slaves

– stimulated by righteous anger – is not a historical constant. After time *t*, in short, agents find it easier to stop doing certain things and to start others than they did before time *t*. All human societies define certain others, who might, in the absence of the prohibition, become such as inappropriate objects of passion: persons of the wrong sex, age, degree of relatedness, social class, ethnicity, or expected future prospects. They are identified to us and their prohibited status explained by appeal to whatever superstitions are in force, or whatever prudential rationales are available. David is caught up in a moment of redefinition, when a certain category of person has abruptly changed in status without his realizing it.

As Williams observes, the Greeks regarded unfortunate events as needing explanation, typically in terms of a responsible human agent in ways that look irrational to modern eyes. According to the system of tragedy, "you can be held responsible by others for what you did unintentionally. Those who have been hurt need a response; simply what has happened to them may give them a right to seek it, and where can they look more appropriately than to you, the cause?"[15] Responsibility was determined for them by outcomes, while the sense of the tragic was maintained by the knowledge of the spectator that, in a causally complex world where we do not know everything, this is in some sense unfair. We moderns understand that causality is distributed, that most causes are contributing and not necessary and sufficient to produce their effects, and that individuals serve as *foci imaginarii* for the origination of actions. To a contemporary social psychologist, the responsibility attributions of the Greeks really are seriously irrational. There is little of value to be drawn from them, and the progressivist view that we are fortunately beyond all that is well warranted.

The novel leaves it unclear whether Melanie was actually harmed by David's successful advances or is merely exploiting a situation to disguise her academic incompetence. She was not coerced, deceived, or abandoned, and she has merely experienced a slightly disgraceful episode of giving in to a man for whom she had no feeling. David's fall is clearly out of proportion to any harm she could have suffered. Yet David is not just the imputed cause of an isolated and rather small misfortune. There has been grave harm, and he is a classic scapegoat who is forced to take on the sins of the world. He suffers vengeance and misfortune entirely out of proportion to the suffering he has personally caused, in accord with the tragic principle that, wherever there is suffering, the costs of redemption must be extracted from some human agent. The institution of which he is a part seizes the opportunity to make an example of him for its own ends, and he is punished for a far larger fraction of the harms to women than he is personally responsible for. Indeed, he is punished, as one of the other characters points out, for crimes that others committed and for which they got off scot-free. As the novel progresses, moreover, David's individuality and the triggering event lose their importance; the story has less and less to do with a reasonably sympathetic but somewhat naïve character who is treated unfairly by an impersonal bureaucracy staffed by persons with petty resentments. To the extent that the novel makes sense to us, we accept its literary-theological-philosophical framework. It is at the same time worth reflecting on the fact that the Greeks, despite what we do share of their worldview, would have been baffled by the novel, and unable to comprehend it as an allegory of justice. The application of the tragic principle to a story involving subject people, animals, and women would not have occurred to them.

3   The Problem of Power

In his celebrated and much-discussed essay "Moral Luck," Williams introduced a fictional character "Gauguin" who "turns away from definite and pressing human claims on him in order to live a life in which, as he supposes, he can pursue his art."[16] He cannot foresee what will happen and he certainly cannot inspect some balance sheet of pains and pleasures. Yet, "if he fails . . . then he did the wrong thing . . . in the sense that . . . he has no basis for the thought that he was justified in acting as he did. If he succeeds, he does have a basis for that thought."[17] This conception invites the question whether David can be read as a Gauguin figure – as an agent who, rather blindly, assumes certain personal risks in the pursuit of an ideal about which he cares strongly, and with whom we sympathize. It also raises the question whether Gauguin can be read as a David figure, as one whose actions, commanded by his own gods, exposed him to the real possibility of moral failure and disgrace.

David is a victim of moral luck; things might have gone well for him as they went well for others before him, but his fancy alighted on the wrong person. Yet David's risky activities are not, as noted, the focus of the narrative. His seemingly private and personal actions propel him into the midst of the political story, in which he finds himself, through no particular action or decision of his own, in the wrong place at the wrong time. He and Lucy come to understand themselves not as individuals but as representatives of groups in morally problematic relationships with other groups: men versus women, light-skinned versus dark-skinned, human versus animal; invader versus native. Both stories presuppose certain common elements of liberty and privilege: male intellectual and artistic talent versus female incompetence; male freedom and mobility versus female passivity and dependence; colonial power versus native submission. David and Lucy, however, lose their comfortable and superior positions because certain ethical values have come into play, whereas Gauguin's lucky outcome has no positive moral significance. Indeed his "success" simply reinforces an imbalanced state of affairs that existed when he assumed his personal risks.

From the perspective of the individual, the moral question is often "I can . . . so why should I not?" The Greek handling of this basic ethical question was, as Williams showed, very different from the modern handling of it. The Greeks were ambivalent about personal power. To be exalted over others, it seemed to them, to have the freedom to do many things and important things, brought gratification and deserved admiration. It was inevitable, on their view, that some persons and some groups possessed more personal power than others, and ethically concerned philosophers were less concerned with equalizing power than with ensuring that it did not fall into the hands of ignorant and impulsive persons. For, those who possessed exceptional degrees of power were acknowledged to be potentially dangerous to others. The presentation of ethical ideals through philosophy, and the presentation of dire consequences through literary tragedy, furnished the terms in which Greek society discussed the problem of power with itself. Tragedy embodied a claim about how the world works: the deployment of excess power, it proposed, stretched capacities to the breaking point and produced exhaustion, resistance, and retaliation. Yet the delights of power were acknowledged at the same time. To be in control of things, to have others do your bidding, to enjoy an excess of leisure as a result – all this was seen as enviable.

The modern approach to power is considerably less ambivalent. As anti-modernists have so often complained, modern institutions aim to capture and contain power, to act swiftly and retributively against its excesses and to reduce the individual's capacity to exercise differential powers by making people as equal as possible. They seek at the same time to reduce or eliminate the effects of chance – including the chance effect of being in a favorable position with favorable qualities. Risk is viewed as capable of mitigation by information – forewarned is forearmed; by sacrifice – avoiding pursuits with a large downside potential; by sharing risks with others though the purchase of insurance; and, when these measures fail, by stepping in with rehabilitative medicines, therapies, and programs. On the tragic view of life that Williams wanted to recover, risk, like differential power, is inevitable, and to be both feared and welcomed. It is inevitable because human foresight is limited and the future is veiled from us. Sometimes information is lacking; sometimes we are given it but in oracular form that we do not understand except in retrospect. Some misfortunes cannot be compensated and cured; they outstrip knowledge and power. Yet by avoiding risky pursuits, we cut ourselves off from the significant experiences that distinguish better and happier lives from less good and happy ones.

These were valuable and much needed insights in the context in which Williams was writing, in which a certain dreariness had overtaken moral philosophy. Yet when it came to explaining the intersection of the personal and the political, Williams found himself on less firm ground. Coetzee was concerned in *Disgrace* with the miasma spread by class power and the emotions it triggers, but also with a condition of disgrace that is experienced by no individual, but that is as objective and real as the shame of the tragic hero.

4   The Evaluation of Social and Political Institutions

The personalities Williams discusses in *Shame and Necessity* have certain characteristics in common. They are "supermen" with unusual capacities, such as exceptional strength, and few inhibitions; Gauguin in turn possesses exceptional artistic talent. Ajax slaughters a field of sheep in a temporary fit of madness; Gauguin abandons wife and children to sail to Tahiti and paint. But where the Greek moral is that the deployment of extraordinary powers tends to bring about a person's downfall or necessitate his self-destruction, Gauguin in Williams's story escapes the fate of tragic heroes and moral condemnation as well. We remember him not for the moral lesson, but for his artistic accomplishments. (The historical Gauguin, who in fact died syphilitic, alcoholic, and alone, is not even held up to young artists as a warning example.)

Williams's model for individual action, one might imagine on the basis of "Moral Luck" and *Shame and Necessity* is this: exercise power where you can, but be prepared to take the consequences. The universe contains many mechanisms that limit the hubris of individuals. Depending on how things turn out, you may delight in the exercise of your powers and capabilities and bring value into the world, or you may rue the day you crossed your threshold, ruining your life beyond repair. The vengeance of whatever gods you offended may be out of proportion moreover to what you actually did, or at least what you thought you were doing and intended to do. These are the cautions to keep in mind when you are feeling overly expansive – not the rigidities of Kantian formulas of duty or the complications of Benthamite calculations. The conception of moral luck implied in these prescriptions suggests an indefinitely revisable past where evaluation is concerned. What happens next may make any given event fortunate or unfortunate and reverse its polarity from one moment to the next. Losing your job is a misfortune, but if it allows you to establish contact with your daughter, it is, after all, a piece of good fortune. Establishing contact with your daughter is in turn good, but if you are set on fire as a result, it is regrettable that you went to see her, though, if you make a decent recovery, it's good after all that you did, and so on. In principle, we observers don't know, and the one who lives the life doesn't know either, whether it is a ruined or a happy life, or indeed nothing special, until the end of that life.

The notion that personal history cannot be evaluated until it is all over with the person prompts a parallel question for institutional history. Might one say that the invention of the institution of Greek and Roman slavery was a misfortune for the slaves, but that, as things turned out, it was fortunate, because the leisure for the educated classes that slavery permitted afforded the benefits of civilization, philosophy, and enlightenment generally, but that these achievements brought their own misfortunes in turn, in part because the philosophy in question was marked by delusory notions of natural hierarchy and biological superiority? Is it possible that the freeing of slaves is fortunate for them, but that it has also brought new misfortunes into the world, including increased levels of conflict, neglect, and insecurity, and that we have yet to appreciate whether, from conflict, neglect, and insecurity, new goods will eventually flow? Perhaps until the end of human history, it will be impossible to assign any particular value to the social and political changes that take place in it, and since we will never be able (and would never want) to stand outside a completed world and judge it, we cannot judge political events in utilitarian terms anymore than we can estimate the moral worth of someone's life to that person "from outside," though we and the agent will in fact react spontaneously with admiration or contempt, with feelings of self-satisfaction or remorse and regret.

If the analogy between personal history and institutional history held, we could experience, collectively, emotions such as regret, relief, remorse, and joy at political events as they take shape. The dismantling of colonial rule, the creation of tribunals to evaluate sexual harassment, the growth of agribusiness and the pet industry, would elicit different responses, even while we recognized that our greatest-good-for-the greatest-number calculations were as likely to be as flawed as our judgments at various times about what was good for us personally. In the absence of knowledge, we would be right to act out of the convictions and passions of the present, projecting ourselves hopefully into an unknown future.

This is not, however, the perspective of substantive moral and political theory, which adopts a standpoint and makes evaluations that are resolutely from outside and that presuppose that the costs and benefits of particular social arrangements like slavery can be satisfactorily assessed right now. If, such evaluations are permissible and indeed necessary, why, one might wonder, should we accept Williams's account of personal morality? Might it not be a kind of duty to think in Kantian or consequentialist terms even if no meta-ethical argument for the correctness of the objective standpoint is available? Might this not correspond to an "ethical stance" that cannot be formally justified but whose worth is proved by experience and history?[18]

In one remarkable essay, Williams did consider an abstract moral ideal – that of equality – from outside, but in a manner that took account of the perspective "from here." This essay, "The Idea of Equality," begins by asking what sort of ideals pertaining to social equality are defensible. Williams notes that there are respects in which all men are alike and respects in which they are not alike. In their skill, intelligence, strength, and virtue, they are different, though in other characteristics – their propensities to use tools, speak a language, live in societies, and interbreed with members of other racial groups freely – they are all the same. They are also all the same in "the capacity to feel pain, both from immediate physical causes, and from various situations represented in perception and in thought; and the capacity to feel affection for others, and the consequences of this, connected with frustration of this affection, loss of its objects, etc."[19] Another universal characteristic is the desire for self-respect, as distinct from the desire for worldly prestige, which varies from person to person. It is, moreover, "certain that there are political and social arrangements that systematically neglect those characteristics in the case of some groups of men, while being fully aware of them in the case of others; that is to say . . . they neglect moral claims that arise from these characteristics and that would be admitted to arise from them."[20] The social or institutionalized mistreatment of others does not stem, Williams points out, from a moral principle to the effect that some persons deserve worse or better treatment, though this may be believed and offered as rationalization, but from a disregard for those moral-reason giving characteristics.

Williams now turns to the notion of respect for others, the attitude that prevents an agent or a group of agents from degrading or exploiting a person or an entire group of others, and he contrasts Aristotelian with Kantian notions of the obligation to respect others, finding both unsatisfactory. Aristotle thinks that moral worth – how good a person is, and also the amount of respect and consideration another is entitled to – can depend on contingencies, on accidents of birth, endowments, or competencies. This conflicts with our sense that moral worth is independent of birth, intelligence, talent, wealth, and other external characteristics. The latter intuition is expressed by Kant, who claims that their common membership in a species possessing rationality and free will is sufficient to ground claims for equal moral worth in all human beings. Yet this is equally unsatisfactory. Even if Kant's view of the species is sustainable, given what we know of the vagaries of human cognition and the determinants of agency, either there is a vast leap from the hypothesis of the possession of certain very abstract qualities to a demand for concrete social equality, or else the qualities of rationality and freedom have been tacitly assigned a kind of transcendental, magical, entitlement-conferring significance.

The ideal of equality, Williams suggests, can best be understood as the injunction to look behind the status men possess under their "professional, social, or technical" titles to their "own views and purposes." "Each man is owed the effort of understanding, and . . . in achieving it, each man is to be (as it were) abstracted from certain conspicuous structures of inequality in which we find him."[21] We are, moreover, capable of standing back from our own roles, and employing "reflective consciousness" to assess our situations and those of others. He now asks whether a stable, hierarchical society could be envisioned in which political inequality was extreme but in which each person was content with (presumably such things as) his unequal share of freedom, worldly goods, and authority, and in which an understanding on the part of others of his views and purposes was not entirely lacking. Such a society is, he argues, unstable, for:

> [W]hat keeps stable hierarchies together is the idea of necessity, that it is somehow fore-ordained or inevitable that there should be these orders; and this idea must be eventually undermined by the growth of people's reflective consciousness about their role, still more when it is combined with the thought that what they and others have always thought about their roles in the social system was the product of the social system itself.[22]

Yet the attempt to think out a blueprint for an appropriately non-hierarchical society is, he insists, fraught with internal tensions and difficulties. Given that some types of liberty, some worldly goods, and, above all, executive authority are limited resources that cannot be possessed by all to the degree that each would like, some allocation mechanism must come into play. To allow each an equal opportunity to bid for them might seem morally correct, but how far should the notion of equal opportunity compensate for the lack of Aristotelian qualities – ambition, intelligence, a supportive family, inherited wealth – which, in an unplanned world, tend to result in the accumulation of more goods? To demand equal respect for persons despite their very different levels of accumulation seems psychologically unrealistic. Moreover, the notion of equal opportunity implies a society that is fiercely competitive, in which no one can depend on his family background, his racial heritage, or his sex to see him through. It is hard to see how notions of equal respect for the person behind his titles can flourish in such an environment. Equality in this distribution of goods is even more problematic in Williams's view, threatening the development of valued skills and ignoring the human desire for special distinction above others. So Williams's pessimistic conclusion is that, while we ought to recognize human needs as equal and strive to fulfill them, we must resign ourselves to an unclear and uncomfortable situation in which we do not know what the ideal of equality really is or understand why it is so desirable.

Some of these points, especially the notion of the development of reflective consciousness about one's place in a hierarchy, are usefully applied to the novel. David and his daughter begin by considering themselves nice, ordinary people with no understanding of their privileged role within the academic and rural worlds they inhabit. They gradually become aware of the emotions experienced by others as a result of their own behavior, ranging from confusion, to demoralization, to parental outrage, to fury, of which they had no idea. That Melanie's plans for her own life might have been vulnerable to disruption, that part of being young involves not having a good grip on reality and firm plans for one's own life, and so being more, not less, vulnerable to a kind of derailing, did not occur to David, who saw her reticence and ambivalence not as indicating a delicate and unformed character but as facilitating his intervention into her young life. Lucy saw Petrus as her factotum and his married life as happening elsewhere, out of her orbit, not as a rightful occupant of the land and one in a position to make viable offers of marriage to persons like herself. Yet the development of more adequate views of the self in relation to others requires more than personal insight of the sort that rains down on Ajax or Oedipus. The movements that inspired the kind of events in the real world that Coetzee fictionalizes depended upon moral philosophy of the generalizing, impersonal sort, the articulation of ideals and reasons without which social movements cannot frame or explain their goals. Even if the exact formulation of the ideals of equality is elusive, we can understand what progress with respect to the condition of women, colonial subjects, and animals amounts to.

In the context of what is manifestly a political novel, David is not merely an individual but also a member of various groups: the class of opportunistic humans versus helpless animals; of invading whites versus indigenous blacks; and of well-protected men versus exposed women. The substitution Williams proposes for referring one's actions to some impersonal standard, namely, assuming risk and being prepared to bear the consequences if things do not turn out well, has no parallel in the case of the group and no lessons are available from tragedy concerning the dangers of hubris. Tragedy is said to teach us that overreaching yourself tends first to provoke violence and pain and then to bring about your downfall. It is important for prospective Gauguins to understand: *You could ruin your own life, as well as some other lives, if you go down that road* before embarking on an adventure. But, where political ethics are concerned, life does not reveal and fiction cannot amplify the notion of built-in cosmic sanctions. Entire classes do in fact assume risks by their aggrandizing actions; in slave revolts, masters are killed, and, under some conditions, masters live in constant fear of their slaves. But there is no sense in which certain men *decided* to become masters and assume the risk of subjugating others, realizing that things could go badly *for them*, but considering that the goals were nevertheless worth striving for. The ancient Greeks could not have thought of themselves as undergoing risks through the institution of slavery and as exposing their society to the risk of failure, injury, remorse, and regret. Nor does it make sense to think of us as undergoing risks by eating large quantities of meat, or by being members of a culture that keeps animals penned up. The notions of personal agency and responsibility do not carry over.

The historical process nevertheless shows us the correction of social hubris, and Coetzee's narrative depicts the crude retaliation that occurs during periods of rapid readjustment of power relations. The ancestors of David and Lucy may or may not have been responsible, along with hundreds of thousands of others, for the conditions obtaining in South Africa, but they did not particularly benefit from them. Their responsibility is purely notional and is derived from their membership in an ethnic group that, historically, oppressed and exploited another ethnic group. Social wrongs are unlike the killing of a man at a crossroads, or the interfamilial violence and betrayal that is the stuff of tragedy. Aggressor and victim, even if they co-exist in the present, may not even be known to one another; without familiarity there can be no empathy, without empathy there can be no remorse or regret. General moral theory, one might argue, seeks to anticipate and preclude crude retaliation. One of its roles is to compensate for the understandable failure of the empathic response to develop and to maintain decent relations when groups are involved that are markedly different in appearance and mode of life.

Williams wanted to remind us that, while there were gains in modernity, there were also losses in its numerous equalizing, power-rebalancing reflexes.[23] Although he was inclined to reject progressivism and to stress the continuities between ancient and modern thought, he was at the same time critical of the too ready acceptance of the necessity of certain arrangements:

> We, now, have no difficulty in seeing slavery as unjust: we have economic arrangements and a conception of a society of citizens with which slavery is straightforwardly incompatible. This may stir a reflex of cultural self-congratulation, or at least satisfaction that in some dimensions there is progress. But the main feature of the Greek attitude to slavery . . . was not a morally primitive belief in its justice, but the fact that considerations of justice were immobilized by the demands of what was seen as social and economic necessity. That phenomenon has not so much been eliminated from modern life as shifted to different places . . . We have social practices in relation to which we are in a situation very much like that of the Greeks with slavery.[24]

Where Williams saw slavery as an arrangement motivated by certain views about social and economic necessity, and as involving an awareness of slavery as a contingent identity, he saw the condition of women as motivated by certain views about essential identity, with modern sociobiology taking the place of Aristotelian anthropology.[25] His considered view was that we are no better off than the Greeks with respect to the oppressive nature of many actual social institutions. The difference is that modern "liberalism demands – more realistically speaking – it hopes – that those concepts, necessity and luck, should not *take the place of* considerations of justice."[26] In articulating this demand and this hope, we moderns have indeed progressed. However, he thought, these demands have not been met and liberal hopes may prove nugatory.[27] There are, in any case, no grounds specifically for shame.

To be sure, this position was consistent with Williams's skepticism about the philosophical grounding and relevance to human life of Kantianism and utilitarianism. But to overlook the connection between modern impersonal moral philosophy, with its rejection of ancient ethical concepts and assumptions, and such social progress as we have observed would be strangely willful. The moral failures of the Greeks were – and by extension those of the moderns are – more than mere imagination-deficits, analogous to our inability fully to envision and realize alternatives to, for example, a fossil fuel-based economy. Coetzee's narrative – though it is fiction and not philosophy – supplies an element missing in the philosophical picture, a sense of how the most disgraceful institutions, that seemed necessary in their time, as well as the most disgraceful personal actions, that seemed compulsory and natural in their time, might bring down something very much like the wrath of heaven as the Greeks conceived it.

Notes

1   Bernard Williams, *Ethics and the Limits of Philosophy* (London: Fontana, 1993), pp. 19, 21.
2   Brian Leiter, "Nietzsche and the Morality Critics," *Ethics* 107 (1997): 250–85.
3   At times, Williams's accusations reminds the reader of the complaints of Dostoevsky's Underground Man, a critic, like Nietzsche, of conformity, domesticity, and hyperrationality, who claims the right to "consciously, purposely, desire what is injurious to himself, what is stupid, very stupid – simply in order to have the right to desire for himself even what is very stupid and not to be bound by an obligation to desire what is sensible" (Feodor Dostoevsky, "Notes from Underground," reprinted in Eric Josephson and Mary Josephson, eds., *Man Alone: Alienation in Modern Society*, New York: Dell, 1962, p. 366). "What does reason know?" the Underground Man asks,

> Reason knows what it has succeeded in learning . . . and human nature acts as a whole with everything that is in it, consciously or unconsciously, and even if it goes wrong it lives . . . You believe in a palace of crystal that can never be destroyed – a palace at which one will not be able to put out one's tongue or make a long nose on the sly. And perhaps that is just why I am afraid of this edifice that it is of crystal and can never be destroyed . . . (Ibid., pp. 366, 371)

4   Martha Nussbaum "Tragedy and Justice: Bernard Williams Remembered," *Boston Review* (October/November 2003).
5   Bernard Williams, *Shame and Necessity* (Berkeley, CA: University of California Press, 1993), p. 13.
6   Sigmund Freud, "The Relation of the Poet to Daydreaming," in *Collected Papers*, vol. 4 (London: Hogarth Press, 1953); reprinted in *On Creativity*

and the Unconscious, ed. Benjamin Nelson (New York: Harper, 1958), pp. 44–54.

7   J. M. Coetzee, *Disgrace* (London: Vintage, 2000), p. 25.
8   Ibid., p. 189.
9   Williams, *Shame*, p. 78.
10 Ibid., p. 70.
11 *Disgrace*, pp. 142–3.
12 *Shame*, p. 45.
13 *Disgrace*, p. 24.
14 Ibid., p. 89.
15 *Shame*, p. 70.
16 Bernard Williams, "Moral Luck," in *Moral Luck* (Cambridge: Cambridge University Press, 1983), pp. 20–29, at p. 22.
17 Ibid., p. 23.
18 On analogy with Bas van Fraassen's "empirical stance," as described in *The Empirical Stance* (New Haven, CT: Yale University Press, 2002).
19 Bernard Williams, "The Idea of Equality," in *Problems of the Self* (Cambridge: Cambridge University Press, 1973), pp. 230–49, at p. 232.
20 Ibid.
21 Ibid., p. 237.
22 Ibid., pp. 238–9.
23 "Throughout his career," says Nussbaum, "Williams gave evidence of being a really serious feminist. He not only defended women's equality in politics and employment, and later their right to be free from sexual harassment in the university, but he also saw the importance of acting in ways that supported women's aspirations" (Nussbaum, "Tragedy and Justice").
24 *Shame*, p. 125.
25 Ibid.
26 Ibid., p. 128.
27 Ibid., p. 129.

7

FACING DEATH TOGETHER: CAMUS'S *THE PLAGUE*

Robert C. Solomon

There's no question of heroism in all of this. It's a matter of common decency. That's an idea which might make some people smile, but the only means of fighting a plague is – common decency.

Camus, *The Plague*

There are two themes of great importance in Camus's novel *The Plague*.[1] The first, immediately suggested by the title, is the high probability of imminent, horrible death. But it is collective death as well as personal death, and so the second theme, at least as important as the first, is our "being with Others," our collective, interpersonal, and social existence. The theme of imminent death also came to the fore toward the end of *The Stranger*, but there it was only a matter of individual death, presented as "absurd." Collective death may also be absurd, but it involves a dimension only hinted at by the abstract metaphor in *The Stranger* – "the brotherhood of men" (all of whom eventually face the same "cold wind" of mortality). In *The Plague*, this brotherhood is everything, and even those who deny it or violate its terms are nevertheless bound by it. It is, accordingly, the best and most moving presentation of Camus's social philosophy, or, rather, the social dimension of his philosophy. Several years later, in 1955, Camus would attempt another, much less moving and much less heroic (indeed, mock heroic), statement of social solidarity in *The Rebel*, where he proclaimed, in yet another parody of Descartes's *cogito*, "I rebel therefore we exist." But in *The Plague*, our existence is both given to start with and collectively threatened. It is in such circumstances, Camus more wisely tells us, that we learn to live – or to perish – together.

An interpretation of *The Plague* largely depends on one's attitude toward Camus, on one's perspective, and on what ideological ax one wants to grind. *The Plague* is, straightforwardly, based on an earlier text about a then recent epidemic, Daniel Defoe's *Journal of the Plague Year* (1722).[2] It is, also straightforwardly, an account of the progress and retreat of an epidemic not unlike the bubonic plague that devastated Europe in the fourteenth century, now set in Camus's romantically remembered, semi-fictional Algeria.[3] But after that, the subject of the novel – and the identity of the plague – is open to interpretation. Camus, as he did with his retrospective comments on *The Stranger*, confuses the issue enormously with his statement of his intentions in this book. In a much quoted conversation with Roland Barthes, he claims that there is no doubt that *The Plague* is a metaphor for the very different sort of pestilence represented by the Nazi invasion and occupation of Europe. And, indeed, Camus wrote the novel in Provence during the occupation.[4] But the analogy between plague and occupation is vague at best, ignoring from the outset the distinction between natural disaster and willful human evil that lies at the heart of Camus's sense of justice. One can, of course, treat willful human evil as just another force of nature, on a par with earthquakes, volcanic eruptions, and floods, but so much is lost by doing so that we find ourselves virtually incapable of thinking that way.

Why did Camus insist that the novel was about the Nazi occupation, a very particular episode in the recent history of Europe, rather than suggest a very general account of human experience in the face of imminent threat? It may be that, as in his later comments on *The Stranger*, he was trying to embellish his own novel and the characters he created with more meaning and a more politically relevant social agenda than he intended at the time. It is true that he started thinking about and writing *The Plague* during and just after the Nazi occupation, but that, I think, would have been a good reason *not* to belabor the obvious but to meditate on the human condition. In his retrospective comments, he may well have been countering the criticism from Sartre and his friends that he was not sufficiently politically *engagé* (despite the fact that Camus, as much as Sartre, employed his literary talents in direct resistance to the Nazi threat[5]). Or he may just have been pulling our collective leg, as authors are often prone to do when annoyed with the question what their writing *means*. It has often been said: an author is in no better position than anyone else to know what his or her work means. But whatever *The Plague* means, it cannot be the reduction of all calamity to blameless catastrophe.

The point of the novel is to focus on a truly blameless catastrophe (with an eye to an even more pervasive and universal catastrophe – death). But even so it is human responsibility that emerges as its major theme. Thus it is properly treated as an "existentialist" novel. Quite the antithesis of a perverse reduction of human behavior to blameless nature, it is a portrait of how even the most ordinary human actions in times of great peril can be heroic and embody an implicit social philosophy.

1   Facing Death

"We are all condemned. We live under a death sentence." This bit of pop shock philosophy is neither profound nor terrifying. It is trite and obvious. And yet we live most of our lives as if it were not obvious at all, as if we would never die, or as if that day is so far off that it could not possibly make any difference to us, at least for now. But then, on a few morbid days, we do have this sense that our whole lives are overshadowed by the brute fact of our mortality, and the question then is: What do we do with this? The realization of our impending death can be paralyzing. Every aim, every pleasure, and every good deed seems to be rendered pointless. Or this realization can be invigorating, impressing upon us the limited amount of time available. Indeed, the realization of one's impending death can be a goad to philosophizing. The German thinker Martin Heidegger did not hesitate to remind us that we are both "being-unto-death" and ontologically "inauthentic," meaning that although death was our "most necessary possibility" we tend to deny this and "fall" back into the forgetfulness of everyday life. But most of us have moments of personally profound reflection, whether or not these count as "authenticity," in which the realization of our own impending death prompts neither panic nor frenzied activity but serious thought and a sincere search for perspective. What has my life amounted to, thus far? What will or could my life amount to, given what time I have left? Have I lived up to my promise? And regarding promises to other people, what promises have I made? Which have I fulfilled? Which have I betrayed? Did those promises make any sense, in terms of who I really want or wanted to be? Have I possibly missed *the way* of my life, perhaps altogether? Who am I really? What does the rambling tale of my life tell me about where I stand in the larger scheme of things, or even in just my own narrative?

These are heavy questions, and asking them is the philosopher's business. They are also are annoying questions, which is why philosophers are considered "gadflies," noxious insects that disturb honest citizens' mundane tranquility. (Or worse.) The novelist has an easier time of it.

By creating fictional characters (or by hijacking real-life stories), the novelist can create a confrontation with death that is both personal and, thankfully, impersonal, in the sense that it is not our person and not our death. We can take up the plight of the fictional character (or not) as our own, but that is our choice, an option, not what Heidegger called our "most necessary possibility." We do not have an "option" with regard to our own mortality. The novelist, by contrast, can consider any number of possibilities, and we as readers can take them to heart or distance ourselves. It is our choice. Thus, unlike the philosopher, the novelist can ask the heavy questions without being too direct or vexatious. And he or she can explore any number of possibilities without hectoring us, as a philosopher would, with the admonition "this is what will happen to you, too."

When the novelist is also a philosopher, the result is, not surprisingly, more philosophical. The questions can still be profound and personal, but they can be asked, as it were, obliquely, and answered indirectly as well. Thus Camus, in several of his novels, asks the question, How will you face death?, but in a crypto-fictional mode. And he gives us an answer so unusual that it is jarring. It is summarized in the odd expression, "a happy death," the title of his first novel, the climactic theme of his famous and still most popular novel, *The Stranger*, as well as in his most morbid novel, *The Plague*, where it is mentioned in the final sentence (in French the final word) of the book. To be sure, there are other fictional (and quasi-fictional) deaths in Camus's work that are not so happy (*Caligula*, *The Misunderstanding*), and the occasional novel that is not about death at all (*The Fall*), but it is a theme that runs through both his fictional and philosophical works (insofar as these can be distinguished at all). Camus had read Heidegger, of course, but he had also confronted death as a child when he contracted tuberculosis and when he lost his father in the First World War. More recently, he had lived through the horrors of the Second World War, the occupation of most of France, and the deportation and murder of the local Jews, so death was no doubt on his mind. As was the innocent happiness that he sought and fantasized about and may have on occasion experienced. But as a philosopher it was the odd pairing of death and happiness that intrigued him, not just as fiction but as a real-life "possibility."

In *The Stranger*, Camus has his character convicted of a serious but pointless crime in order to force him to confront his imminent death. Meursault is to be executed by guillotine, and although in his final hours he muses on the desirability of a "loophole," he is quite clear that death could not be more certain. But Meursault, "strange" character that he is, faces this certain death more or less philosophically, asking the crucial questions ("Did I live right?" "Was my life meaningful?") and giving shockingly glib answers ("Yes, because it does not matter how one lives" and "Yes, because life itself is life's only meaning"). But if the second answer is straight from Camus, the first emphatically is not. Does it matter how one lives? Yes, and *nothing else* matters. Camus broke with Sartre and the left because they condoned a violence he could not abide. In a famous essay, he urged us to be "neither victims nor executioners," to live in such a way that we condone neither violence nor resignation in the face of violence.[6] He wrote eloquently against the death penalty because he found in it the ultimate crime in which we are all complicit.[7] Thus while Camus may or may not identify with his character Tarrou, in *The Plague* he clearly uses him as a spokesman for some of his most heartfelt moral opinions. Death is the worst thing, and complicity in killing is the worst crime of all.

Of course, one can question this, and I will suggest that Camus gives us a good reason for doubting that death is the worst thing of all. What is so terrifying about the plague is not just death but the manner of death. Death by plague is disfiguring, humiliating, disgusting. Nothing so clean and clinical as the guillotine. And is killing (or complicity) the worst crime? It is with good reason that the most vindictive murderers in history have preferred slow and mortifying means of killing, which is why torture has become so reviled throughout the civilized world. But for Camus, with his desperate affirmation of life, it is life itself that is meaningful, and death is the ultimate enemy. Nothing other than life is worth our attention. It is often said that death is "part of life," but it is not. It is simply its cessation. So, too, death is to life not life's "opposite" but its end. It is therefore the enemy of all enemies. So Camus perversely insists (in *The Myth*) that the "quality" of life is no substitute for "quantity" of life. There is no compensation for loss of life or wrongful death. It is not clear how this view is compatible with the "happy death" that he touts in other works. What Camus seems much more concerned with is happiness *in* life, which would seem to me to be just what "quality of life" is all about. Or, perhaps, what concerns him is the happiness we ought to have about just being alive. (Caligula screams, in his final seconds of life, "I'm alive!") But insofar as happiness is an issue about life then one might argue that it must be an issue about death as well. Against the background of the plague, individual happiness is what the novel is about. The characters of the novel struggle to come to terms not so much with imminent death as with their own happiness and how it conflicts with their sense of obligation.

2   Individuals and Shared Destinies

The plotline of *The Plague* is certainly not about happiness. It is about death. Plague breaks out in Oran. It is at first apparent only in the large and inexplicable deaths of the rats in the city. Then people start dying, and it quickly becomes an epidemic, forcing the authorities to close the city, quarantine many people, and create emergency mass mortuaries. And then it passes, or seems to, as quickly as it came. Against this background narrative, however, individual happiness is what the novel is about. The story traces the interweaving fates (and an occasional fortune) of Dr Bernard Rieux, who is the dominant figure in the novel (and, we eventually find out, its narrator), Jean Tarrou, an endearing smart-ass moralist and an occasional spokesman for Camus, Raymond Rambert, a journalist in love with a woman in Paris who has gotten trapped in Oran when the city gates closed, a quite ordinary man ironically named Joseph Grand, a priest/preacher named Father Paneloux, and a scoundrel named Cottard. All of them struggle to come to terms, not so much with imminent death but with their own sense of obligation in conflict with what they really want for themselves, what it would take to make them happy. Rieux, for example, throws himself into his work, in part to distract himself from the absence of his wife, who is suffering from tuberculosis. Rambert, who is also painfully separated from his beloved, spends most of the novel trying only to get out of the city, but then finally joins the cause. Cottard, by contrast, uses the plague for all that it is worth, taking advantage of the situation to make a small fortune by smuggling. In each of their cases, too, there is something like a resolution to "start over again," just as Meursault, facing death at the end of *The Stranger*, reflects on his mother, ready to "start life all over again." We are reminded, of course, of Nietzsche's fantastic "test" of life affirmation, the "eternal recurrence of the same." But one is also reminded (as suggested by Stephen Kellman) of Sisyphus in his endless toil, starting (with each roll of the rock) all over again. But in *The Plague*, at least, the "starting over" is in every case a resolution to be happy, to "get it right" this time around.

The unusual example here is the scoundrel Cottard, who, before the start of the plague (at the beginning of the novel), attempts suicide, fails, and survives. By the time the plague arrives, he has already "started over again," and in many ways has a much clearer sense of how to live under plague than the others. He also has the benefit of a somewhat lessened sense of vulnerability, having already escaped one encounter with the grim reaper. So he more than anyone (any other major character, that is) tries to live his life to the fullest, by which he means enjoying the luxuries and extravagances still available in Oran. It is said, however, that "it is an ill wind that blows no one good," suggesting that some will benefit from even the worst tragedy. It allows Cottard, first of all, to avoid arrest, and then it provides him with the means to profit from the burgeoning black market. He shows no inclination to join the others in their efforts to halt the plague, for it "suits him quite well" and he sees "no reason to stop it."[8] But it also allows him to join in the feeling of solidarity, because the reprieve from his fear of arrest allows him to live as part of society, even soliciting the good opinion of others. Cottard may be a scoundrel, a crook, and a criminal, but he has a charm that captivates even the moralists around him. Grand, not surprisingly, seems attracted to his glamour. Tarrou at one point insists that "the plague has done him proud."[9] (Camus gives a somewhat mixed account of the citizens' general sense of indulgence, suggesting at one point that they all become short-term hedonists and at another that they give up on pleasure altogether. No doubt this is indicative of their schizoid reaction to the plague rather than narrative inconsistency on Camus's – Rieux's – part.) But like Sartre's war profiteers and collaborators Cottard takes advantage of the horror all around him, and though he is despicable he does not come off as a villain, at least not until the end of the novel, when the end of the plague signals the end of his advantages as well, and he goes berserk and starts shooting people.

There are also many minor characters (including the entire population of Oran), whose place in the novel is either to act as the absent partner of one of the main characters (Rieux's wife, Rambert's girlfriend, Grand's ex-wife) or just to put faces and features on the victims and give them names. (We remember from *The Stranger* how alienating it is when the Arabs remain nameless while the Europeans are called by their first names.) Some, like Rieux's medical colleague Castell and the magistrate Othon, who also loses his son in the most tear-jerking passage in the entire novel, fill out the portrait of the officialdom of the town. One, Dr Rieux's mother, plays a peculiarly personal role in the novel. She is a specter that hovers on the margins of the story, and she is a poignant presence although she says hardly a word. She reminds one of Camus's own mother, who was deaf and had a speech deficiency, a powerful presence in the author's life who also played a central role in his posthumous novel, *The First Man*. So we are not surprised to see that she is treated respectfully, even reverentially, by Rieux (and by Camus), despite the fact that she is a marginal figure in the story.

They all display the various ways that individuals face the horror of the plague, just as (we might add, without giving away too much to Camus's retrospection) the French citizens of Provence displayed many different strategies in facing the horror of the Nazi occupation, captured well in Philip Hallie's superb 1978 book, *Lest Innocent Blood be Shed*.[10] This is a topic that Sartre pursues in some detail in his mid-war tome, *Being and Nothingness*. Some Frenchmen joined the resistance. Some tried to go on as usual. Some hid. Some wrote books, novels, and memoirs. Some collaborated. Some used the drastically altered circumstances to profit from others' misfortune. Some maintained their sanity by continuing old habits. Others used the new and terrible circumstances as an excuse to break habits. In *The Plague*, Camus gives us a similarly varied account of the personalities and responses of the citizens of Oran, but I do not think that the individual biographies should be allowed to eclipse the main point of the book, the collective solidarity to which they all contribute, if only in their own peculiar ways.

With this in mind, we can ask the awkward and perhaps juvenile question: Who is the "hero" of the novel? (It is Camus, via Rieux, who forces this question upon us.) Because it is a dumb question, it is also self-serving, for Dr Rieux is clearly the central character of the novel, the one who seems to make the greatest sacrifices, the dynamic engine that maintains the "resistance" – however ineffective. But because he asks the question (to which the answer would seem obvious), he also feels compelled to answer it, in a disingenuous way that is meant to hide its self-aggrandizing nature. So he comments that if anyone is the hero of the story, it is the most unlikely character Grand, who is, one might say "a hero of everyday life," a phrase that Camus borrows from the Russian poet Mikhail Lermontov in his opening epigram to *The Fall*. But Grand is a joke (or as close as anything in *The Plague* ever comes to being a joke). Even his name is obviously ironic, and his job title is ludicrous. He is assistant temporary clerk, a job he has held (without a promotion) for 30 years. Yet his wife left him, he tells us, because he was so caught up in his career. His project throughout Camus's novel, however, is the most ludicrous bit of all. Throughout *The Plague*, he struggles to write a novel, despite the fact that he is almost always (in his own words) incapable of coming up with the words. So after years of writing, he is still working on the first sentence, which he rewrites and rewrites and rewrites. (Speaking of futile Sisyphusian labors!) Some hero! Dr Rieux is obviously trying to put one over on us (a point that many commentators seem not to notice).

For this reason, and for several others besides, I found myself quite put off by the heroic Dr Rieux. I found him to be something of a cold fish and a moral prig. While Rambert cannot think of anything but his woman, Rieux seems hardly ever to think of his wife. He has no evident sense of humor, a fact thrown into ironic relief by his name, which more or less means "one who laughs." Although he is devoted both to the ultimate helping profession and to the immediate task of building solidarity in his community, he is portrayed as a self-righteous, isolated man. He treats the other characters in an "arm's length" and coolly formal manner. Even Tarrou, who comes as close as anyone to being Rieux's friend, is addressed in an oddly self-righteous way. I think that this is true even in the most light-hearted scene in the narrative, when the two of them slip off and enjoy an illicit swim in the sea. Even there, Rieux comes off as stuffy and officious.

I also found Rieux's constant insistence on the truth to be tiresome, and also somewhat dubious, especially when we find out, as if we hadn't suspected it all along, that he is the coy narrator of the journal. The "objective" medical perspective may be appropriate to the novel, to be sure, but I think that we can detect here some of Camus's own defensive self-righteousness as a writer, perhaps thus expressing his discomfort in the presence of such self-righteous and sophisticated pundits as Sartre and his friends. (As Rousseau no doubt felt in the presence of the Parisian courtiers two centuries before.) In Camus's other work, too, his characters, for instance Clamence in *The Fall*, proclaim themselves champions of the truth, and this, of course, was how Camus retrospectively interpreted his character Meursault in *The Stranger*. But the truth is by no means easy to tell, if by that we mean "the whole truth and nothing but the truth." Every truth is told from a particular perspective, and the very nature of perspectives is such that there can be no capturing "the whole truth," and it is highly unlikely that one will be able to discern the peculiarities of one's perspective in order to guarantee "nothing but the truth."

Doctors, perhaps, have a better claim than most of us to insist on truthfulness, compared to the prevarication and evasions regarding illness and disease that are so prevalent among their patients and the public figures who have the unwelcome task of announcing epidemics. (It is Rieux who first dares to pronounce the word "plague," to the horror and objections of his medical and political colleagues – although his elderly colleague Castell beats him to the diagnosis.) But Rieux's insistence on the truth, too, readily strikes the reader as overly cold and clinical, a common fault among physicians to be sure. What is missing from Rieux's journal is real feeling, and what makes reading Camus's novel so alienating is not just the gruesomeness of the plot. It is its detached and unfeeling descriptions, which Rieux (but I doubt Camus) confuses for the truth. If he unifies the story and gets credit for the solidarity that emerges by Part IV of the novel, Rieux nevertheless provides us with an odd and uncomfortable "hero," whose dedication to fighting the plague is compromised by its futility and his own self-righteousness.

But this, many readers of Camus will be fast to object, is just the point. Rieux, like Sisyphus (and debatably like Meursault), is "the absurd hero," fighting futilely but relentlessly against an unbeatable foe, whether this is conceived to be death or rather the meaninglessness of the universe. And, indeed, interpreting the plague as either death or the Absurd is a superior because far more philosophical account of the novel than Camus's own retrospective interpretation of it as a metaphor for the Nazi occupation. But this is where I think that the concept of the Absurd gets overdone in Camus interpretation. It is indeed a striking image, and it certainly did capture the wartime "sensitivity" that Camus sensed around him in the early forties. But I think that in *The Plague* he was trying for something much larger than that individual confrontation with the indifferent universe. What is important about Rieux's quixotic mission is not its futility but the zeal itself, the "resistance" he displays despite its lack of effectiveness, and the solidarity he forges among the citizens, at the very least a way of giving them the all-important feeling of doing something as opposed to just waiting as victims for fate to make its decisions. True, one might well interpret this as just a continuation of the Absurdist philosophy captured in *The Myth*, but I think Camus was already well on his way toward the themes of *The Rebel*, still several years off: rebellion and resistance. And if I think *The Rebel* is a seriously flawed book, even a mistake, it is because of the pathos of Camus's defensiveness against Sartre and his friends, not because I find fault in the themes or the psychological insight that motivates the themes. That is what makes Camus an "existentialist" (despite his denial). It is this emphasis on doing something, on making life meaningful, despite its futility or its consequences, and quite apart from any moral "principles" that might be operative.

Jean Tarrou, in contrast to Rieux, is full of personality and humor, although his jocularity never seems to help the humorlessness of the novel. Tarrou can be annoyingly solicitous, but he can be profound as well. As I suggested earlier, he is more of a spokesman for Camus than any of the other characters, including Dr Rieux. Nevertheless, he has an erratic presence in the story, appearing from time to time, often with just a *bon mot*, and we do not really get to know him at all until toward the end of the novel, when he dies of the plague. He says that he aspires to be "a saint without God," a pretentious aspiration, to be sure, but loaded with philosophy. Steven Kellman suggests that the philosophy is distinctively post-Nietzschean, but if that is so it must be said that Tarrou (perhaps like Camus) is still very much caught up in "the shadows of God." In many ways, he anticipates Clamence in *The Fall*, although with none of the cynicism and resentment. He is a profound moralist, and although he is dedicated to one particular cause (the abolition of the death penalty) it is clear that he has larger quasi-theological issues in mind – innocence, guilt, and redemption. He keeps his own journal of the plague, which (we gather) is far less matter of fact and far more whimsical than the one we read by Rieux (and I have sometimes wondered what the impact of this alternative *Plague* might have been). He also throws himself into the project of fighting the plague second in dedication only to Rieux, although he manages to maintain a sense of humor and an Absurdist perspective that always seems to be just out of reach for the doctor. It is another irony that he falls victim to the plague, but his death is anything but the gruesome and tragic scene that we have seen for so many other characters. His, perhaps alone, is a "happy death," and the reason seems to be that he takes it – and the plague – not all that seriously. Is this, possibly, the real lesson of the book? If so, did Camus himself ever manage to take it to heart?

Raymond Rambert, by contrast again, is a Parisian journalist assigned by his newspaper to look at health conditions in Oran. Another irony. The assignment obviously turns into something else. He isn't much of a character but he provides a different kind of poignancy to the story. Whereas for most of the characters death and plague are the immediate issues, for Rambert the only issue is love and separation. He is desperate to get back to his wife in Paris but is prevented from doing so by the quarantine, and so he exhausts himself consorting with various shady characters trying to get smuggled one way or another out of the country. The plague, in short, is not his problem, just the cause of his problem. It is for this reason that he is never a candidate for the authorship of the journal (that non-mystery that Rieux teases us with), despite his writing and reporting abilities. But here we might note that it is a curious sub-theme of *The Plague* that so many folks seem to be writers, an unlikely avocation for people in such dire circumstances. Rieux is the coy journal author/narrator, Grand is slaving away at his novel, Tarrou has his journal, and even Father Paneloux is working on an essay when he dies. But Rambert, the journalist, never seems to get around to writing anything.

But Rambert also illustrates a problem that obsessed Camus, the idea of "exile," even though Rambert is caught *in* the city rather than exiled *from* home. But one might rightly argue that these are just two ways of viewing the same dilemma, the idea of being trapped away from "home." Camus makes his own "exile" from Algeria one of the repetitive themes of his work, although one might ask not only to what extent exile in Camus's case is self-chosen but more profoundly, whether we are all in "exile" and not "at home" whether we know it or not. Might it not be the "modern condition," emphasized famously by Heidegger in his early work? (Although it should be pointed out that actual homelessness in Germany after the First World War was the highest it had ever been.) All of us are in a society that is not "our own," although, again, we should note that Camus describes Algeria here as in *The Stranger* as if it is nothing but a European colony. In *The Stranger* the Arabs who make up most of the population don't have names, but in *The Plague* they don't seem to have deaths either, except, perhaps, in the statistics, although the death toll among the native population must have been much worse than what we see among the Europeans. So the "exile" problem may in fact be much more serious than Camus lets on. It is not just a question of being caught away from home. It is a matter of refusing to see and acknowledge the people with whom one actually shares one's existence.

Rambert illustrates yet another point that obsessed both Camus and Sartre, the idea that one is an "exception." Taking oneself as an exception, we might note, is a central concern of Immanuel Kant's moral philosophy. One is, to keep it short, not supposed to do it. The "categorical imperative" is defined to be universal, to make no reference to any particular persons, and reference to self is, of course, the most egregious violation of morality. But considering oneself as an exception will play a curious role in Camus's own later novel, *The Fall*. There, Clamence tells a story about a Jewish prisoner in a German death camp, who complains "But my case is different. I am innocent." Thus it is of particular significance that Rambert, in the end, declines to escape from the city and joins Rieux and the others in their heroic but futile effort to blunt the tide of the plague. In the end, in other words, he realizes that he is not an exception after all.

Finally, there is Father Paneloux. His role in *The Plague* is rather straightforward, and is in a way familiar to us already from the figure of the prison chaplain in *The Stranger*. He is the reminder that wherever there is tragedy, the theology of the "problem of evil" is never far away. "Why is this happening to us?" and the unpleasant answer is, "because of something you have done." This is the central theme of the Hebrew Bible, and it is the subject of Father Paneloux's first sermon. "Calamity has come on you, my brethren, and you deserved it."[11] Camus, of course, does not put much stock in this. His atheism and his philosophy of the Absurd preclude it. If there is no divine, there can be no divine retribution. But, nevertheless, there is still guilt and, one might argue, if we acknowledge Nietzsche's "shadows of God" idea, sin. Tarrou, who aspires to be a saint without God, makes this point expressly. In Camus's terms, Paneloux is guilty of "philosophical suicide," but so, too, are we all guilty, of complicity in injustice and murder (according to Tarrou), of indifference to life, according to Camus himself. But there is a change in Paneloux towards the end of the novel, when he gives a second sermon, this one admitting the incomprehensibility of the tragedy, in fact even echoing Camus on the Absurd. But of particular significance here, pointed out by Kellman, is the shift from the second person "you" in the first sermon to the first person plural "we" in the second, suggesting a transformation in the priest, too, from righteous accuser to a participant in the emerging solidarity of the community. And yet, when Camus has him die of a fever that is not clearly that of the plague, his place in that doomed community is thrown open to question.

3   Rats! A Note on Plague

What is plague?[12] Camus learned a good deal from Defoe and from accounts of earlier plagues in England and Europe, in particular the bubonic plague of 1347 (called "The Black Death" in England, because of the black spots that were one of the symptoms of the disease). Surprisingly, Camus evidently did not spend much time reading about or discussing the deadliest plague in history, the worldwide flu epidemic of 1918, which occurred in his lifetime (when he was five). As a sometime enthusiast of the classics, he may have done some reading on the Great Plague of Athens, in 400 BCE, recently dubbed the "Thucydides Syndrome," which was probably a flu with secondary bacterial infections.[13] He may not have known that the outbreak of bubonic plague in Europe was imported via Italian merchant ships from China, where there had been a deadly outbreak in the early 1330s. This might have provided Camus with an alternative exotic setting, but it is worth noting, as in *The Stranger*, that although the setting of *The Plague* is Algeria there are no named Arab characters, no one speaks Arabic, and the novel could actually have been set just about anywhere. (It is thus disingenuous that Camus said, in his Nobel acceptance speech, that he had "never written anything that was not connected, in one way or another, to the land where I was born.")

In the fourteenth century, the devastation in China, and then in Europe, was horrendous. Twenty-five million Europeans died in the five years between 1347 and 1352. An eyewitness from Sicily in those terrible years reported, "Fathers abandoned their sick sons. Lawyers refused to come and make out wills for the dying. Friars and nuns were left to care for the sick, and monasteries and convents were soon deserted, as they were stricken, too. Bodies were left in empty houses, and there was no one to give them a Christian burial." The Italian writer Boccaccio, who referred to the plague in his *Decameron*, wrote that its victims "ate lunch with their friends and dinner with their ancestors in paradise," so quick was the death that struck many people. After the most horrible years, smaller outbreaks continued for years, indeed for centuries. Medieval society never recovered. Europe lived in constant fear of the plague's return, for it tended to "go underground" for periods of time (when the fleas from the rats go into hibernation) and then return again. It is not hard to imagine that the characters in Camus's fictional Oran continued to be traumatized for many years as well. But it is also easy to imagine, as in Europe six centuries before, a second-order epidemic of denial and distraction. We do not live easily with the possibility of death.

The "problem of evil," made famous by the Enlightenment philosophers of the seventeenth century (not all of them very religious), was but a burp of evil compared to the plague. The devastation of the Lisbon earthquake is not to be dismissed, of course, but that was sudden, communal, unanticipated death and destruction. The plague, by contrast, was ongoing, brutally present but unpredictable, demanding not retrospective philosophical commentaries but ongoing coping strategies, whether Dr Rieux's commitment to keep busy or Paneloux's increasingly accusatory sermons. It is Paneloux who raises these classic issues in *The Plague*, how a good God could wreak such havoc on an innocent people. His answer was the answer that had dominated since the tales of the Old Testament, that the people must not have been so "innocent" after all. It is worth noting that Camus is not at all sympathetic to Paneloux, even though in his novels *The Stranger* and *The Fall* he makes innocence and guilt a dominant theme. But in this novel, which so much seems to invite some theological speculation or at any rate some serious consideration of the justice of the situation, Camus is remarkably silent. Dr Rieux simply reports the deaths of children and scoundrels alike, with no suggestion of desert at all.

The plague is both invisible, in that its transmission is mysterious, and grotesquely visible in the horrible symptoms that announce its full arrival. Camus makes much of this, and the contrast with the hands-on violence of the Nazis is worth noting. Plague causes a painful swelling of the lymph glands called buboes (how the bubonic plague gets its name), and red spots appear on the skin that then turn ghastly black. There is vomiting and all sorts of other gruesome signs of the disintegration of the bodily, so even if death comes quickly it is not a "happy" death.

4   *The Plague* as Horror

In *The Plague*, in contrast to *The Stranger*, we all face death, or, rather, everyone in the novel faces death together. And it is a horrible death, with nothing like the clean blade of the guillotine. *The Stranger* forces us to confront the idea of imminent death; *The Plague* is, by contrast, a horror novel, a novel designed to evoke horror in its readers. People die horribly, and Camus like Defoe details their death agonies for us. And people do not just die together, as they might in an earthquake or a flood, nor just as individuals, like a single criminal facing execution, but nevertheless the citizens of Oran die collectively as individuals, each at his or her own time, no matter how many at a time and no matter how untimely their deaths may be. They all know that they could take ill at any moment, regardless of their age, their health, their habits, their virtues, their vices. So their anxiety is as awful as the death itself. It is what individuates them, as their deaths as such do not. And they do not die quietly or with dignity either, again, as a victim of the guillotine might manage to do. They writhe in agony. They vomit and defecate violently. They turn all sorts of gruesome colors. And people do not just die together *as people*, either. Their demise is prefigured and accompanied by the death of the most despised of all mammalian creatures, the rats. Their conjoined demise is a source of special horror, depriving death of the human dignity it might want to claim.

Horror is a special kind of emotion. Horror is not fear or anxiety. Fear provokes action, no matter how aimless, useless, or incompetent. Anxiety creates confusion, insofar as one does not know what threat to protect oneself against. But horror is fully aware of what it sees and what threatens; it just cannot do anything about it. Moreover, horror fascinates. Drivers slow down and "gawk" at a dismembered body on the highway, despite their knowing how much this will upset them and despite their utter inability to help out the victim in any way. We are fascinated by what horrifies us. And plague therefore fascinates. That fascination is what stokes our persistence through the gruesome monotony of Camus's novel. The appearance and death of the rats, the more or less detailed descriptions of the final behavior and then the devastated bodies of the victims, the medieval accounts of mass quarantines (incarcerations) and mortuaries provide us with an escalating sense of the horrific, which, like all of Camus's novels, has no "happy" ending.

Camus has a number of devices, as did Defoe, for distancing us from the characters and their plight. Not least of these distancing mechanisms is the fact that *The Plague* is a novel and, unlike Defoe's *Journal*, a piece of fiction. It presupposes our willing sense of disbelief, which, given the gruesome subject matter, may require some persistence. Another distancing device is the quasi-journalistic style, which, like *The Plague* itself, plods on at a dreary and increasingly gruesome pace with only anxious anticipations of what is to come. We become accustomed to the slowly building horror. Moreover, there is no character with whom we get so involved, or with whom we could easily get involved, to draw us into the novel. In that sense, it is the least phenomenological of all of Camus's novels. We read the characters only through their behavior, not through their experience. And, finally, there is the character of Dr Rieux, the narrator and author of the journal. He is something of a cold fish, a phenomenological dud, and his uncritical insistence on telling the objective truth and nothing but the truth, however important that may be in a journalist, further removes us from the poignancy of the situation. Moreover, Rieux plays coy with us throughout the novel, not even telling us who the author/narrator is and thus forcing us to step back and try to guess, distracting us from the catastrophe fictionally unfolding before our eyes.[14]

The danger is that the many deaths in the novel remain merely "objective" to us, in the sense dismissed by Kierkegaard and Heidegger as utterly "inauthentic," and not indicative of "our own" deaths at all. As readers, there is nothing we can do but watch. We do not empathize. That is the nature of horror, and in that sense it already contains a built-in distancing mechanism.[15] But for the citizens of Oran, too, there is little that they can do. For them too the experience is one of horror rather than fear. They feel helpless. And that, of course, is the point of the novel. With regard to impending death, there is little that one can do. One can try to slow it down for a while. One can hope and even try for a cure or a palliative. One can make the dying more comfortable. One can keep a journal. Or one can simply indulge oneself in being horrified (an emotion that Dr Rieux never seems to display). Thus the plight of the characters in the novel is not so different from the situation of the reader, one of horror and helplessness, except for the all-important fact that we, at the moment, are not facing the plague.

Just a few decades ago, however, many Americans found themselves among people in several countries who were confronting a real but equally mysterious epidemic, first referred to only as "gay cancer" but then identified as HIV/AIDS, which turned out to be indiscriminate as to sexual orientation or gender, or for that matter indiscriminate as to age, as more and more babies were born with the disease. In the late 1980s, as the number of infections and deaths increased exponentially, the panic in America approached epidemic proportions. A few physicians and social scolds recommended that people stop having sex altogether, even within monogamous marriage and despite their use of protection. But more illuminating was the fact that an accompanying sense of reck-lessness escalated, displaying just the desperate polarity described by Camus. Here was young America, confronted with death. Hysterics advised abstaining from sex altogether while rock bands like Nirvana celebrated and even invited the grim reaper to their parties. Hoping desperately for some sort of vaccine or cure, whether they were more careful or more careless in their sexual behavior, young Americans watched with horror and a sense of utter helplessness. But both care and carelessness were responses to the epidemic, and we do not understand the psychology of *The Plague* unless we appreciate both reactions.

The analogy has its limitations. Except for the babies and recipients of contaminated blood transfusions, the victims of HIV/AIDS were at least a little bit complicit in their infection (although suggestions of complicity have almost always accompanied epidemics, as the preacher Paneloux makes quite clear in *The Plague*). And, as in Camus's novel, modern medicine kept alive some hope that human intervention might actually succeed where it had not in the plagues of earlier centuries. Of course, the HIV/AIDS epidemic did not fade away, and it continues to ravage Africa and many populations in Asia. Even in the United States young people, especially, continue to be infected and to die at an alarm-ing rate. But even more than in Camus's fictional Oran, and over a longer period of time (now more than 20 years), Americans lose focus and interest. They find it easier to convince themselves that the threat is past, or that it can no longer affect them, or that modern medicine – which has indeed made serious advances in treatment – will take care of it if they ever should get sick. But, at least for a few years, younger American readers had no difficulty at all identifying with the characters in Camus's novel. The horror was all very real to them.

The combination of identification and distancing is what makes *The Plague* so effective. This is the key to horror, from Camus's most gruesome novel to the trash 1950s "horror films" that can still be seen on late-night television. If there were no identification with the victims, horror would become no more than abstract sadism, pity, or indifference.

If there were no distancing oneself from the horror, then one would become a victim, and the horror would be pushed aside by the more exigent emotions of fear and anxiety. There is no doubt that, for Camus, the people of Oran were like people he knew, which made the identification even more poignant. And, for us, the specific names, descriptions, and conversations of the characters help us to identify them, as we could not, for example, the nameless Arabs in *The Stranger*. But the fact that *The Plague* is a piece of fiction that Camus was writing in a different place and in the face of a very different horror provides him with the necessary distancing for his work to remain philosophical rather than, as for Dr Rieux, a matter of "truthful" reporting. Both the fiction and the exotic location provide the distancing for us. This is not a story of any particular plague, nor an allegorical history of the Nazi invasion and occupation. The horror that Camus describes is nothing less than the human condition. No matter how happy our lives may be, there is an awful fate that lies at the end of them, for all and for each and every one of us.

5   Facing Death Together: Being-with-Others

In *The Plague*, the people of Oran do not face death alone. Nor, insofar as we identify with their fate, do we. It is true, as Heidegger reminds us (with more profundity than the point is worth) that each of us must die his or her own death. But in plague we face a collective death, or at least we all face a similar cause of death that threatens us all at more or less the same time in more or less the same horrible way. This changes everything.

What is the difference between individual death and collective death? Robert Jay Lifton describes the horrific phenomenon of the "second death" experienced by the victims of Nagasaki and Hiroshima, in which their own individual deaths were evidently accompanied by the death of their entire world, making individual death all the more horrible. It is one thing to face your own death. It is something quite different to face at the same time the deaths of your loved ones, the deaths of your friends, the deaths of your neighbors, the deaths of your entire community, the death of your society and your culture. In such circumstances, one could, of course, continue to focus only on one's own death and hope only that oneself might be saved, whatever happens to the others. But such a person would be an ass, a cad, something inhuman. Most of us, social and caring creatures that we are, would care as much (or more) about the deaths of at least some other people. Whether or not we were to die at exactly the same time, our deaths would no longer be individual, and we would *not* each die only our own individual death. And if it were the entire community, the entire populace of a substantial city that was so threatened, the possible death of all around us would not be a mere abstraction, despite the small number of people we actually know. It would be very much like a "second death," the death of our world.

But death in *The Plague* is yet more complicated and confusing. It is not just individual death, although there are a great many individual deaths. The plague of Oran is not the sudden death of an entire world, all at once, as in nuclear holocaust. Death in *The Plague* is collective but not simultaneous, not everyone at once. And some people will surely survive (as in just about every other known plague in history. Some people, remarkably, have immunity.) As unimaginable as the loss of one's whole world is – and as uncomfortable as the idea of the continuation of the world *without me* might be to some people – the uncertainty of death by plague further increases the anxiety and adds to collective death a curiously competitive element. To understand the peculiarity of plague death, we have to understand this peculiar form of irrationality.

Added to the desperate irrationalism that often defines thoughts and behavior regarding impending death, there is an additional ingredient, the idea of *either you or me*, an idea that may not be warranted by our knowledge of epidemics, but is almost unavoidable anyway. Knowing, for example, that 30 percent of the population are likely to die of a sufficiently lethal plague, it is hard not to think about whether or not one is included in that 30 percent, and if not, who is. Thus the thought *maybe me, maybe not*, is oddly competitive and empathetic at the same time. Thus the importance of Dr Rieux's constant insistence that "we fight the plague together," whether or not there is anything effective that we can really do. Forging solidarity and with it empathy is an essential part of the battle. Death is the ultimate enemy, but, in *The Plague* at least, the fragmentation of society emerges as a close second. Facing death in *The Plague*, Being-with-Others turns out to be one of the ultimate values.

A more familiar form of irrationality is to be found in the accusations of complicity and other sorts of blame that often accompany the threat of death, as when long-term smokers are blamed for their cancers and, appallingly, gay men were originally blamed for HIV/AIDS. This is one more manifestation of the "blaming perspective," which pervades the whole of Judeo-Christian thinking. (Talk of forgiveness already presupposes the blaming perspective.) In a competitive situation, or in a situation that is, however irrationally, thought to be competitive, the blaming perspective will be all the more pronounced. It serves as rationalization ("Well, yes, so-and-so died but he drank the water," or "He didn't say his prayers," and so on). As I have argued in my account of *The Fall*,[16] this form of rationalization is surprisingly effective, and therefore also quite widespread. It is not about blame for the sake of blame. It is about blame as a source of hoped-for immunity, exception, or salvation. ("I did not drink the water." "I do pray.") It obviously contributes to the competitiveness and to the fragmentation of the community and therefore has to be countered.

The blaming perspective is not the whole story, of course, although people like Paneloux struggle to keep it alive (allowing Camus one of his few bouts of black humor in a grim novel). But the very idea that whether or not one comes down with the plague has anything to do with either luck or blame encourages the divisiveness that is the second mortal enemy of the novel. The struggle in *The Plague*, as opposed to the supposedly heroic struggle to "keep the Absurd alive" that defined Camus's philosophy just a few years earlier, is a social struggle. It is not so much a struggle against death as a struggle for solidarity. It is only by sticking together, Camus is suggesting, that we can make any headway against our ultimate common enemy. But even if there is no avoiding death, we can, by appreciating our common fate, transcend the isolation that can make "strangers" of us all.

Notes

1   Albert Camus, *The Plague*, trans. Stuart Gilbert (New York: Random House, 1948). I have benefited from reading Steven G. Kellman's book, *The Plague: Fiction and Resistance* (New York: Twayne, 1993).

2   The real epidemic was in 1665 in England, when Defoe was five years old.

3   Camus learned a lot from Defoe and from accounts of earlier plagues in England and Europe. Oddly, he does not seem to have spent much time grappling with "the deadliest plague in history," the worldwide flu epidemic of 1918, which would have occurred in his lifetime (when he was five). See John M. Barry, *The Great Influenza: The Epic Story Of The Deadliest Plague In History* (New York: Viking, 2004). See also the review, Barry Gewen, "Virus Alert," *New York Times Book Review* (March 14, 2004): 10–11.

4   An excellent account of that part of France in which Camus was living and writing, is Philip Hallie's superb book, *Lest Innocent Blood be Shed* (New York: Harper and Row, 1978).

5   Camus edited a paper aggressively called *Combat*. Sartre, of course, founded and edited *Les Temps Modernes*. Camus originally accepted assignments from Sartre.

6   Albert Camus, *Neither Victims nor Executioners*, introduced by R. S. Kennedy and P. Klotz-Chamberlin (Philadelphia, PA: New Society Publishers, 1986).

7 Albert Camus, "Reflections on the Guillotine" in *Resistance, Rebellion, and Death*, trans. Justin O'Brien (New York: Knopf, 1961).

8 Camus, *The Plague*, p. 145.

9 Ibid., p. 176.

10 Hallie, *Lest Innocent Blood be Shed*.

11 Camus, *The Plague*, pp. 86–7.

12 On plague, see again Barry, *The Great Influenza*. Robert Sullivan's *Rats* (London: Bloomsbury, 2004) is eye-opening, as is the review by Sue Halpern, "City Folks," *New York Review of Books* (May 13, 2004): 13–15.

13 A. Langmuir et al., "The Thucydides Syndrome: A New Hypothesis for the Cause of the Plague of Athens," *New England Journal of Medicine* (October 17, 1985): 1027–30.

14 For more on this, see Kellman, *The Plague*.

15 See Robert C. Solomon, "Real Horror," chapter 5 of *In Defense of Sentimentality* (New York: Oxford University Press, 2004).

16 Robert C. Solomon, "Pathologies of Pride in Camus's The Fall," *Philosophy and Literature* 28/1 (April 2004): 41–59.

Part IV
Visual Art, Artifacts, and the Ethical Response

8
STAYING IN TOUCH
Carolyn Korsmeyer

1 Three Examples

1   In early July of 1863, Confederate and Union soldiers fought in an area of farms and woods in eastern Pennsylvania near the little town of Gettysburg. After three days of combat there were close to 51,000 casualties, and over 7,000 men lay dead in the mud of the devastated fields. Plans to dedicate the area as a memorial to the fallen began as early as 1864, and eventually in 1933 it was taken over by the National Park Service. Over the years the perimeter of the recognizable battlefield altered as land was purchased and buildings erected; trees have grown where once there was pasture. The long-term battlefield rehabilitation projects are aimed to "return the Gettysburg landscape as close as possible to its 1863 appearance." The stated goal of the memorial is "to preserve the park and to provide you, the park visitor, with a fulfilling experience."[1]

2   Part of the Historical Museum of the City of Krakow, the branch known as "Silesian House," occupies a set of buildings that in 1939 was taken over by the Gestapo. In one group of small rooms located half-underground, Poles who were arrested on suspicion of anti-Nazi activities were detained, interrogated, tortured, and sometimes put to death. On the cement walls of these cells are more than 600 inscriptions scratched by prisoners who left their names, their prayers, their protests, and their final messages to family and friends. Over time those marks have faded, and the caretakers of the museum have redrawn some of them so that they are still readable. On portions of the walls that have not been so kept up, one can discern only faint traces.

3   Frank Lloyd Wright built his most elaborate prairie style home for Darwin D. Martin and his family in Buffalo, New York, between 1903 and

1905. It comprised five adjoining and connected buildings, including the main residence, a secondary residence, a garage-stable, conservatory, and long pergola. After the family left the house in the 1930s, portions of the complex were sold as separate properties, and the remaining buildings stood empty for years. In 1960 a developer demolished the pergola, conservatory, and garage and erected two apartment buildings on their site. Restoration efforts began in the 1990s, and by 2005 the newer apartments had been removed. Projects are underway to restore the entire architectural complex to its original specifications. Those specifications include the preservation, restoration, and where necessary replication of Wright's signature art-glass windows.

All three of these examples refer to sites that have recognized historical importance, manifest in the fact that they have been accorded museum or landmark status that now protects them. All three have undergone change and damage, such that they are not "the same" as once they were. And with all three, retaining aspects of their original condition is deemed important to their preservation, their value, and the relationship they bear to those who visit – including to the experience that the visitor expects, achieves, and takes away. In other words, the elements of these examples that count as "original" or – a related but not identical concept – as "genuine" are among their valuable features. It is my task to show that genuineness is a feature that has both ethical and aesthetic valence.

This approach to investigating the relationship between moral and aesthetic properties of art is somewhat different from the way that philosophers often address the topic of ethical criticism. Participants in this debate tend to focus on narrative arts, which more obviously have moral content by virtue of plot, dialogue, reference, and portrayal of subject – a content that may or may not be presented with subtlety, lyricism, complexity, coherence, or other familiar artistic virtues. Approaching the issues this way tends to assume that the features of a work of art that count as "moral" are different from those that count as "aesthetic." For example, perhaps the seductive portrayals of base and lowly themes make Baudelaire's famous poems in *Les Fleurs du Mal* putatively "evil," but their cadence and fresh language render them aesthetically accomplished. Or: the rule-abiding clarity of the social worlds depicted in Jane Austen's fiction may add an ethical dimension to aesthetic features such as the neatness of her plot structures and witty language, blending moral vision with artistry. The question then becomes, does the moral valence of a piece of literature contribute to its aesthetic value, such that the moral dimension itself becomes an artistically valuable quality (or alternatively the moral dubiousness compromises artistic quality)? Or are they two independent sets of values that happen to operate side-by-side in certain works?[2]

To a degree the terms of this debate involve disagreement over the scope of the term "aesthetic." If "aesthetic" is taken to refer only to those properties of art that are by definition *not* morally relevant, as for purposes of clarity many theorists have maintained, then what counts as "artistic" worth is either purely aesthetic, setting moral matters aside; or "artistic" value refers to an expanded set of qualities that might include both aesthetic and moral virtues. The relation of the latter two would still be a matter of contention. But if one and the same property has both ethical and aesthetic salience, the gap between "aesthetic" and "ethical" considerations could be closed. This is the idea I shall pursue. I hope to show that one and the same feature of a work – its "genuineness" – is the ground for both aesthetic and moral significance, that what is morally important about this quality is also aesthetically important.[3] The examples that propel my thinking are not narrative, at least not in any ordinary sense; furthermore, they cross the conventional borders between art and non-art.

Genuineness, originality, authenticity, and so forth are overlapping values commonly invoked in debates over forgery, but I have purposely avoided examples where fraud or fakery operate. Moral issues there are obvious because they involve deliberate deceit, and that is not the case with my three examples, since all of these sites publicly state the conditions of their displays. Nonetheless, the possibility of deception of some sort will be a relevant consideration in the course of my argument.

It might seem at first that only two of the opening examples elicit moral considerations. The Gettysburg Battlefield remembers those fallen in a conflict that divided a nation and a people; visiting the site prompts consideration of the rival values of that war, the blunders and brilliance of its leaders, and its horrendous casualties. The Silesian House museum stands as a memorial to victims of the Nazi occupation of Poland. The evidence they left behind demands reflection on one of the most painful chapters of human history. With both these cases, their histories of violence and suffering constitute part of the presentation of the sites. Therefore, the Silesian House museum and the Gettysburg Battlefield have clearly historical and ethical significance. Their aesthetic impact is powerful, but they are not by any means standard examples of either aesthetic objects or works of art.[4]

The Darwin Martin House is clearly of artistic and aesthetic importance, but here the ethical dimensions are less readily evident. There was no war, no torture, no more than the ordinary daily suffering that is the lot of every person. Moral complexity would not seem to be what one seeks when visiting works of domestic architecture anyway, even extraordinary examples such as this one. In the absence of wartime tragedies or deliberate cruelties, the destruction involved with the Wright House and its subsequent repair and restoration might occupy an aesthetic, artistic, and historical realm, but not an ethical one. However, this is what I hope to challenge with my pursuit of the idea that certain features of objects are simultaneously ethically and aesthetically salient.[5]

All three of the central terms of this analysis – aesthetic, ethical, and genuine – are open to a degree of interpretation. I think that my usage will become clear in the course of discussion, but here are some initial working definitions. The notion of "aesthetic" I employ includes the immediate, sensed grasp of the properties, the meaning, and the value of an object. This is a sense of "aesthetic" that was introduced, along with the term itself, at the advent of the eighteenth century, though as philosophies of taste developed in the course of the modern period, their concepts of the aesthetic tended to emphasize a distinctive type of pleasure. Pleasure will not be central to my use of the concept, but the affective understanding that issues from imaginative engagement with an object – whether pleasurable or not – will subtend the analysis of all of these guiding examples. My argument thus proceeds from a "cognitivist" reading of the aesthetic, which interprets the nature of aesthetic engagement to include singular insight that would be unavailable or dimmed unless the experience is the result of a direct, affective encounter with an object.[6]

The notion of the ethical refers not to the manner of apprehension of a situation but to its meaning insofar as it includes such matters as suffering, cruelty, loss; or valor, endurance, or achievement – acts and character traits situated in the domain of ethics. (For my purposes, the distinction sometimes drawn between moral theory's focus on right action and ethical theory's focus on the good is not salient. Therefore, I use "moral" and "ethical" interchangeably.) When such matters are apprehended through aesthetic encounters, they are felt with a particular intensity, directness, and focus. While an aesthetic encounter might lead to action according to some recognized moral imperative, in many cases the apprehension concerns events from so long ago that they are now inaccessible to action.

Because conditions for applying the term vary with the type of object, the concept of "genuine" resists general criteria, as is the case with similar terms such as "authentic," "original," or "real." Geographic location, for example, is indispensable for a battlefield; Gettysburg cannot be relocated. Location may or may not be as necessary for a building; it is not at all necessary for many paintings. And so forth. Therefore, I shall not try to specify in principle what "genuine" means in all cases, trusting to particular examples to manifest its importance clearly enough in order to probe the relationship of the ethical and aesthetic dimensions of the genuine.

There are those who would doubt that "genuine" refers to an aesthetic feature of an object at all, since often it is not a property that, strictly speaking, can be perceived. Hesitation over including genuineness among aesthetic values will be considered in the discussion to come. But as Peter Railton notes, "valuing enters the picture when *mattering* does," and I argue that being genuine matters.[7] Indeed, the property of being genuine is multivalent, possessing a significance that can be cognitive, historical, artistic, aesthetic, and moral.[8]

The complexity of the concept of the genuine is dramatized by the choice of examples which are not entirely in their original condition, and where the features that are being preserved or restored vary in kind. The perimeter of the Gettysburg area where the fighting took place is not the same as that marked out today as the edges of the Military Park, and because the land is no longer farmed, the terrain looks different from the way it did at the time of the Civil War. In order to rehabilitate the battlefield, the Park Service must remove trees that have grown up for more than a century so that the fields more closely resemble their condition in 1863. In Krakow the poignant messages left by prisoners are renewed periodically by the hands of others. They scrupulously preserve the messages, but they must do so with their own marks and their own inks. (Some of the originals were written in blood.) When the Wright complex is completed, some of the stunning windows – 394 in all, including glass-fronted cabinets and skylights – will be the ones that originally hung in the Martin House.[9] Others will be recreated using, as far as possible, the same processes that the Linden Glass company used to produce Wright's designs in the early years of the twentieth century.

From one point of view, these examples are little more than complicated instances of the classic philosophical problem of identity through time. Change is inevitable, and hence it is always doubtful that anything whose existence extends over a (reasonably long) period of time remains the same. Landscape changes with use and natural growth; boundaries erode and expand; and while catastrophe is not inevitable, woodworm as well as war can bring down buildings. Complex objects with long histories are never identical in every respect with the entities that originally bore their names.

The problem of identity through time presents an urgent practical problem for preservationists and others charged with art restoration. Because artworks are also historical documents, retaining sufficient qualities of the "original" version such that the item still counts as "genuine" (indicating again that those terms are not always coextensive), is critical for insuring whenever possible that in the course of care "the right object has survived."[10] I shall not pursue questions of ontology here, although there are intriguing puzzles to be explored. Their various possible solutions will not resolve the question of the relationship between ethical and aesthetic properties. For the inevitability of change does not foreclose either the moral or the aesthetic questions prompted by considering genuineness, authenticity, and what counts as "the right object."

2   Sameness of Experience

The viewing public, of course, is usually not in a position to judge the authenticity of an article on display. For that matter, even experts, unless they are engaged at the moment in professional analysis, may not be sure about matters of restoration, repair, and replication. One purpose of skillful restoration is to render objects such that the apparent continuity with their past seems to resist the more destructive changes that time brings about. Perhaps what is important, as the remarks quoted above from the Park Service about the Gettysburg Battlefield indicate, is that one be able to have the fullest *experience* possible of the object, and often that requires replacing broken parts, removing discolorations, trimming trees, and so forth. Such restorative activities are deemed successful if they insure the possibility of full, affective experience, including aesthetic insight made possible by presenting an object that appears to be close to its original condition. Such practical and sensible considerations complement a theoretical position that locates the aesthetic value of artworks entirely in the experience they prompt.

Locating the fully realized work of art in all its value in the experience it affords is the view John Dewey promoted when he insisted that art "has aesthetic standing only as the work becomes an experience for a human being."[11] A number of current theories also defend the primacy of experience in their accounts of aesthetic and artistic value as well. As Malcolm Budd puts it:

> [T]he experience a work offers is an experience of interacting with it in whatever way it demands if it is to be understood – reading it, looking at

it, listening to it, performing it or in some other way appreciating it. For you to experience a work with a (full) understanding your experience must be imbued with an awareness of (all) the aesthetically relevant properties of the work – the properties that ground the attribution of artistic value and that constitute the particular forms of value the work exemplifies.[12]

Budd is addressing philosophy of art, but his emphasis on experience can be extended to other types of artifacts where experiencing them includes a strong affective impression that is possible only in their immediate presence.

Whether genuineness is counted among the aesthetically important features of an object turns out to be quite contentious for approaches that stress experience, because it can be argued that genuineness is not itself a perceptual property.[13] When genuineness is immediately noticed, it is apprehended inferentially on the basis of qualities such as worn edges, characteristic workmanship, faded colors, and so forth. However, if there can be two visually indiscernible objects, one of which is real and the other a careful copy, and if aesthetic properties are by definition manifest in experience, then it is hard to argue that genuineness is an aesthetically important property. While much of the argument over this point has concerned the aesthetic value of forgeries (in contrast to their moral, economic, or historical value), it is easily extendible to the kinds of examples in question here, where preservation and restoration fix damage and reinstate an object that at least seems to be the genuine article. If in the absence of deception there is no moral disvalue, then what does it matter if the "real" thing is lost and good substitutes remain? If both yield similar experiences, it might seem that there should be no sacrifice of aesthetic value.

An approach that emphasizes "experience" so conceived is in fact enacted in certain decisions that museums make with the objects under their care. Many museums are increasingly substituting visually indiscernible replicas to display in place of fragile artifacts and are supplementing exhibits with teaching tools such as virtual tours and interactive videos. Hilde Hein observes that these decisions not only have the obvious practical importance of safeguarding rare items, but they also indicate a changing attitude about the concept of the museum and its function.

> Museums have always prized the authenticity of "the real thing," and professed to find it in objects that are genuine or original instances of their kind. Used in this context, the term "real thing" designates a singular entity and has an altogether different connotation from the reality or genuineness of an experience (which might well be initiated by an illusion.) . . .

> [T]oday's museums are engaged in an entirely new enterprise aimed chiefly
> at eliciting thoughts and experiences in the public. That objective is not
> exclusive of assembling collectibles, but it takes collection as a means rather
> than an end – and by no means the only means to that end. The end is
> the achievement of a certain type of experience that is genuine.[14]

The use of visually indiscernible replicas to prompt appropriate experience is no doubt heuristic and harmless in many situations, but I believe
that the examples under study here dramatize why an exclusive focus on
experience of perceptual properties is not adequate to capture either the
aesthetic or the ethical elements of encounters with these artifacts.
Experience is inseparable from what it is "about," and how one experiences an object is partly determined by that object. Of course, one can
be fooled, as with any perceptual encounter. But being fooled constitutes
a flaw in the experience itself – albeit the flaw is not always recognized.
Hence I doubt that a "genuine" experience can be "initiated by an illusion." Matthew Kieran makes a similar point regarding the compromised
aesthetic value of both forgeries and non-deceptive simulacra of works
of art:

> The crucial point is, even if we did have perfect copies, we would still have
> reason to value the originals more than the perfect copies. It is neither irra-
> tional nor sentimental to do so, since the reason runs very deep indeed.
>   What is the reason then? It concerns the essentiality of origin. What this
> opaque phrase picks out is the idea that what matters regarding our atti-
> tudes to something is not just a function of what its inherent qualities are,
> but also a matter of the relations in which the object stands to us.[15]

In terms of its phenomenal quality, the relation between a genuine artifact and a perceiving subject, and the relation between a replica and the
perceiving subject, might at first seem to be indistinguishable. The evidence presented to the senses, after all, would be the same, wouldn't it?
If you can't see a difference, then isn't the insistence that there is an
aesthetic difference either stubborn ideology or pretentious snobbery?
I believe it is not. First of all, it is by no means clear that we can be
sure that perceptual experience is either stable or predictable. Nelson
Goodman makes an acute cautionary observation when he argues that
forgeries – and by extension copies in general – are, in principle, aesthetically
flawed: no matter how skillful, copies always admit the possibility that
eventually someone will be able to discern their falseness. And this fact
itself, though non-perceptual, is aesthetically relevant. As he says:

Although I see no difference now between the two pictures in question, I may learn to see a difference between them . . . And the fact that I may later be able to make a perceptual distinction between the pictures that I cannot make now constitutes an aesthetic difference between them that is important to me now.[16]

What is more, as a rule the argument on behalf of "experience" alone is conducted implicitly with the distance senses in mind: vision and hearing. These are the primary senses for the perceptual experience dictated by museums and other institutions in which valuable artifacts are housed. However, I contend that part of the relationship between object and subject includes the relationship of proximity – even of contact – between the two, where that contact is literal and physical, where it implies the possibility of *touch*. Pursuing this line of thought adds further support to the argument against detaching the value of experience from the genuineness of its object.

3   Touch, Contact, Nearness, Presence

Touch is not the usual sense that informs consideration of the display of artworks or museum artifacts. Under the institutions of art with which we are now most familiar, one is simply not supposed to touch the objects. There are good conservation reasons for this, because even the merest brush of the finger can leave skin oil on a surface; the moisture from one's breath can be damaging to some materials. The prohibition on touch puts objects ahead of the audience, for while we may desire closer contact, that contact compromises the endurance of objects. We pass through their space. They endure far longer than we, and banning touch implies that their persistence is more valuable than our moments of intimate contact.

What is more, the prohibition on touch is usually not considered much of a sacrifice, for touch is not one of the traditional aesthetic senses. Where artworks require sense experience, it is vision and hearing that they usually address. Except in cases where crafts with practical functions are elevated to the condition of fine art, as is the case with quilts which are snatched off beds and hung on museum walls, one supposedly can grasp all the sensory aesthetic qualities of a work with the eyes and the ears, with the help of the imagination and relevant background understanding. Still, even if one refrains from touching, the possibility of touch, and even the synaesthetic experience of touch (what we might call implicit touch), can be crucial to the experience of an artifact.

The displays of the Silesian House are not works of art, but I believe that reflecting on their powerful effect bears on our understanding of art and the occasional coincidence of its aesthetic and ethical traits. These messages are historical records, personal laments, and – now – memorials. That the wall-inscriptions are the exact marks made by prisoners is part of their impact. Stepping close to the wall, close to those scratches, the visitor is moved to retrace the marks with her own fingers – to touch that which was first inscribed under circumstances one painfully struggles to imagine. (And in this particular case, there is no prohibition on so doing.) There is a sense of continuity in touching what others have touched. Touch provides – or seems to provide – an intimate contact that is closer and more direct than vision.[17]

I say "seems to provide," because while the deceivability of vision is familiar, touch is sometimes thought to be the more reliable sense. It is the outstretched hand that determines if a hallucination is real or not. But we can be just as mistaken or misled about the authenticity of the object of touch as we are about anything else, and here lies one nexus of the aesthetic and the ethical value of the "genuine object." Implicit touch imparts a sense of being in the presence of something unusual, special, or unique. Being deceived or mistaken about such an object – and therefore of such an experience – is not trivial. David Davies has argued that there are a number of salient evaluative properties that are not directly perceivable but that affect experience because one is aware of them as a condition of the immediate encounter.[18] I agree, and would argue that genuineness is a presumptive property that makes a profound difference to the quality of experience.

Another display at the Silesian House dramatizes this point. Upstairs there is a large room with vitrines full of objects from the Nazi occupation. One of them holds a collection of grisly detritus from the camps, including a set of dice made by a prisoner from lumps of bread; and a gold-embossed cigarette case made from human skin.

One cannot tell that the case is made from skin just by looking. It could be any pale leather. But it is crucial to the experience of this item that one believe that one is in the presence of the real thing – a frivolous object made from a fragment of what once was a living person. Of course, one can be deceived that this is so; only the label testifies to the authenticity of the material. But the point is that no simulated-skin cigarette case – nothing presented as a simulacrum – could possibly have the same impact.

When face to face with a horror such as that cigarette case, there is no doubt of the moral resonance of the object. Making a replica so that the observer might imagine what the real thing would look like would be out of the question, almost disgraceful. Only the genuine object can bear witness to itself. But this is an artifact made by an act of inhuman cruelty, and it may seem as if the moral significance of its genuineness is a consequence of the cruelty that brought it into being. If so, the genuineness of something made without such vicious intent might not possess moral valence. It might not even be important to the experience at all. To test this surmise, let us move away from examples where the ethical weight of the object is indisputable to those where it might be overlooked.

I once visited a Swedish natural history museum because I'd heard of a display of the carcass of a baby mammoth recently released from glacial ice. I found the mammoth resting in a huge climate-controlled plexiglass cube. He was black and rubbery looking, collapsed on his side and rather squashed. It was a peculiarly moving experience, and I stood vigil for a while. Although as far as I could see he might have been made from a deflated inner tube, I trusted that I was in the presence of a creature so old and rare as to be now nearly unique. And what put me in the presence of the mammoth was the possibility of reaching out and touching it – which I would have done had the glass barrier not prevented it, just as I traced the names on the walls in Krakow.

Suppose I was wrong. Suppose the Swedish caption to the display (which I could not read) announced that the actual mammoth carcass was still in a freezer somewhere, and what lay before me was a polymer replica. (Implicit in this supposition would be a replica of a refrigeration unit as well for added verisimilitude.) Would my experience change if someone translated the caption for me? Undoubtedly. Would it have been the same if I had known about the substitution from the start? Absolutely not.

Sometimes there is interest, charm, and enjoyment in viewing a good reproduction of something important, such as a work of art, and often a reproduction is as close as one can get. Indeed, sometimes copies are themselves "works." (Think of all the Roman versions of Greek statuary.) But I can't imagine why one would ponder a lopsided lump of dark plastic trying to imagine what the remains of a mammoth look like. In a case such as this, a display that isn't the thing itself could arouse only mild interest – as part of a diorama of an archeological dig, perhaps. But discovery that one had been fooled, whether deliberately or not, would surely provoke a let-down and a sense of being cheated. The experience aroused from encountering the thing itself is not the same experience as would be occasioned by a replica.

But the question may be pressed: *how* are they different? After all, if the delusion were to persist, one would continue to value it. Does not this prove that the experience must be the same, and that any resentment upon discovery is merely retrospective revaluation of the *object* rather than legitimate reassessment of the *experience*? I think we can see that this distinction, which attempts to separate conceptually the "object" component from the "experience of the object," is insupportable. To make this case, I borrow an argument from Ronald de Sousa's analysis of emotions, which illuminates the importance of the genuine object and amplifies Kieran's comment about the relation that an original bears to the perceiving subject.

With the objects of some emotions, de Sousa notes, it is their properties that are the relevant triggers for those emotions. For example, when one feels fear when encountering a snake while hiking, it is the property attributed to it of being dangerous – which includes being poisonous, fast, and ready to strike – that accounts for the justified arousal of fear in its presence. Another snake with similar properties would arouse similar fear. Therefore, while the fear has a particular intentional object, any similar snake with similar properties in similar circumstances would be frightening. However, there are other emotions, such as romantic love, where the object of the emotion does not seem to be the *properties* of the object so much as the *object itself* which possesses those properties. Consider Alcmene, the loving and faithful wife of Greek myth, whom Zeus seduced by taking on all the perceptible characteristics of her husband and fooling her about his identity. Why should Alcmene care that the object of her love was not really her husband Amphitryon, asks de Sousa? After all, the transfigured Zeus had all of his properties – and therefore her experience with Zeus was the same as would be the experience with her husband. Nonetheless, Alcmene would be rightly affronted to discover that it was Zeus beside her rather than Amphitryon, even though the two were, for a night, perceptually indiscernible. This demonstrates that some emotions, including love, are directed not just to objects with certain properties but also to non-fungible (that is, non-substitutable) objects possessing those properties.[19]

This conclusion regarding love squares with common usage; few would think that marrying one identical twin is prudent because if he dies the other is available as a spare, even if they were virtual clones of each other. The loss of a spouse, friend, or child is not even faintly redressed by the gain of another, no matter how similar his or her traits. The emotional phenomenon of non-fungible objects is reflected in the values we ascribe to persons. The conceptual habits and intuitions that govern responses to artifacts are not so entrenched.[20] What is more, there are plenty of artifacts and even works of art that are fungible – that permit substitution with no loss of value. Copies of literary works or musical scores or recordings are obvious. But even physical artifacts such as lithographs or structures built to plan may be fungible objects of more or less inter-changeable value.

The examples discussed thus far are not fungible. If one discovers that they are not genuine, the experience fades. Irritation, dismay, or a sense of betrayal replaces aesthetic absorption. Here is clearly a merger of aesthetic and ethical sensibilities. What is more, even if the labels on displays openly state that the object before one is a replica or a substitute, the effect is dimmed. I can't imagine being transfixed by a mammoth made from plastic, or meditating upon a field that looks just like Gettysburg but happens to be in Montana, or even being moved by a stretch of wall that merely duplicates the final pleas of prisoners, copying them down in another place. Being in the presence of the genuine objects – within touch-ing range – is required for their affective power to be felt.

Windows, however, are replaced all the time, as are bricks, boards, stones, moldings, plumbing, nails, roofs, locks, and many of the other elements that make up a building. These sorts of things seem *prima facie* to be uncontestably fungible objects. So let us turn now to the Darwin Martin House to see to what extent aesthetic and ethical valences remain attached to the property of genuineness with this example. I focus on the windows designed for the house both because the entire architectural com-plex is too extensive to consider here, and also because windows – highly breakable and importantly functional elements of a building – present us with especially challenging test cases for the value of the genuine.

4   Wright's Windows

The Martin complex was intended as a home not only for Darwin Martin, his wife Isabelle, and their two children, but also for his sister and brother-in-law. In fact, the first structure built on the site was the Barton House for the latter. The remaining buildings were linked struc-tures spread over a very large lot[21] (Plate 8.1). The main residence fronted onto one street; the Barton house faced a street that was at a right-angle to the main residence; and in between were the garage-stable and a con-servatory (Plate 8.2). The latter occupied the end of a long pergola such that one could look from the living quarters of the main residence down 100 feet of pergola into the conservatory (Plate 8.3).

Wright designed not only his houses but also their furniture, fixtures, tiles, carpets, and utensils, and he was particularly interested in windows.

Plate 8.1: Panoramic view of the Darwin Martin House. The main residence is at far left; the Barton House appears at far right. In between are the long pergola and conservatory. The roof of the garage-stable may be seen just over the latter.
Source: University Archives, University at Buffalo, State University of New York.

The windows he conceived for his prairie style homes departed from the styles of leaded-glass windows popular at the turn of the last century, abandoning figurative images for geometric arrangements of many pieces – sometimes hundreds – of colored, frosted, and clear glass, secured by delicate vertical webs of cames. (Cames are the thin metal borders that are the hallmark of so-called leaded glass. They hold the glass pieces in place and mark off the edges of the designs.[22]) Wright conceived of his windows partly in terms of these divisions. In a letter to Darwin Martin he stated, "We haven't designed 'leaded glass' for you, we have designed a dainty metal grille with glass insertion."[23] With nine primary patterns, the Martin House contained more distinctive window designs than any of his other domestic buildings.[24]

Wright called his windows "light screens," and they were designed for the purpose of both separating spaces and integrating them by means of the views they afforded and the patterns of light they cast. One commentator states

> Through his screen-like patterns, he sought to "bring the outside in," to eliminate the impression of boxy enclosure of the traditional house by making the exterior visible. Yet he maintained the separateness of interior and exterior, setting them off by the delicate pattern of leadlines in his

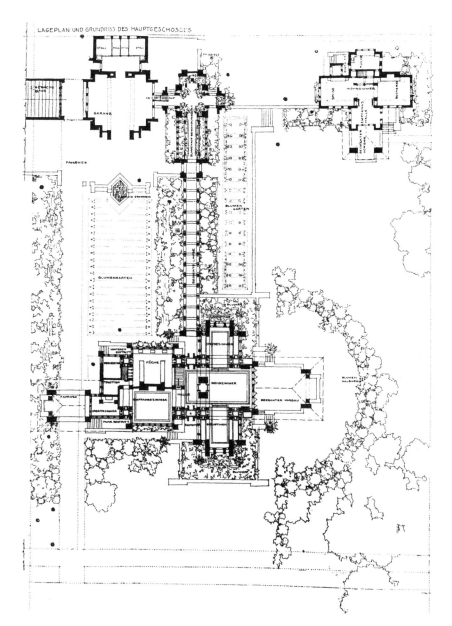

Plate 8.2: Groundplan. The main residence is drawn at the bottom of the image, the Barton House at the upper right, the garage-stable at upper left. The conservatory appears at the end of the long pergola attached to the main residence.

Source: University Archives, University at Buffalo, State University of New York.

Plate 8.3: Photo: Henry Fuermann. View from the main residence down the pergola.
Source: University Archives, University at Buffalo, State University of New York.

windows, which retained the sense of the building's structure but rendered it permeable, almost diaphanous. In all these aspects of his use of it, decorative glass was integral to Wright's architectural vision of a newly continuous living space.[25]

The extensive correspondence between Martin and Wright regarding window design and placement confirm that for Wright, his windows were indispensable for the integrity and the very life of his buildings. Elsewhere he wrote:

> By means of glass, then, the first great integrity may find prime means of realization. Open reaches of the ground may enter as the building and the building interior may reach out and associate with these vistas of the ground. Ground and building will thus become more and more obvious as directly related to each other in openness and intimacy; not only as environment but also as a good pattern for the good life lived in the building.[26]

When the back buildings of the Martin complex were destroyed in 1960 to make way for development, some of their windows were removed. Others fell victim to the wrecking ball, and the long pergola and its terminus, the "jewel-like conservatory at the heart of the composition," were obliterated[27] (Plate 8.4).

The summer before reconstruction of the pergola and conservatory was to begin, I learned from Jack Quinan, curator of the Martin House, that he was conducting a dig on the site before the new foundations were laid, looking for any remains of the original buildings that would help to guide the restoration project. There wasn't much expectation of great discovery, as the area had already been bulldozed twice. Seizing the opportunity to step onto a road not taken, I asked if I could help, and thus one sizzling afternoon I picked my way across the construction site and skidded into a trench. I was handed a hard hat and a claw and directed to a corner of the dig. After an hour of hacking that turned up only tree roots and small shards of clear glass, beginner's luck struck. A glinting fragment of conservatory window, tiny amber beads still secured between the twisted cames, fell into my hands.

It was, of course, thrilling. But why, exactly? I had become bored with turning up bits of the thin clear glass from the ceiling that littered the area, but they were just as "original" as this piece. (And in fact, though I did not know it at the time, Wright chose the method of manufacture for his clear glass with great care.[28]) The leaded glass with its colored design was prettier, or at least had been before demolition. But was that all?

Plate 8.4: Photo: Henry Fuermann. Conservatory of the Darwin Martin House.
Source: University Archives, University at Buffalo, State University of New York.

The case I make for the importance of the genuine has made use of the question of fungibility, and windows are an interesting test for this gauge. As a rule, windows are fungible items. To the degree that the same pattern can be replicated, even Wright's art-glass windows may seem to be fungible. But if we care that they are the very windows that the Martins looked through, the ones their maids washed, the ones that let in air and light – the continuity with the past is missing when the windows are replicas. They fail the test of implicit touch. This is a less important factor in this case than with the others adduced earlier, but it is still a failure, and it indicates an aesthetic difference between what will be a splendidly reproduced conservatory window and the damaged relic I dug up. It might be the only value the latter retains, but it is one that the reproduction will not share.

For this type of building, elements that are largely functional in other houses are central to the artistry of Wright's architecture. He exerted his designer's eye often at the expense of the convenience of his clients, although he conceived of his domestic buildings not only as their homes but also as extended expressions of their own personalities. As Quinan says, "The prairie house was not . . . merely a new domestic prototype to be doled out to waiting customers as so many variations on a theme. Instead, Wright considered it something personal and intimate, like an article of clothing."[29] In other words, though his windows were manufactured and (within serious practical limits) could be – and sometimes were – replaced within a few years of original construction, they also constitute individually designed and selected artistic elements that are intrinsic aspects of the architecture. Their destruction, therefore, is obviously an artistic loss. Their approximate replication is possible because of remaining originals, extant drawings, photographs, and a few left-over fragments.

How great a loss it is that replicas try to redress is very much a matter of degree. We replace windows all the time, but a "replacement" window is clearly a fungible item. Only a special window is worthy of a "replica." A replica is not a replacement. A replacement window assumes the simple role of window, but a replica retains a reference to something of still greater value. This suggests that for certain kinds of artifacts there is a state between fungible and non-fungible that needs to be investigated alongside the value of genuineness. A replacement is fully fungible, and the values of serial replacements are likely to be equivalent. A replica is itself fungible and can be replaced without loss of value with another replica. (Barring those cases where the replica itself becomes a significant historical artifact, which certainly can happen.) But while a replacement is fully fungible, a replica stands in for a non-fungible item.

I have argued that genuineness is a presumptive quality that subtends the perceptual and affective experience that is labeled "aesthetic." It admits of degrees of significance depending on the conditions of origin and meaning, and these vary with objects too radically to permit useful generalization. With two of the guiding examples that opened this essay, the Gettysburg Battlefield and the objects of the Silesian House museum, genuineness is also required for the ethical task of manifesting that which should not be forgotten, of bearing witness. (It probably has something in common with the values ascribed to religious relics, a comparison I shall not pursue.) The Darwin Martin House is not of this sort, neither its windows nor the entire structure. However, there is a sense in which this work and any other particularly innovative work of art can be said to bear witness – to a way of life and to a distinctive artistic achievement. The loss of the genuine article is therefore a loss of that achievement. A replica reports what was achieved; it does not supplant, nor does it reenact, the achievement.

The moral valence of the Martin house is slight compared to the other two examples. Ethical significance, however, is not altogether absent. At the very least, its destruction was a wrong done to the artist, so to that extent one can see restoration as an effort to right that wrong (although its intended purpose is usually more to reinstate something important for the living). What is more, destruction of art also wrongs its audience. That it is a loss to culture is obvious, and insofar as the scope of the ethical is conceived to include a "good" life as a whole, important cultural losses are ethically meaningful. But I believe we can discern a more specific type of wrong when considering the experience of replicas. Experiencing artworks, just as experiencing the other sorts of artifacts discussed here, affords an opportunity to extend our present worlds backwards in time. We are presently attuned to values of cultural diversity and to arguments that we should expand our points of view to include the perspectives of others with whom we share the planet. With globalization, many of the markers of identity that once distinguished one culture from another – such as foods, market systems, attitudes towards elders, and so forth – are diminishing, and the loss of such distinctive habits and products is frequently regretted. These losses extend into both ethical and aesthetic domains.

They extend into the past as well, for something of the same loss occurs with the destruction of art and other artifacts whose impact is wrought through aesthetic encounters. Once that destruction occurs, a restoration effort is the only way to reinstate something like the accomplishment of the past, and that is good. At the same time, while responsible restoration announces itself and does not deliberately deceive, replicas tempt *self*-deception. That indeed is their very purpose – to induce an experience of something with an approximate something else. This is a pheno-menon with both aesthetic and ethical substance. Replicas are likely to be successful in cases such as the Darwin Martin house. With the other examples, they utterly foreclose experience in both aesthetic and ethical directions. The continuity that can be seen among the examples I have discussed here (and there are many others one could add) advises that the value of genuineness is widely important. And genuineness is a value that falls simultaneously within several normative categories, including the aesthetic and the ethical.

It may seem as if I am heading to a cumbersome practical conclusion: never destroy; only preserve. However, such a directive would be impossible as well as ill-advised, and while my argument bears on practical considerations, those have to be determined in the particular instance. Change is inevitable and often good, and not even great achievements are meant to be preserved forever, no matter how non-fungible they may be. At the same time, objects whose genuineness matters exert a claim on us, and a failure to attend to that claim is both an aesthetic and an ethical fault. When they are destroyed, so is the apprehension that is attainable only in the tangible presence of that which has endured.

Notes

The images of Frank Lloyd Wright's Darwin D. Martin House appear courtesy of the University Archives, University at Buffalo, State University of New York.

For his generous consultation about Wright and the Martin complex, I thank Jack Quinan, Curator of the Darwin D. Martin House. For their perceptive suggestions on earlier drafts, I also thank Ann Colley, David Hershenov, Ken Shockley, and Joe Zeccardi. I am grateful to John Edens and Bill Offhaus of the University at Buffalo Archives for their kind assistance with the images.

1 Gettysburg National Military Park website, http://www.nps.gov/gett/home.htm.

2 For a review of the many versions of ethical criticism, see Noël Carroll, "Art and Ethical Criticism," *Ethics* 110/2 (January 2000): 350–87.

3 As I hope to make clear in the course of argument, this is not the same as claiming that moral merit is *pro tanto* an aesthetic merit, as some have argued. See Berys Gaut, "The Ethical Criticism of Art," in Jerrold Levinson, ed., *Ethics and Aesthetics: Essays at the Intersection* (Cambridge: Cambridge University Press, 1998), pp. 182–203.

4 Arthur Danto has pointed out some ways in which battlefields are like works of art. His moving essay "Gettysburg" is indispensable reading for understanding the complexity of the "experiences" this battlefield can afford. See

Philosophizing Art (Berkeley and Los Angeles, CA: University of California Press, 1999), 233–50.

5   As Marcia Eaton notes, "There may be assessments that require *both* aesthetic and ethical reflection simultaneously" ("Aesthetics: The Mother of Ethics?" *Journal of Aesthetics and Art Criticism* 55/4 (Fall 1997): 355–64, p. 356).

6   The use of "cognitivist" differs somewhat in aesthetics, ethics, and emotion theory, and since I engage all three areas there may be some confusion about this term. Here I use the term to indicate that it is the nature of (at least some) aesthetic encounters to impart a type of insight or understanding. Although I am sympathetic to the view that all aesthetic experiences are to some degree cognitive, the argument here only presumes that some of them are: that included among the possibilities of aesthetic encounters is the achievement of understanding following from direct acquaintance with some particular object.

7   Peter Railton, "Aesthetic Value, Moral Value, and Naturalism," in Levinson, *Aesthetics and Ethics*, p. 62.

8   For an analysis of the relation between historical value and art value that includes "age-value," see Alois Riegl, "The Modern Cult of Monuments: Its Character and Its Origin," trans. Kurt W. Forster and Diane Ghirardo, *Oppositions* (Fall 1982): 21–51.

9   Jack Quinan, *Frank Lloyd Wright's Martin House: Architecture as Portraiture* (New York: Princeton Architectural Press, 2004), p. 114.

10   David Carrier, "Art and Its Preservation," *Journal of Aesthetics and Art Criticism* 43/3 (1985): 291–300, p. 299. The identity of artifacts through time is discussed by Randall R. Dipert, *Aesthetics, Art Works, and Agency* (Philadelphia, PA: Temple University Press, 1993), chapter 7.

11   John Dewey, *Art as Experience* (1934; reprint, New York: Capricorn Books, 1958), p. 4.

12   Malcolm Budd, *Values of Art: Pictures, Poetry and Music* (London: Penguin, 1995), p. 4. See also Alan Goldman, "The Experiential Account of Aesthetic Value," *Journal of Aesthetics and Art Criticism* 64/3 (Summer 2006): 333–42.

13   There are major differences in approach to the scope of aesthetically relevant properties, the extremes of which are represented by Frank Sibley, "Aesthetic Objects," *Philosophical Review* 68 (1959): 421–50 (who treats aesthetic properties on a perceptual model) and Arthur Danto, *The Transfiguration of the Commonplace* (Cambridge MA, Harvard University Press, 1981) (who argues that a number of aesthetically relevant properties are perceptually indiscernible).

14   Hilde Hein, "Museums – from Object to Experience," in Carolyn Korsmeyer, ed., *Aesthetics: The Big Questions* (Malden MA: Blackwell, 1998), p. 108.

15   Matthew Kieran, *Revealing Art* (London: Routledge, 2005), p. 14.

16 Nelson Goodman, *Languages of Art* (Indianapolis, IN: Bobbs-Merrill, 1968), pp. 103–4.

17 "Knowledge of the most profound and intimate emotions is literally conveyed by touch" (Christopher Perricone, "The Aspiration to the Condition of Touch," *Philosophy and Literature* 30/1 (April 2006): 229–37), p. 233. See also Constance Classen, "Touch in the Museum," in Constance Classen, ed., *The Book of Touch* (Oxford: Berg Publishers, 2005), pp. 275–86.

18 David Davies, "Against Enlightened Empiricism," in Matthew Kieran, ed., *Contemporary Debates in Aesthetics and Philosophy of Art* (Malden, MA: Blackwell, 2006), p. 28.

19 Ronald de Sousa, *The Rationality of Emotions* (Cambridge, MA: MIT Press, 1987), pp. 8–9, 97–8, 130–32. A similar line of thought is presented by Mark Sagoff, "On Restoring and Reproducing Art," *Journal of Philosophy* 75/9 (September 1978): 453–70.

20 R. A. Sharpe suggests that responses to art and to persons may be comparable, in "The Empiricist Theory of Artistic Value," *Journal of Aesthetics and Art Criticism* 58/4 (Fall 2000): 321–32.

21 The Barton house was designed first, and then the garage-stable and conservatory, the pergola, and the main residence were constructed. An additional building for a gardener's cottage was designed in 1905 but not built until 1908. (It is still standing, with an addition built by a private owner before the structure was reacquired as part of the Martin Complex.) A commercially designed greenhouse was inserted between the garage and the gardener's cottage sometime around 1907–8, added because Martin felt the conservatory did not provide sufficient growing space. Wright wrote that he would embellish the greenhouse with architectural design, but there is no evidence that he did so. The greenhouse is not part of the restoration project. (Jack Quinan, private correspondence.)

22 The cames of "leaded glass" windows need not be made from lead. Wright preferred using lighter, hollow cames made of zinc, copper, or brass. See Julie L. Sloan, *Light Screens: The Leaded Glass of Frank Lloyd Wright* (New York: Rizzoli, 2001), p. 29. The Darwin Martin House windows are set in brass. See Jack Quinan, ed., *Frank Lloyd Wright: Windows of the Darwin Martin House* (Buffalo, NY: Burchfield-Penney Art Center, 1999), p. 9.

23 Quoted in Sloan, *Light Screens*, p. 29.

24 Ted Pietrzak, "Foreword," in Quinan, *Windows of the Darwin Martin House*, p. 7.

25 Sloan, *Light Screens*, p. 23.

26 Quoted from Wright's autobiography by David G. De Long in his Introduction to Sloan, *Light Screens*, p. 18. Compare a comment Wright made some years later about windows in his religious architecture: "Perhaps more important than all . . . is that by way of glass the sunlit space as a reality becomes a more useful servant of a higher order of the human Spirit" (quoted in Sloan,

Light Screens, p. 145). It should be observed that Wright's conception of the "good life lived in the building" was not always shared by his clients. Isabelle Martin objected to many aspects of his design, including the windows, the original placement of which she felt obscured the view.

27   Theodore Lownie, "Introduction," in Quinan, ed., *Windows of the Darwin Martin House*, p. 8.
28   Sloan, *Light Screens*, pp. 30–31.
29   Quinan, *Wright's Martin House*, p. 33.

9

SUSAN SONTAG, DIANE ARBUS, AND THE ETHICAL DIMENSIONS OF PHOTOGRAPHY

David Davies

1 A Baby with a Hand Grenade

Norman Mailer, one of her better-known subjects, wrote of Diane Arbus that to give her a camera was "like giving a hand grenade to a baby."[1] This rather complex simile seems to rest upon two distinct comparative claims: (1) that a camera, like a hand grenade, is something which has the potential to damage people if used without due care, and (2) that Arbus, like a baby, was naïvely unaware of the damage that such a device can do. Arbus's best-known critic, Susan Sontag, shared Mailer's general concern about the harm that can be done by the taking and receiving of photographic images, and agreed that Arbus is especially notable as a cause of such harm. But Sontag offered a much less charitable diagnosis of the psychology that underlies Arbus's photographic work. A baby, after all, could not be held morally or legally responsible for the damage it caused with a hand grenade, but Arbus's photographs, for Sontag, manifest a cruelty and a moral irresponsibility that reflect both on her professional ethics and, perhaps, on the artistic value of her work.

Sontag's scathing ethical criticism of Arbus's work,[2] originally published in a critical response to the Arbus retrospective organized in the wake of the artist's suicide, still colors critical responses to that work. There is an abiding tendency to read the work psychoanalytically, and to characterize Arbus's vision, as expressed in her work, as "cruel," compassionless, and insensitive to the individuality of her subjects.[3] In light of such critical responses to the 2005 international Arbus retrospective at the

Metropolitan Museum of Art in New York, it is perhaps time to look more closely at Sontag's criticisms, some of which apply more generally to photography, and at the issues they raise about the moral dimensions of the medium. The plethora of biographical material on Arbus now made available by Doon Arbus, the artist's daughter and the guardian of her estate, and published in the voluminous catalogue to the 2005 retrospective, casts doubt upon at least some of the psychological lore on Arbus that more recent critics seem to have inherited from Sontag. More interesting, however, are those deeper questions that the latter raised: first, about the responsibility of the photographer to her subjects – a matter of professional ethics; and, second, about the ethical dimensions of a medium that seems to engage us with the world outside the work in an immediate way that other arts are unable to. Is Sontag correct in characterizing the act of taking photographs as "predatory" and "voyeuristic," and the act of receiving them as something that threatens to blunt our moral "vision"?

I shall begin by locating these ethical concerns about photography in the context of other, broadly epistemological and artistic, challenges to the medium. I shall then summarize Sontag's claims, about photography in general and about Arbus in particular, sketching at the same time some salient facts about Arbus's oeuvre. On the basis of this, I shall distinguish a number of distinct ethical issues raised by Sontag and some of Arbus's more recent critics. After briefly calling into question assumptions about Arbus's life and motivations that ground some of the ethical criticism of her work, I shall further explore the different kinds of moral questions posed by that work and Sontag's critical responses to it.

2   Implications of a "Causal" Medium

From the very beginning of philosophical reflection upon photography, the "causal" or "mechanical" nature of the process whereby a standard (i.e., non-digital) photographic image is formed has raised concerns about the medium. It has been widely assumed that the relationship between a photographic image and what is imaged differs from the relationship between a painting or drawing and what is imaged: while the intentionality of the artist plays a particular kind of determining role in the latter, it plays no analogous role in the former. In at least one sense, what a standard photographic image presents or represents is whatever was before the camera at the time of taking the picture and caused the image to offer to the viewer a particular visual array. This is sometimes put in counterfactual terms: had what was before the camera differed in those visual properties falling within the range of the lens, then, *ceteris paribus*, the visual array presented by the image would have differed in some corresponding respect. In the case of a painting or drawing, on the other hand, it is the beliefs of the artist concerning what is before her that at least partly determine the visual array presented by the image and thus what the image is of.

One proposing such a distinction can grant that the intentional states of the photographer play some part in determining what the subject of a picture is by deciding which parts of the world to put within the scope of the lens. But the difference in etiology between photographic and pictorial images has been seen by some as entailing other salient differences in ontology, epistemology, and aesthetics. André Bazin, for example, has been taken by some to argue for an ontological difference between photographs and paintings or drawings: in a photograph, the entity, light rays from which are causally responsible for producing the visual array, is somehow present in the image itself.[4] Kendall Walton has offered a less startling reformulation of Bazin's claim, arguing that the difference is properly viewed as more epistemological than ontological.[5] While paintings and drawings are representations of their subjects, photographs, like mirrors or telescopes, are ways of indirectly seeing their subjects: we see the subject through the photograph, which is in this sense "transparent," and this explains the kinds of evidential and emotional significances that we ascribe to photographs but not to paintings.

The supposed "transparency" of the photographic medium has been claimed by some to be incompatible with the idea that photography, like painting, can be a representational visual art. The most widely discussed contemporary proponent of such concerns is Roger Scruton.[6] In the case of paintings, he argues, we look at them in a way that is deeply informed by our awareness that they are the products of representational acts on the part of their makers. We take it that the manifest properties of the image are ones that were intentionally conferred upon it by the artist, and we therefore regard the painted canvas as an expression of thought about its subject. This enters into our engagement with a picture in two ways. First, we do not look through the canvas to what it represents, but rather take its representational content to be determinable only by scrupulous attention to the painted surface itself. Second, we attend to how the subject has been rendered, and thereby treat the painting as the perceptual embodiment of a "thought" about its subject.

This allows us to take a properly artistic interest in the representational content of painting. If a properly artistic (*qua* aesthetic) interest must be an interest in something "for its own sake," then a properly artistic interest in a representational artwork must be an interest in inherent properties of the representation, rather than an ulterior interest in the thing represented. The representational content of a painting enters into our assessment of its artistic value because a properly artistic interest in a representational painting is always an interest in how the representation renders the subject, in two distinct senses: first, it is an interest in the "thought" expressed about the subject – the "thought-content" of the representation; and second it is an interest in the manner in which this thought-content has been expressed through the manipulation of the medium.

However, so Scruton argues, no such account can be given of our engagement with a photographic image. For, so he claims, there are two crucial differences between painting and photography in this respect, both of which derive from the essentially causal nature of the process whereby photographic images are generated. First, because we know that what is imaged in a photograph must have existed in front of the camera when the image was generated, we are led to look through the image to its subject and to take an interest both in the existence of the subject and in the truths about it revealed by the photograph. Photographs therefore serve not as things in which we are interested for their own sakes, but rather as entities in which we have an ulterior interest parasitic upon our interest in their subjects. Second, a properly artistic interest in the content of a photograph is impossible because we cannot see how the subject is represented (in either of the above senses) by looking more closely at the photograph. For many of the details of a photographic image are determined by the world, given the causal process whereby the image is produced. While the photographer is able to arrange details of the subject, and indeed to choose what to photograph and the perspective from which the photograph is taken, none of this, according to Scruton, can be determined by the receiver who more closely scrutinizes the image. At best, the viewer can take the image as a sign from which certain representational intentions might be inferred.[7]

3   Ethical Concerns about Photography

Unsurprisingly, the causal relationship between a standard photographic image and what it images also underpins some of the ethical questions about photography raised by Sontag, and, thereby, her critical response to the work of Arbus. Our knowledge of the causal process whereby a photographic image is produced leads us, she claims, to treat such images very differently from the way we treat verbal descriptions or handmade images of the world. For, while we recognize the latter as interpretations of their subjects, we treat the photographic image as part of the world rather than as a construal of it. This, for Sontag, explains the kinds of evidential and justificatory roles ascribed to photographs – like bear-tracks in the wood, we might say, they are taken to testify, even in a distorted way, to what actually happened. But photographs, she further claims, thereby deceive us, in that "in deciding how a picture should look, in preferring one exposure over another, photographers are always imposing standards on their subjects. Although there is a sense in which the camera does indeed capture reality, not just interpret it, photographs are as much an interpretation of the world as paintings and drawings are."[8] This, as we shall see, is crucial if we are to hold the photographer accountable in certain ways for the images she produces.

Sontag raises two more specific ethical questions about photography, one pertaining to the activity of taking photographs and the other to the activity of looking at them. First, the act of taking a photograph of a given event E is one among a number of possible responses one might make to E, and excludes other possible responses that would involve intervening so as to affect E's occurrence in some way.[9] Nor is this merely a matter of passivity: to elect to photograph E is to have an interest in E remaining unchanged at least until the photograph has been taken. Sontag further charges that the act of taking photographs is "predatory:" "To photograph people is to violate them, by seeing them as they never see themselves, by having knowledge of them that they can never have, it turns people into objects that can be symbolically possessed."[10] This rather Kantian criticism of photography – that it treats its subjects solely as means rather than as ends in themselves – is one to which we shall return when we examine the ethical relationship between the photographer and those people who serve as subjects for her pictures.

Second, she questions the effects of photographs on those who view them. She grants that much work by serious photographers has had the morally laudable aim of presenting the suffering and misfortunes of others in order to help bring about some kind of redress of a social wrong. This applies in particular to the work of Lewis Hine, which facilitated the enactment of legislation against child labor, and the work of Roy Emerson Stryker's 1930s Farm Security Administration Project whose photographs of migrant workers and sharecroppers again played a role in shaping public policy.[11] However, Sontag maintains, looking at photographs has the potential to corrupt rather than purify consciousness, since familiarity with the sufferings of others may lead to a lessening of our tendency to feel compassion for them. As with pornography, she argues, familiarity with a certain kind of image may deaden our responses so that only even more horrific images can move us. This claim might profitably be related to the claim, by Iris Murdoch, that "moral seeing" plays a crucial role in moral agency – that a truly good person sees the events unfolding before her in "thick" moral terms, and is immediately prompted to act in the right way by what she perceives.[12] Literature, according to Murdoch, is particularly effective at removing our moral blindness and sharpening our moral vision. Sontag, however, might be taken to be suggesting that familiarity with certain sorts of photographic images can blunt our ability to see things in terms of their moral aspects, or perhaps undermine the connection between moral seeing and moral agency. As we shall see, Sontag feels that Arbus's work is particularly susceptible to such criticism.

4   Sontag's Critique of Arbus

Sontag contrasts Arbus's work to a tradition of American photography that sought, in different ways, to fulfill a Whitmanesque conception of the proper goal of photography – namely, to bring out the particular beauty or value in all things, including those that seem most trivial and even vulgar. The humanist ideals underlying Edward Steichen's 1955 "Family of Man" exhibition represent one of the final manifestations of this tradition, and stand in stark contrast, for Sontag, to the next photography exhibition at the Museum of Modern Art to engender similar attention, the 1972 Arbus retrospective. Where the images selected by Steichen seek to express, in different ways, a shared human condition, Arbus's images, she claims, suggest a world in which everyone is alienated and isolated. She describes the content of the images as follows: "The Arbus show lined up assorted monsters and borderline cases – most of them ugly, wearing grotesque or unflattering clothing, in dismal or barren surroundings – who have paused to pose and, often, to gaze frankly, confidentially at the viewer."[13] This is a far from neutral description of the works, generalizing from pictures of what Arbus herself termed "freaks" or "eccentrics" to pictures of "ordinary" people shot in a distinctive style – square images, often in close-up, the subject looking directly at the camera, in a large format that revealed great detail in a very sharp manner. But, so Sontag argued, Arbus's way of presenting her subjects "could insinuate anguish, kinkiness, mental illness with any subject . . . Anybody Arbus photographed was a freak."[14]

What Sontag finds morally questionable in Arbus's work is not simply that the chosen subjects are suffering or troubled. Rather, it is the manner in which such subjects are presented, the absence of "the compassionate purpose that such a project is expected to serve." The latter, for Sontag, is evident in the fact that images of people who are "pathetic, pitiable as well as repulsive"[15] fail to arouse in us any compassionate feelings, where this is presumably taken as evidence as to how the pictures are intended to strike the viewer. As to why we are not moved by these images, Sontag's analysis seems to rest on the fact that, rather than display an awareness of "how grotesque they are,"[16] Arbus's subjects pose as if cheerful and accepting of their lives. So presented, they are not possible objects of our compassion or pity, for we cannot comprehend what kind of inner life could underlie the visual appearances: they simply strike us as "other," as "strange."

The charge that Arbus's pictures of her marginalized subjects lack compassion is expressed in even stronger terms by some more recent commentators. Most critical is Germaine Greer who recounts her own experience of being photographed by Arbus.[17] Rejecting as "nonsense" talk of Arbus's empathy with her subjects, and of her pictures as capturing "the unique interior lives of those she photographed," Greer maintains that the emotion expressed by each of Arbus's iconic images is "a relentless, all-encompassing loathing" for her subjects. Her subjects, unlike those in the tradition of "freak photography" are nameless, Arbus having no interest in them as individuals: "She reduced her subjects to generic phenomena by the names she chose for them: Jewish Couple, Puerto Rican Housewife, Albino Sword-Swallower . . . Feminist in Hotel Room." Even critics more favorable to Arbus's work concur with Sontag in talking of Arbus's "sublime cruelty with the camera," and of the style of presentation of her subjects as one which "in [its] unsparing detail made all but the most beautiful subjects look stark and ugly."[18]

As may be clear, such criticisms of Arbus's work seem to run together two distinct moral charges. One charge is that the works lack compassion for their "pathetic, pitiable" subjects, presenting them in such a way as to prevent our feeling pity for them. On at least some views of artistic value, such a moral failing in the images may count as an artistic failing in the works. But a quite separate charge addresses not the experienced qualities of Arbus's images, but the actions of Arbus herself in creating those images – not the compassionless nature of the images but the compassionless nature of the photographer responsible for creating them. If, as we surely must, we separate what a work expresses about its subject from what the creator of the work felt about that subject, it is important to distinguish between these two charges. In fact, Sontag's most influential criticisms of Arbus involve speculations about the psychology of both the artist and those drawn to her work, and the ascription of moral failings to Arbus in virtue of her psychological states vis-à-vis her subjects. The issue, here, is more one of the professional ethics of the photographer – her responsibilities to her subjects – than of the moral qualities of her work.

Sontag thinks that many have taken Arbus's suicide as an indication that her work was sincere and compassionate rather than voyeuristic, and as showing that her engagement with such difficult subjects was coura-geous. But Sontag rejects Arbus's own comparison of her activity with that of a war correspondent, and then identifies as "what is finally most troubling in Arbus's photos" not the subjects portrayed but "the cumul-ative impression of the photographer's consciousness, the sense that what is presented is precisely a private vision, something voluntary."[19] Sontag proceeds to offer an analysis of the psychological states she takes to motiv-ate Arbus and those who are drawn to her work. Arbus, she claims, is not, like some romantic artists, someone driven to self-destruction through the exploration of their own pain, but, rather, someone who sought out and collected images of others' pain. This, she suggests, was motivated by the desire to demonstrate an ability to confront life's horrors without blanch-ing, although the photographer's and the viewer's relationship to these horrors is always that of the spectator, the tourist. She traces such a desire to Arbus's childhood, in which, Arbus once regretted, there had been no need to face adversity. Arbus, she further maintains, used her camera as a way of procuring vicariously the sorts of experiences she had been excluded from, "the shock of immersion in experiences that cannot be beautified, the encounter with what is taboo, perverse, evil."[20] Her interest in "freaks" "expresses a desire to violate her own innocence, to undermine her sense of being privileged, to vent her frustration at being safe."[21] Once again, it is worth noting that this sort of psychoanalytic approach to Arbus is still prevalent in the critical response to her work. Adam Phillips' review of *Revelations*, the catalogue to the 2005 Arbus retrospective, traces Arbus's thematic interests to her sense of "exclusion" and her sense of "thwarted closeness" in her attempts to befriend "freaks" and others she encoun-tered in her work.[22] Phillips' concluding observation is that "what is truly odd about Arbus's work is not her subject matter, but how difficult it is to conceive of not talking about it in psychological terms."

While this exercise in psychoanalysis is intended to be specific to Arbus, Sontag believes that the more general motivation for looking at that which is horrible – to suppress or reduce what is regarded as a "bourgeois" moral and sensory queasiness – is a more general feature of capitalist high art, and of particular concern in photography given the general worries about the latter set out above. For, she maintains, in changing our level of tolerance for looking at representations of that which is shocking or painful, we change our level of responsiveness to the shocking and painful itself. Applying her earlier comparison between pornography and photography in general, she writes that such experiences with pictures make "one less able to react in real life. What happens to people's feelings on first exposure to today's neighborhood pornographic films or to tonight's televised atrocity is not so different from what happens when they first look at Arbus's photographs."[23]

5   Some Difficulties with Sontag's Analysis

The more one reads Arbus's personal papers, comes to learn about her personal and professional life, and looks at the full range of her photographic oeuvre, the less plausible, or, where plausible, the less relevant Sontag's more speculative criticisms become. This is not, however, something that can be argued here: the interested reader is referred to the extensive body of "evidence" contained in *Revelations.* In her afterword to this volume, Doon Arbus comments that, while her earlier strategy had been to try to protect the photographic legacy from "an onslaught of theory and interpretation" by holding back on various papers and other documents that had been preserved following her mother's death, her new strategy is to make as much of this material as possible available without any accompanying commentary or interpretation. Her hope in providing such a repository of material is that "this surfeit of information and opinion would finally render the scrim of works invisible so that anyone encountering the photographs could meet them in the eloquence of their silence."[24] Whether the strategy succeeds I must leave to the reader's individual judgment.

What can be addressed, however, are certain internal difficulties in Sontag's analysis, and her more general claims about the ethical accountability of Arbus's work in particular, and photographic works in general. An initial point that rewards consideration is an apparent tension between Sontag's widely repeated judgment that the images that Arbus presents to us are "horrific" – essential if we are to accept her further claim that it is a desire to look unblanchingly at the horror of life that motivated both Arbus's taking of such images and our eagerness to look at them – and her explanation of why the images themselves do not express any compassion for the "pathetic, pitiable . . . repulsive" individuals portrayed. She maintains, we may recall, that, while the subjects of Arbus's photographs are pathetic, pitiable, and repulsive, they display no sign of emotional distress and appear to be quite accepting of their lives: they pose as if for a traditional portrait, seemingly unaware, as Sontag puts it, of "how grotesque they are," appearing "not to know that they are ugly."[25] Thus, rather than feeling compassion for the subjects, we are struck by their strangeness and otherness, their psychological impenetrability. As Phillips suggests, we cannot refrain from asking what their psychology must be like.

There is an underlying assumption here, concerning the conditions under which we can feel compassion, that might be questioned: the assumption, as Peter Schjeldahl puts it, is that "people who look or behave in unusual ways merit sympathy from the rest of us only if they visibly assent to our disgust with them."[26] But, more significantly in the present context, it is difficult to reconcile this explanation of why the pictures fail to arouse compassion with the claim that we and Arbus are attracted to the images by the horrific nature of what is depicted. For, in the first place, if that were indeed the motivation – a desire to stare the horror of life in the face – then it would surely be necessary that the images show the subjects to be aware of their suffering and the pitiable nature of their condition. Conversely, if the images really did strike us as horrific, it is difficult to believe that the subject's apparent failure to register the nature of their condition would prevent us from feeling compassion for them. This suggests that, without having recourse to the phenomenology of our own individual encounters with Arbus's images, we have reason to question Sontag's diagnosis of what is going on in such encounters.

Sontag's error, I think, is that she both relies upon yet fails to properly respect the distinction canvassed earlier in the sketch of Scruton's argument against representational art in photography – the distinction between the subject of a photographic image (the entity that stands in the relevant causal relation to that image) – and the manner in which that subject is represented. Sontag relies on this distinction in order to contrast the "pitiable" nature of Arbus's subjects with the distinctive way in which Arbus presents them, both stylistically and in terms of the "thought" about them that is embodied in pictorial form. (Recall also her remarks about the necessarily interpretive nature of photography in general.) But, once we allow that distinction to be made, and once we accept that a properly artistic interest in a photographic image concerns itself not with the subject but with the manner of representation of the subject, it is clear that, if our interest in looking at Arbus's images is artistic – and their being displayed in art galleries suggests that it usually is – then our response is to be explained not in terms of the subjects, abstractly construed, but in terms of how those subjects are represented in the image. Thus, for the purposes of explaining our interest in looking at the images and the way in which they affect us, their content is not properly characterized in terms such as "pathetic, pitiable . . . repulsive," since, as Sontag admits, this is not how the subjects are represented by Arbus. This is not to deny that some might be drawn to look at Arbus's images purely out of an interest in their subjects – although, as just suggested, one so drawn might prefer images of subjects more obviously in distress. But this is no more an objection to the artistic pretensions or value of the photographs than would be the objection, to the artistic value of some Renaissance paintings, that "serene" portraits of the martyrdom of saints may be objects of prurient interest on the part of those who wish, for whatever reason, to dwell on the visual representation of the suffering of others.

6   The Ethics of Taking a Photograph

There is a deeper conceptual point here, however, given that Sontag also wants to raise moral questions about Arbus's failure to act responsibly towards her subjects, to treat them as "ends" rather than solely as means, or, recalling Greer's sharper formulation of this criticism, as merely generic entities. The charge, here, is best seen as one of professional ethics. The assumption is that the photographer has a responsibility to the people she photographs, even if, as Sontag believes, photographers like Arbus try to deny that responsibility. Arbus, she claims, sees her camera as "a kind of passport that annihilates moral boundaries and social inhibitions, freeing the photographer from any responsibility toward the people photographed."[27] But under what conditions can the photographer be said to have any such professional responsibility? It will be instructive here to consider a related question about the professional ethics of the artist – the responsibility, if any, that a writer of fictions has to any real persons upon whom she bases, in some degree, her fictional characters. This largely ignored issue is discussed by Felicia Ackerman,[28] and a brief sketch of her analysis will help to clarify the issues with respect to photography.

According to Ackerman, the writer of fictions is morally constrained in basing her characters on real people because the latter can be harmed in various ways by such actions on the part of the writer. She lists a number of forms such harm can take. Some rest upon the possibility that readers may identify the person S serving as the model for a character. This may harm S either because readers thereby acquire various true or false beliefs about S that cause him distress, or because the character based upon S is presented in a degrading light. Even if readers are not able to recognize S in the character based upon him, S may be harmed in that he feels betrayed by the writer, A, who is a friend, acquaintance, colleague, etc. Ackerman argues that, while a general requirement for "informed consent" on the part of those used as models for fictional characters would seriously harm the practice of writing fiction, and thus deny us the many benefits that we may gain from the fruits of such practice, such a requirement is appropriate in cases where there is a pre-existing personal relationship of some kind between A and S. In such cases, if A fails to obtain S's informed consent, she may violate *prima facie* moral duties, such as the duty not to betray a friend or the duty to keep a promise.

Ackerman's account might seem to involve a suspicious mixture of consequentialist and deontological considerations, given the initial analysis in terms of the relative harms and benefits of basing a fictional character on a real person, and the subsequent analysis in terms of *prima facie* duties. But presumably the appearance of conflict can be resolved by reconstruing talk of harms and benefits in deontological terms – we have, it might be argued, a *prima facie* duty not to harm others, and our overall obligations are always to be determined by balancing different *prima facie* duties rather than by balancing consequences. But it is worth noting an alternative way in which this issue might be set up – in terms of a Kantian duty always to treat other people as ends in themselves and not merely as means, a duty presumably violated if an author uses another person as a model for her fiction without considering ways in which that person's capacity for autonomous agency might be compromised by such use. This may remind us of Sontag's charge that the act of photographing someone is always predatory because it involves treating the other as an object, and of Greer's charge that Arbus took no interest in the individuality of her subjects.

Can Ackerman's account of the moral responsibilities of the fiction writer to those who serve as models for her characters be applied, *mutatis mutandis*, to the issues about the professional ethics of the photographer canvassed by Sontag? How we answer this question will depend in part upon how we respond to an apparent disanalogy between the two cases. Where a character in literary fiction is based upon a real person, it seems clear how it is the person who is in some sense presented in the fictional work and who might be harmed by being so presented. The aspects of S that serve as a model for a fictional character C are closely tied to our intuitive conception of what individuates us as persons in the actual world – our distinctive personality, character, "style," or achievements. It is in virtue of sharing these kinds of characteristics, for example, that the character Skimpole, in Dickens's *Bleak House*, was modeled (somewhat unkindly) by Dickens on Leigh Hunt. These aspects are abiding features of a person: they are very much part of one's sense of who one is, even if not (on at least some accounts of personal identity) modally necessary features of who one might be. But, it might be thought, all that is presented by a photographic image is the transitory appearance of a person, not the person herself: our individuality does not reside in how we look at a given moment. Thus the subject of a photograph is not presented in a photograph in the same way that a real person is presented in a fictional character modeled on him: it is merely their appearance at a given moment in time that is there.

It is interesting to note, here, some remarks by Doon Arbus in the afterword to *Revelations*. In defending the manner in which she has exercised her guardianship of her mother's personal and artistic estate, she appeals not to a duty to protect her mother's memory, but to a duty to protect her mother's work and those who served as subjects for it. While the latter had volunteered to be in the images, they had not bargained, in doing so, on "getting diagnosed by strangers as mere symptoms of someone else's hypothetical state of mind." But, she maintains, her responsibility is not to the people themselves, but to the "aspects of them that continue to exist in the pictures."[29] The question raised in the previous paragraph is how those "aspects" are to be conceived. How we answer depends, yet again, on how we respond to the Scrutonian claim that a photographic image, unlike a painting, is incapable of expressing a determinate "thought" about its subject, and serves merely to draw our attention to the subject itself. If we accept this view, then it is indeed only the momentary appearance of a person that "exists," and may "continue to exist," in the image. Of course, appearances can be revealing, but they can also be deceptive. We may take the look of someone at a given moment, as captured by a photographic image, as evidence of some more abiding quality of character or personality – especially if they are captured apparently engaging in some action of moral note – but, to the extent that the photograph merely performs the function of pointing to or "freezing" that momentary appearance, we can hardly hold the photographer responsible for making us aware of what was already there to be seen.

Suppose, on the other hand, that we reject Scruton's claim and hold that genuinely artistic representation is a mark of the sort of use of the photographic medium at which someone like Arbus is adept. In this case, we can say that Arbus's photographic images present not merely a person's momentary appearance but also the person themselves in a certain light – embody a thought about them in pictorial form – using their appearance, as causally implicated in the forming of the image, as a means of identifying the person in question. Photographic images, then, are analogous to paintings and drawings, or, perhaps, to the work of a caricaturist. The momentary appearance is chosen both to identify the person to the viewer and to represent something about enduring qualities of their personality or character. It is these qualities, ascribed by the photographer to the subject in virtue of the way in which she has manipulated the photographic medium, that "continue to exist" in the images, in Doon Arbus's words. And in this case, a real person may be said to "exist" in the images in a way similar to how a real person may be said to be presented in a fictional character. Thus some of the issues of professional ethics raised by Ackerman seem to arise for photographs: by representing a person in a certain way, the photographer may harm that person, or breach a friendship, or in some other way act in a morally questionable way.

Only if we reject the Scrutonian account of the content of photographic images can such issues concerning Arbus's professional ethics plausibly be raised. If photographs merely present the momentary appearances of subjects, then, if Arbus is indeed guilty of "cruelty" for presenting her subjects in a stark and unflattering light, this is a matter of her character but does not in an essential way involve her activity as a photographer. But, of course, Arbus's very choices as to how to use the medium – the square, high-resolution format and the close-ups – which are instrumental in the proclaimed "cruelty" of her images – are essential features of her photographic activity. The resulting image is not merely what one might have seen without the photographer's intervention. I have argued elsewhere[30] that photographers are indeed able to manipulate the medium in such a way as to embody, in their images, determinate thoughts about their subjects that are graspable by the receiver. But, even without rehearsing my reasoning, it should be clear that only if this is the case can the sorts of issues identified by Sontag with respect to Arbus's professional ethics in producing such images be raised.

But is Arbus plausibly viewed as acting unethically in producing these images? In the first place, as Sontag admits, in the vast majority of cases Arbus not only obtained the consent of her subjects, but also befriended them and won their trust before taking their pictures. Furthermore, she kept in touch with many of her subjects.[31] As Sontag again admits, the self-confidence with which Arbus's subjects confront the camera testifies to their willingness to present themselves in this way to the viewer. Thus at least one of Ackerman's conditions on using real people as models for fictional characters is satisfied. Furthermore, the publications that commissioned Arbus's photo essays, which provided the framework for most of her iconic images, insisted not only that the subjects consented to publication of the image, but also that they were made fully aware of the general thematic material with which their images were to be associated. In a letter to Arbus in February 1961, Harold Hayes, her commissioning editor at *Esquire*, cited "a legal ruling that under no circumstances are we entitled to publish photographs of people under any conditions other than those represented to the subject. That is, you can't take a picture of someone for the purposes of showing him as an 'eccentric' unless that person knows he is being shown in that light."[32]

Might it nevertheless be said that Arbus's subjects were still unaware of exactly how they would be represented – of the unflattering nature of the images through which their appearance was captured, or of the "compassionless" way in which their situation was presented, or of the "loathing" for the subjects which Greer finds in all of Arbus's iconic images? As noted above, to some extent the answer to this question depends upon whether one agrees with Arbus's critics in finding these qualities in the images. Of the "loathing" of which Greer speaks I find no evidence in the images, nor in any of Arbus's writings collected in *Revelations*. And if the pictures fail to arouse compassion in us for the subjects, this is a professional failing in Arbus only if the subjects merit from us compassion rather than, perhaps, an attempt at comprehension, or a recognition of the possibility of value to be found in moral and existential choices different from the ones we ourselves have made. Sontag writes that "to the painful nightmarish reality out there, Arbus applied such adjectives as 'terrific', 'interesting', 'incredible', 'fantastic', 'sensational',"[33] and further remarks that in "photographing an appalling underworld (and a desolate, plastic overworld), she had no intention of entering the horror experienced by the denizens of those worlds."[34] But Sontag's charge requires that we acquiesce in her description of the lives of Arbus's subjects as "painful," "nightmarish," "horrific," rather than put our trust in the way in which the subjects present themselves in Arbus's photographs, as self-confident and accepting of their lives. Compassion is properly given only to that which merits it, and Arbus's subjects, as she represents them and as they present themselves, are not asking for compassion.

7   The Ethics of Viewing a Photograph

I have argued that Sontag's criticism of Arbus's professional ethics pre-supposes that photographic images do not merely present their subjects, but represent them in a certain way in virtue of the ways in which the photographer has manipulated the medium. I have also argued that, given this perspective, the charges of professional irresponsibility in her activity as a photographer are at best moot. But what of Sontag's other principal charge against Arbus and against photography in general, that the reception of photographic images, and in particular of the kinds of images offered by Arbus, can be morally corrupting? Fortunately, given the length of this chapter, I think this charge can now be quickly disposed of. In the first place, insofar as we disagree with Sontag's char-acterization of the subjects of Arbus's pictures as "horrifying," we will not be concerned that looking at such images will render us insensitive to that which is truly horrible in the world.

More significantly, however, even if we were to agree that the subjects themselves are "pathetic, pitiable . . . repulsive," Sontag's charge, if leveled at an acknowledged photographic artist such as Arbus, is mis-conceived. For it rests, yet again, on a failure to take proper account of the distinction – necessary for Sontag's own critique – between the sub-ject of a photographic image and the way in which that subject is repres-ented by the photographer, and to recognize how this distinction bears upon the reception of photographic works. As noted earlier, a properly artistic interest in a representation is always an interest not in the subject *per se* but in how the subject has been represented, in two distinct senses: first, it is an interest in the "thought" expressed about the subject and second it is an interest in the manner in which this thought-content has been expressed through the manipulation of the medium. If Arbus's images are works of representational art, then the focus of our appreciative attention will not be on the subject matter *per se*, but on how it has been rendered in both of these senses. This is why the analogy with looking at pornography or televised scenes of violence is misconceived. Suppose, for the sake of argument, we grant that, in the latter cases, the reception of images may indeed morally harm us in the ways Sontag describes. The harm attends our engagement with the subjects represented – the viewer of pornography treats the image as transparent, as a window onto cer-tain events experienced as arousing. But, to the extent that we are con-cerned with Arbus's images as representational artworks, this is precisely how we must not engage with them. Of course, as noted earlier, artistic images can be treated "pornographically," and, if there is evidence that many people are so treating such images, perhaps this is grounds for imposing some restrictions on the kind of access permitted to those images. But to condemn the works as immoral because they can be misused by a minority requires much more in the way of argument, and, in any case, is not the claim that Sontag is making.

In conclusion, then, I think we should resist the sort of moral questioning of Arbus's work that takes its lead from Sontag's criticisms. The latter, I have argued, rest upon a failure to think coherently and consistently about the nature and functioning of photographic images, and about how such images engage us as artworks. It is time that Arbus's visually arresting images and experimentation with the medium are freed from the cloud of ethical suspicion, so that, as Doon Arbus says, we can encounter those images "in the eloquence of their silence."

Notes

1 Cited in Sean O'Hagen, "Review of the Exhibition Diane Arbus: Revelations," *The Observer* (October 16, 2005).
2 In "America, Seen Through Photographs, Darkly," and also, passim, in the other essays in her *On Photography* (New York: Picador USA, 2001).
3 See, for example, Adam Phillips, "Thwarted Closeness," *London Review of Books* (January 26, 2006); Germaine Greer, "Wrestling with Diane Arbus," *The Guardian* (October 8, 2005); O'Hagen, "Review of the Exhibition."
4 See André Bazin, "The Ontology of the Photographic Image," in *What Is Cinema?* vol. 1, trans. Hugh Gray (Berkeley, CA: University of California Press, 1967), pp. 9–16. For a critical discussion of Bazin, see Noël Carroll, *Philosophical Problems of Classical Film Theory* (Princeton, NJ: Princeton University Press, 1988), chapter 2. For an alternative interpretation of Bazin, see Jonathan Friday, "André Bazin's Ontology of Photographic and Film Imagery," *Journal of Aesthetics and Art Criticism* 63/4 (2005): 339–50.
5 Kendal Walton, "Transparent Pictures," *Critical Inquiry* 11/2 (1984): 246–77.
6 See Roger Scruton, "Photography and Representation," in his *The Aesthetic Understanding* (London: Methuen, 1983). For a lively critical discussion of earlier proponents of such arguments, such as P. H. Emerson, see Patrick Maynard, *The Engine of Visualization: Thinking Through Photography* (Ithaca, NY: Cornell University Press, 1997), pp. 269–77, 290–93; and Carroll, *Philosophical Problems of Classical Film Theory*, pp. 20–29.
7 I argue against Scruton in David Davies, "How Photographs 'Signify': Cartier-Bresson's 'Reply' to Scruton," in Scott Walden, ed., *Philosophy and Photography* (Malden, MA: Blackwell, 2008). For the purposes of this

chapter, however, what matters is that, as I shall argue, Sontag's criticisms of Arbus generally seem to presuppose that Scruton is wrong, and that we can take a properly artistic interest in the representational content of photographs. My contention will be that if Scruton is indeed wrong, then none of Sontag's principal criticisms, of Arbus in particular and photography in general, hold up.

8   Sontag, *On Photography*, pp. 6–7.
9   Ibid., pp. 11–12.
10   Ibid., p. 14.
11   Ibid., pp. 61ff.
12   Iris Murdoch, *The Sovereignty of Good* (London: Routledge, 1970).
13   Sontag, *On Photography*, 32.
14   Ibid., pp. 34–5.
15   Ibid., p. 33.
16   Ibid., p. 36.
17   Greer, "Wrestling with Diane Arbus."
18   O'Hagen, "Review of the Exhibition."
19   Sontag, *On Photography*, p. 40.
20   Ibid., p. 43.
21   Ibid.
22   Phillips, "Thwarted Closeness."
23   Sontag, *On Photography*, p. 41.
24   Doon Arbus et al., *Diane Arbus: Revelations* (London: Jonathan Cape, 2003), p. 299.
25   Sontag, *On Photography*, p. 36.
26   Peter Schjeldahl, "Review of the Exhibition Diane Arbus: Revelations," *New Yorker* (March 21, 2005).
27   Sontag, *On Photography*, p. 41.
28   Felicia Ackerman, "Imaginary Gardens and Real Toads: On the Ethics of Basing Fiction on Actual People," *Midwest Studies in Philosophy* 16 (1991): 142–51.
29   Arbus et al., *Diane Arbus*, p. 299.
30   Davies, "How Photographs 'Signify'."
31   See, for example, Arbus et al., *Diane Arbus*, p. 168.
32   Ibid., p. 156.
33   Sontag, *On Photography*, p. 41.
34   Ibid., p. 42.

10

ETHICAL JUDGMENTS IN MUSEUMS

Ivan Gaskell

A hand-painted roadside sign in rural Massachusetts reads:

> For Sale
> Rabbits
> Pets
> or Meat

The stark disparity between the invitation to affection on the one hand, and butchery on the other, gives the motorist speeding past on the country road a shock. The commodity on offer has two incompatible matter-of-fact uses, one sentimental, the other brutal. The sign starkly evokes the human propensity to put something to more than one use. This applies not only to rabbits, but to many, if not most, of the tangible things that we encounter in the world. A person can use one thing in various ways. Different people can use the same thing in different ways, either contemporaneously or successively. Some of these varied uses admit of others, while others do not. One person's god is another's idol, which, to yet another, is an archaeological find, and to yet another, a work of art. One person's pet is another's dinner.

1 Respecting Sacred Objects: Some Difficulties

In this chapter I shall discuss how this basic observation can affect how we approach a shifting, variable kind of object: those things that some people, at least, whether some or all of the time, regard as sacred. We might begin to define a sacred object as one that affords its users access to a transcendent realm. In consequence, they consider it to be worthy of veneration. They may consider it to be capable of agency within both the quotidian and the transcendent realms, and may think of it as imbued with the quality of being animate in some sense. We might also bear in mind that there are several variations or categories of the sacred. All are numinous.

At the outset we should acknowledge an underlying difficulty. In some communities of thought and belief there is a sense in which the term sacred has lost its purely descriptive character. It has acquired an aura of approval: that is, if something is sacred, it is good. Properly speaking, sacred objects can indeed be good, or be a means of trying to do good, for instance to honor deities or spirits, cure disease, bring rain, or encourage crops. Yet in the eyes of their communities of users, sacred objects are not necessarily benign. They can also be indifferent. They can even be maleficent. Numinous things can be made and used purposefully to celebrate evil or to do malicious harm to other people. Increasingly, scholars in museums and universities, responding to the often legitimate concerns of indigenous peoples and religious groups, have become faintly self-congratulatory in their propensity to honor the sacred objects of subaltern cultures. In doing so they tend to confine their attention to those sacred objects with broadly benign associations. I do not wish to denigrate the sensibilities of people who have done a great deal to resuscitate the sacred use of sacred things, but – to be honest – this is easy. It is not difficult to entertain sympathetically those prior claims to objects in museums that imply their beneficent use – for the free exercise of Native American religions, for instance. There may be good arguments that other, competing, claims on those objects – such as museological use – are superior and should prevail, but even some proponents of this view would concede that religious use, while it may be deluded, is not in itself harmful, except, perhaps, to the objects themselves, which may be a cause for regret, or even outrage. (There are others, of course, who would say that religion *per se* is harmful, for it perpetuates unjust social relations.) I wish to consider some objects that may cause us to question what I fear is in danger of becoming a complacent sympathy. I propose to discuss some things that are not quite so lovable as the majority of those objects repatriated to Native American nations in compliance with US Federal law (specifically the Native American Graves Protection and Repatriation Act of 1990: NAGPRA).

In 1999 a curator in Luxemburg told me about an exhibition she was organizing on the history of witchcraft. It was to be held the following year at the Musée d'Histoire de la Ville de Luxembourg. In the course of her research she had located a group of contemporary objects used in black magic. They were in the collection of the French national folklore and popular culture museum, the Musée National des Arts et Traditions Populaires in Paris. In conversation she gave me the following account of these objects.[1] In 1981 an exorcist in Bordeaux had mailed a group of black magic paraphernalia to the museum. The objects included a small doll, a wooden hand, and several items pierced with pins. A second consignment from the same source followed in 1982, including a number of objects, such as a glove, covered with owl feathers. Why did he do this? We are familiar with the claim that museums are purely secular sites in which sacred objects lose their numinous potency, or at least are treated as though they have none. Apologists of the sacred often make this claim in an accusatory manner, bemoaning this neutralizing effect as impoverishing and deleterious. This may indeed be justifiable in the case of predominantly beneficent or non-maleficent sacred objects. The exorcist who sent the black magic paraphernalia to the Paris museum would seem purposefully to have been exploiting the capacity of such an institution to contain or to neutralize the numinous quality of sacred objects. He had been faced with a problem: how to get rid safely of potent, maleficent objects recently used in sorcery. Interestingly, he saw the museum as a site where these things might be lodged safely. Here we see a person deeply involved in handling numinous artifacts exploiting that very mechanism of secularization for, in local terms, good ends. The exorcist sought to harness the museum's secularizing capacity in an attempt to neutralize terrible, powerful things that could not safely be destroyed or otherwise disposed of.

What was the museum to do with such things? One of the first things the curators did was to try to find out more precisely what they might be. Those sociologists and anthropologists who work on contemporary European witchcraft are inevitably largely dependent on participant informants: practitioners. The museum appealed to one such informant, a woman from Nevers fully conversant with black magic. She examined all the objects that had been received, and classified them according to her perception of their numinous efficacy, declaring several to be deadly (*meurtre*). The presence of these reputedly potent and harmful things became widely known within the museum. A number of the staff became very disturbed by them. In particular they upset the preparators, who are responsible for transferring objects from one part of the museum to another and readying them for conservation, packing, and exhibition. Such was the fear they inspired among the preparators that the senior staff reportedly had to reach an agreement with them that these objects, which the preparators regarded as magically potent and malignant, should remain isolated in storage, literally untouched. The Musée d'Histoire de la Ville de Luxembourg wanted to borrow these objects for its projected exhibition on witchcraft. I was told that the Paris museum acceded to the request for their loan, but with a stipulation that is very unusual in museum practice. Such was the fear they inspired among the French museum staff that representatives of the Luxemburg museum would have to collect them, and even pack them. These objects may have been lodged in a secularizing, neutralizing setting, but even for some of those who worked there, their malign potency prevailed.

I saw the exhibition in question, *Incubi-Succubi: les sorcières et leurs bourreaux jusqu'à nos jours*, in the summer of 2000.[2] I think these contemporary witchcraft objects would have troubled me even had I not known how they were treated in Paris, and how they had come to Luxemburg. On seeing them I have to admit that I felt a frisson of fear, just as I had when I stumbled upon the remains of a ritual rooster sacrifice in an isolated hilltop grove in Italy some years before. For all the normalization of the New Age movement, religious relativism, and anthropologists' demystification of contemporary suburban witchcraft cults – in, for example, the work of the anthropologist, Tanya Luhrmann[3] – I nonetheless found the tangible evidence that people today practice black magic to be viscerally disturbing. While I admit that I may be irrationally susceptible, I nonetheless maintain that if there are such things as ethically bereft objects, these are they. What are the responsibilities of museums in respect of such things?

There are those who eloquently propose that museums holding certain categories of objects – particularly sacred objects – are under an obligation to return them to their original users or such descendents who have demonstrated the veracity of their claims. Let us bear in mind that until now those who maintain that museums should return objects for sacred use have assumed that those uses are good, or at least lie beyond proper ethical scrutiny by members of the dominant culture. While there are many and various conflicts over sacred objects throughout the world (and in the United States such discussions largely concern the disposition of Native American objects) this claim holds generally. In the case of Native American claims such proponents hold that the obligation is not merely legal, but ethical, and would exist irrespective of the existence of NAGPRA. This is the view of, for example, Martin Sullivan, who has commended the actions of the Peabody Museum of Archaeology and Ethnology at Harvard University for its return of the sacred pole of the Omaha before the enactment of NAGPRA.[4] His own actions conform to his stated principles. In 1989, also before NAGPRA enactment, when he was director of the New York State Museum in Albany, Sullivan was instrumental in arranging the return of 12 wampum belts from the museum to the Onondega Nation.[5] (Lest there be any doubt in consequence of my argument below, I should state that I am broadly in sympathy with this view, and applaud the Peabody Museum's embrace of the opportunities afforded by NAGPRA to return objects to indigenous nations, and to enhance stewardship relations with their representatives.) However, in the light of the example of the black magic paraphernalia in the Musée National des Arts et Traditions Populaires, should we regard any such obligation as absolute?

Suppose for a moment that the original user or users of the witchcraft paraphernalia now in the Musée National des Arts et Traditions Populaires came forward and reclaimed these objects, stating that they were necessary for the practice of their religion. Would the museum be under a moral obligation to return them even though they might once again be used to cast malign spells and possibly cause at least mental injury or anguish? If we say yes, and release these things into the active world of black sorcery, real harm may result. That harm may be no less real in its effects for being merely imagined by sorcerer and victim (if that is indeed the case). If we attempt to treat all numinous objects consistently, we would be trapped into producing what might be a truly bad result. Yet if we say no, and maintain that the museum must retain these objects, we would be tacitly admitting that the criteria for recognizing a moral obligation in respect of such things does not depend upon their sacred or numinous quality, but rather upon an ethical judgment on quite other grounds. That is, we could no longer claim that the repatriation of numinous objects to Native American peoples is right solely because of those objects' sacred character. Rather, we would have to recognize that it is right because the responsible representatives of the dominant culture approve of those peoples' use of those objects. In these circumstances, therefore, in spite of all the claims about obligations to return sacred objects, we would find, after all, that the institutions of the dominant culture, including its museums, were doing so because they sanction those people to behave in certain ways. If the dominant culture acquiesces in the retention of the black magic paraphernalia, it can be seen, in spite of hand-wringing guilt, firmly to be retaining its initiative to prescribe and proscribe the behavior of subaltern and subcultural groups irrespective of the status of the sacred. The sacredness or otherwise of an object is not the operative criterion. That criterion is, rather, approval or disapproval of behavior.

NAGPRA is, properly speaking, not an ethical instrument, but rather it is consequential. It cannot be stressed firmly enough that the aims of

NAGPRA were originally to give substance to the American Indian Religious Freedom Act of 1978 (AIRFA), and nothing more. Certain categories of things covered by NAGPRA, notably objects that would be used by a federally recognized tribe in contemporary Native American religious observance that originated in the same cultural group or a direct predecessor thereof – that is, sacred things – are effectively open-ended, and potentially all-embracing. For example, as Michael F. Brown reports, the Hopi Tribe, represented by the Hopi Cultural Preservation Office, requests the repatriation of all Hopi artifacts on the grounds that anything made by Hopis is sacred. As one representative is quoted as saying, "Even something like a digging stick could have a ritual use, but we're not about to say what it is."[6] And so the sacred becomes all-encompassing, and the effective criterion claimed for repatriation is that of broad cultural identity.

I am not doubting or contesting the Hopi claim that all their artifacts have numinous qualities, but am rather seeking to point out two possible consequences. The first is that some might suspect that such claims are specious, and designed to exploit white guilt at the treatment of a subaltern culture. It is hardly surprising that earnest and politically astute subaltern groups might seek to exploit NAGPRA, and other mechanisms in other countries, as far as possible in pursuit of restitution, with unanticipated effects. Second, some might come to see that in some cultural circumstances, at least, the Western distinction between the sacred and the secular has no meaning, and that the places of things in the world can vary conceptually in ways that the categories available to Western thought have difficulty in acknowledging.

2   Alternative Grounds for Respect: The Historical and Aesthetic Properties of an Object

How are scholars from the dominant culture – historians, philosophers, and curators – to address these issues? One possibility would be to find and use practical analogues to the numinous within the terms of the dominant culture in respect of the objects concerned. I want to discuss how this might be achieved in the context of museums of various kinds that hold collections of objects from subaltern cultures. The key attitude on the part of those who remain responsible for such objects is one of demonstrable respect towards them, and their origins, however skeptical one might be of the possibility of true respect existing in inequitable conditions.[7] That respect – however qualified and circumscribed – can find expression in various ways, but the ones I want to consider in particular, and that can serve as analogues to the numinous, concern history and aesthetics respectively. To accord an object historical and aesthetic standing is to respect it, and, by extension, its makers and first users. I want to illustrate this from my own studies within one vast field: Native American basketry.

Several tribes in northern California, including the Hupa, Yurok, and Karuk, perform religious dances as part of what have been termed world renewal rites. One such rite is the Jump Dance. The dancers hold shallow, long, and narrow twined baskets constructed around two bowed sticks, laid parallel and bound together at both ends with strips of animal hide. The opening that runs the length of the sticks is so pinched that its contents (dried grasses or other fine stems and leaves) would seem to be permanently inaccessible. The Berkeley anthropologist Alfred L. Kroeber and his colleagues studied the Jump Dance, and the rites of which it is a constituent, during the first half of the twentieth century.[8] Dance regalia items were highly prized, and included objects acquired by long-distance trade, such as dentalium shells from Vancouver Sound, which had compensatory value in settling disputes. By the end of the nineteenth century the Jump Dance had apparently taken on the character of a competitive display among such wealthy men as owned the regalia.[9] Items of regalia were individually owned, heritable, and alienable within each tribal group, but would seem to have been regarded by their users as ultimately the property of the numinous forces evoked by the dancers. They were, and remain, in effect "spiritually entailed,"[10] and, as such, subject to repatriation under NAGPRA from US museum collections under two headings: as objects used in religious ceremonies, and as cultural patrimony.

Such a basket was repatriated to the Hoopa Tribe, with other dance regalia, by the Peabody Museum of Archaeology and Ethnology at Harvard University in 1998. I was able to study it in the museum, where it was displayed in the Hall of the American Indian prior to its return, and, thanks to the kindness of David Hostler, the tribal elder responsible for dance regalia, and director of the tribal museum, I was able to study it again in storage at the Hoopa Valley Tribal Museum on the Hoopa Reservation in California in the summer of 2002.[11] Unlike many other baskets from this region, the Jump Dance basket was most certainly not made for the colonial market, nor for contemplation by museum visitors. It is an item for ritual use made anonymously, presumably in a male society sweat lodge. Even though its form may be a post-contact innovation imitating the elk-horn purse used to hold dentalium shell money, it remains, obviously, a sacred item in respect of the purpose for which it was made, and the use to which it was put.[12] However, it may also partake of the numinous on the grounds of its making and its materials. As Marvin Cohodas has recently described, all baskets made by Native American weavers in these northern Californian valleys share numinous character- istics that derive from their materials, and the process of making. They embody a part of the natural world from a specific set of times of the year when their materials were gathered and prepared, in harmony with the human creativity of the weaver. Such objects – even if seemingly purely utilitarian, or made for the white market – acquire a numinous quality akin to animation. This most likely accounts for the regular visits of a Native American woman to the Clarke Memorial Museum in Eureka, California, which has a large collection of mostly Yurok and Karuk baskets, to sing to the baskets in order to assuage their loneliness.[13] Thus utilitarian baskets, while not sacred in the sense of the Hupa dance bas- ket, are, nonetheless, numinous. This is a perception widely held among native peoples.[14]

My own recent work on baskets has focused on the work of Chitimacha weavers in southern Louisiana. The revival of Chitimacha basket weaving is a complex story that I can only touch on here.[15] It was due primarily to the work of two women: a Chitimacha weaver, Clara Darden, and a white woman, Mary Bradford. Clara Darden (or Dardin) was born in 1829 or 1830 and spent her life on the small Chitimacha reservation on the shore of the Bayou Teche, west of New Orleans. By the end of the nineteenth century few families lived on the reservation, and Clara Darden was the sole surviving practitioner of the art of split cane basketry.[16] This was when Mary Bradford, who lived about 20 miles to the west at Avery Island, became involved with Clara Darden and the Chitimacha. Prompted by her observation that the Chitimacha "are a respectable, deserving people, very poor, and totally without education,"[17] her admiration for Clara Darden's artistry, and the Euro-American basket-collecting craze that played on sentimental interest in – as the title of an article in *Harper's Bazaar* in 1899 expressed it – "The Last Industry of a Passing Race," Mary Bradford contrived to ensure that Clara Darden's skills should be passed on to others in the tribe.[18] In 1899 she commissioned Clara Darden to make baskets in all the forms and designs known to her. She recorded the names of the designs, and offered prizes to younger women to learn weaving skills.[19] Within five years, Clara Darden and her students had woven no fewer than 72 baskets.

Mary Bradford made shrewd use of the contemporary basket-collecting craze in order to further her aim of establishing an "industrial school" for the Chitimacha.[20] The 72 baskets were exhibited at the Louisiana Purchase Exposition in St Louis in 1904. Otis Tufton Mason discussed and illustrated a selection in the book that became the bible of basketry studies, *Indian Basketry: Studies in a Textile Art without Machinery*, published in the same year.[21] Mary Bradford tried to take advantage of the exposure to sell the collection to a museum in order to raise money for a Chitimacha industrial school. Only the Peabody Museum and the Field Columbian Museum, Chicago, expressed interest, but neither would meet her modest asking price of $150. She appealed to Neltje Doubleday, wife of the publisher of Otis Tufton Mason's book, who raised the purchase price through the New York chapter of the Sequoya League. The League then presented the collection to the Hampton Normal and Agricultural Institute in Hampton, Virginia (now Hampton University), a college originally intended for liberated African American slaves that since 1878 had extended its program to include Native Americans.[22] Hampton had adopted Indian crafts as a way of improving Native American prospects, and in 1902 had appointed a Cherokee weaver, Arizona Swayney, to teach basketry.[23] The baskets by Clara Darden and her Chitimacha students were to serve as patterns in Arizona Swayney's classes. They are now in the collection of the Hampton University Museum.

Mary Bradford retained, or, before Clara Darden's death in 1910, acquired, 11 further baskets by her. Aware of her own mortality, and of her unfulfilled promise to the aged weaver that she would erect a headstone at her grave, Bradford sold these 11 baskets for $50 – "less than they cost me" – to the Peabody Museum in 1932.[24] Only then was she able to commission a tombstone (the Chitimachas, long under French rule, were Roman Catholics), and install it with the participation of the entire tribe.[25]

Clara Darden's double-weave river-cane lidded baskets are objects of extraordinary beauty. They represent the survival of a tradition of artistry by a whisker. None is sacred in the sense that the Hupa dance basket is sacred, but they partake of the numinous in the manner Marvin Cohodas (in the case of northern Californian baskets) and Sarah Hill (in the case of Cherokee baskets) both describe. How, then, should they be treated within museums? I want to describe first how I believe they should *not* be treated.

In its gallery devoted to Eastern Woodlands Indians, the American Museum of Natural History, New York, takes a thematic approach. Among the subjects of its displays is basketry. Among the 21 baskets displayed are three described as Chitimacha, and a fourth as probably Chitimacha. Others in the group are identified as Choctaw, Iroquois, Penobscot, Ojibwa, and Delaware: in other words, from widely dispersed peoples from Maine to Louisiana. Five are placed directly on the floor of the vitrine, which is covered in crumbled cork to resemble pebbles; the remaining 16 are affixed to the backboard without any visible means of support, together with several basket-making tools. Figures painted on the backboard are depicted preparing splints and weaving a basket. Texts discuss the essentials of technique. The display presents basket making as timeless, without history, and as culturally undifferentiated, except in respect of the availability of materials. The Chitimacha baskets, like the others, are presented as specimens, their individuality ignored. Their very means of display – deprived of the exercise of their proper means of support, and affixed invisibly to the backboard – deprives them of their basic dignity. This is a hazard of one type – the dominant type? – of ethnographic gaze. Those responsible for the display do not appear to value the artifact for its own qualities, but rather as a representative example, implicitly interchangeable with many others. Disrespect for objects, their makers, and first users is not inevitable in ethnographic display. I infer respect for objects, their makers, and first users in Margaret Mead's Hall of the Pacific Peoples in the same museum. A successful, respectful display of an object or group of objects must incorporate one or other or both of two factors that depend upon the uniqueness of the object: recognition of its place in human history, and recognition of its amenability to aesthetic attention.

The four Chitimacha baskets displayed in the American Museum of Natural History deserve the respect that being explicit about their place in history – Native American history, Euro-American history, and their intersections – engenders. They deserve the respect that acknowledging their unique aesthetic qualities should elicit. They are, presumably, by Clara Darden or her students. This deserves acknowledgement, and explanation. To allow the makers to slide into the abyss of the past, to present their production as "timeless" and hence subtly inhuman, to allow their particular characteristics to be subsumed by an implicit statement that one can stand for any, are all behaviors that promote disrespect for the object and their makers. The acknowledgement that history and aesthetics are the Western analogues of recognition of the numinous qualities of an object, and that such an object should be presented so as to encourage or at least permit attention in these terms, promotes respect.

These values – historical and aesthetic significance – are closely entwined with monetary considerations. Unique artworks, which instantiate historical and aesthetic values most clearly, are expensive, whereas specimens, which do not, are cheap. In 1932 the Peabody Museum was willing to pay only $50 for 11 baskets by Clara Darden: less than they had cost Mary Bradford, on her own account. Two years later, in 1934, the Peabody Museum could pay just under $150 dollars for no fewer than 91 Paviotso or Northern Paiute items supplied by an ethnologist in the field.[26] Here we see a true classificatory contrast between two distinct models of object-making and their correlated sets of expectations concerning terms of acquisition. Mary Bradford clearly regarded Clara Darden's baskets as the highly valued products of an experienced and aesthetically skilled individual. Donald Scott, of the Peabody Museum, was used to the acquisition of ethnographic specimens from unidentified and unacknowledged makers for very small sums of money (for example, $1.50 for a Paviotso basketry parching tray). Of all those ambiguities that envelope Native American basketry, affecting and shaping classification and taxonomy – the recognition or not of individual skill, of tribal peculiarity, and of Native American distinctiveness separate from white involvement (other than as ultimate consumer) – that between specimen and unique artwork is at the very heart of the paradoxical position they occupy for the historian. It is clear that the practice of treating artifacts as specimens alone – ignoring their history and aesthetics – is a prime cause of offence among those who view such things as numinous. Acknowledging an object's unique place in history, and its unique aesthetic character is the dominant culture's equivalent of recognizing its numinous quality. Both imply and engender respect.

In conclusion, some things regarded as sacred by various constituencies will quite properly leave museums to be used in religious contexts. Others will remain in museums, and, indeed, I believe should remain in museums. Museums can be effective repositories for harmful numinous artifacts, such as the French black magic paraphernalia discussed above; but they can also be suitable sites for the maintenance and use of allegedly beneficent objects, so long as they are treated with respect that acknowledges the numinous character ascribed to them by those with non-museological interests in them. Ideally, museum scholars should strive to emulate the Peabody Museum in acknowledging and incorporating the concerns of other interested constituencies in both their practical care of the collections and their scholarship. However, we should always bear in mind the human propensity to use objects for purposes other than those for which they appear to have been intended. Such is the variety of human use of objects, and the ingenuity displayed in thus using them, that there is no compelling reason to assume that the original purpose for which an artifact was made – when it can be identified – should necessarily take precedence over other uses. To suggest otherwise would be to limit human behavior – notably for both problem solving and creative inquiry

– intolerably. Were we to acquiesce in allowing artifacts to be used for their original purpose alone, museums, and the forms of inquiry they permit, would not exist, for the museological use of objects is usually an unforeseen use subsequent to purposive use. This is as true of a painting by Rembrandt as it is of a Hupa Jump Dance basket. If we disallow museological use, entire kinds of object might be condemned, and our opportunity for historical and other forms of understanding accordingly diminished. For instance, the disturbing items I saw in Luxemburg could apparently only be used for the performance of black magic. However, the very circumstances in which I saw them suggest otherwise, for they were being used for quite another purpose: within a museological discourse exposing the current practice of malign magic in contemporary western Europe. The museum concerned might even have been said to have redeemed the objects by containing their malignancy (as the donor seems to have intended), and by putting them to this demonstrative use. All this, though, is conditional upon use epitomized by a single word: respect. The demonstration of respect, by acknowledging the history and aesthetics of things, accommodates the numinous, opens dialogue with other interested parties, and paves the way for the enrichment of understanding that is the goal of scholarship.

Notes

I undertook the research for this chapter while enjoying sabbatical leave positions simultaneously as visiting curator for research at the Peabody Museum of Archaeology and Ethnology, and as senior fellow at the Center for the Study of World Religions, both at Harvard University, in 2003–4. I presented an earlier version at the Center's Fellows' Seminar, and benefited from discussions with other fellows, notably Martin Sullivan.

1   Two written requests for confirmation or correction of this account, in 2000 and 2004, elicited no response from the curator concerned.

2   The exhibition was accompanied by a substantial publication, which concentrated on historical matters: Rita Voltmer and Franz Irsigler, eds., *Incubi-Succubi: Les sorcières et leurs bourreaux jusqu'à nos jours* (Luxemburg: Musée d'Histoire de la Ville de Luxembourg, 2000).

3   T. M. Luhrmann, *Persuasions of the Witch's Craft: Ritual Magic in Contemporary England* (Cambridge, MA, and London: Harvard University Press, 1989).

4   See Robin Ridington, *Blessing for a Long Time: The Sacred Pole of the Omaha Tribe* (Lincoln, NE: University of Nebraska Press, 1997).

5   Martin Sullivan, chief executive officer and executive director of the Historic St Mary's City Commission, Maryland, is a particularly effective advocate in

the field of cultural property. He served as chair of the NAGPRA Review Committee between 1992 and 2000, and chair of the President's Advisory Committee on Cultural Property between 1995 and his resignation in 2003 over US conduct in Iraq.

6   Michael F. Brown, *Who Owns Native Culture?* (Cambridge, MA, and London: Harvard University Press), 2003, pp. 20–21.

7   Some theorists are highly skeptical of the possibility of members of a dominant culture according a subordinated culture true respect, and doubt that members of a subordinated culture are necessarily willing to accept professions of respect in such circumstances. I should like to thank Homi Bhabha for thoughts on this matter expressed in conversation.

8   Alfred L. Kroeber and Edward W. Gifford, "World Renewal: A Cult System of Native Northwest California," University of California *Anthropological Records* 13/1 (1949): 1–155. For an indigenous account of the Jump Dance, see Byron Nelson, Jr., *Our Home Forever: The Hupa Indians of Northern California* (Hoopa, CA: Hupa Tribe, 1994), pp. 33–5.

9   Marvin Cohodas, *Basket Weavers for the Curio Trade: Elizabeth and Louise Hickox* (Los Angeles, CA: University of Arizona Press and Southwest Museum, 1997), p. 94.

10 This is the term I coined in my discussion of the repatriation of Hupa/Hoopa dance regalia in my "Sacred to Profane and Back Again," in Andrew McClellan, ed., *Art and its Publics: Museum Studies at the Millennium* (Oxford and Malden, MA: Blackwell), 2003, pp. 149–62.

11 It is unlikely that the basket could ever be used, not because of its fragility, but because of treatment at the Peabody Museum in the early twentieth century to destroy and deter infestation. Indelible poisons were employed, so it, and other objects like it, can only be handled using suitable precautions. This was the case with the dance regalia returned to the Hoopa, and discovery of this state of affairs has caused tribal members distress and occasioned anger and resentment. I wish to thank David Hostler, the Hoopa tribal elder responsible for the dance regalia, and director of the Hoopa Valley Tribal Museum, for his hospitality and generosity in showing me the regalia, discussing issues related to them, taking me to sacred dance sites, and inviting me to attend a sacred dance ceremony during my visit to the Hoopa Nation in August 2002.

12 Cohodas, *Basket Weavers for the Curio Trade*, p. 94.

13 As described to me by Pam Service, director and curator of the Clarke Memorial Museum, during a visit in August 2002.

14 In August, 2003 I was generously entertained by Fran Sark, widow of the hereditary chief of the Lennox Island Band of the Miq'mak Nation, Prince Edward Island, Canada, who allowed me to examine the collection of baskets he had formed. Mrs Sark, though a good Roman Catholic, regarded the baskets as numinous and in some sense animate.

15 I give a fuller account in my chapter, "Some Cherokee and Chitimacha Baskets: Problems of Interpretation," in Paul Taylor, ed., *Iconographies Without*

Texts (London: Warburg Institute; and Turin: Nino Aragno Edittore, forth-coming) from which the following, abbreviated, account derives.

16 Mary Bradford to F. W. Putnam, Peabody Museum, October 28, 1904 (Peabody Museum of Archaeology and Ethnology, Harvard University [PMAE] accession file 32-18-10/30, 32).

17 Ibid.

18 Ada Woodruff Anderson, "The Last Industry of a Passing Race," *Harper's Bazaar* 32 (November 11, 1899): 965. The most succinct account of the later nineteenth and early twentieth-century basket collecting craze is by Dorothy K. Washburn, "Dealers and Collectors of Indian Baskets at the Turn of the Century in California: Their Effect on the Ethnographic Sample," *Empirical Studies of the Arts* 2/1 (1984): 51–74, who cites and quotes Anderson's article (p. 58).

19 John R. Swanton, "Indian Tribes of the Lower Mississippi Valley and Adjacent Coast of the Gulf of Mexico," *Bureau of American Ethnology Bulletin* 43 (1911): 347–48.

20 Mary Bradford to F. W. Putnam, Peabody Museum, October 28, 1904 (PMAE accession file 32-18-10/30, 32).

21 Otis Tufton Mason, *Indian Basketry: Studies in a Textile Art without Machinery* (New York: Doubleday, Page, & Co., 1904), p. 292, plate 133.

22 Mary Bradford to Mrs. F. N. Doubleday, April 5, 1905; Mary Bradford to President Howe, Hampton Institute, August 14, 1934 (Hampton University Archives: copies in PMAE accession file 32-18-10/30, 32).

23 Susan H. Hill, *Weaving New Worlds: Southeastern Cherokee Women and their Basketry* (Chapel Hill, NC: University of North Carolina Press, 1997), pp. 213–19.

24 Mary Bradford to Donald Scott, Peabody Museum, August 27, 1932 (PMAE accession file 32-18-10/30, 32).

25 Mary Bradford to Donald Scott, Peabody Museum, July 24, 1934 (PMAE accession file 32-18-10/30, 32).

26 Willard Z. Park to Donald Scott, Peabody Museum, October 18, 1934 (PMAE accession file 34-114-10/3938).

Part V
Music and Moral Relations

11

COSÌ'S CANON QUARTET

Stephen Davies

The *opera buffa Così Fan Tutte* followed *The Marriage of Figaro* and *Don Giovanni* and was composed about two years before Mozart's death. The plot concerns a wager between Don Alfonso, a "cynical philosopher," and two men, Ferrando and Gugliemo, confident of the faithfulness of their fiancées, Dorabella and Fiordiligi. Under Alfonso's direction, and with help from Despina, the ladies' maid, the men are disguised and court each other's former lover with such success that the bet is lost. When all is revealed, mutual forgiveness prevails and the couples marry.[1] These events supposedly take place within the span of 24 hours.

The opera was dismissed in the nineteenth century as immoral and in the twentieth as irretrievably silly. Perhaps it is because he shares this latter view that Peter Kivy attempts to save the music by treating it as separable from the dramatic context when he declares the work to be a *sinfonia concertante* for voices. He writes:

> Its "characters" therefore are not Fiordiligi, Dorabella, Gugliemo, Ferrando; they are *the* soprano, *the* mezzo-soprano, *the* heroic tenor, etc. They are instruments in a *sinfonia concertante*, instruments with proper names . . . Like the characters of *opera seria*, the characters of *Così fan tutte* are as close to being character types as they can be without ceasing to be characters at all.[2]

Despite these reactions, I argue that the work is no less dramatically interesting or successful than its predecessors. I claim that the key to understanding the dramatic theme of this *opera buffa* is revealed in Mozart's treatment of the work's enigmatic canon quartet.

1   Gugliemo's Non-Participation in the Canon

In the finale of the last act of *Così* there is a magical moment of divinely beautiful music when the action freezes. The four main protagonists sing a canon or round in A-flat major to words proposing a toast. Or, at least, Fiordiligi, Ferrando, and Dorabella take their turns with the melody but, when it comes to Gugliemo's, the theme is passed again to Fiordiligi while Gugliemo mutters discontentedly.

Why does Gugliemo not take his turn? Mozart's operatic music almost always serves or creates a dramatic point, so it is in this direction that one most naturally seeks an answer. Gugliemo's confident trust in Fiordiligi has only recently been betrayed. Ferrando, Fiordiligi, and Dorabella have had longer to acknowledge and accept the reversal of affections on which the opera's plot hinges. The music indicates that Gugliemo has yet to accommodate himself to the new situation. Were one to look for a precedent, it might be found in the last act finale of *Abduction from the Seraglio*. There the main characters one by one sing the verse of a strophic song (with short chorus) praising Pasha Selim. Osmin, who is unhappy with the outcome, begins the verse but breaks off in a fit of pique. (Mozart quotes here Osmin's aria in Act I, which he famously discusses in the letter of September 26, 1781, addressed to his father.)

This account is perhaps not entirely convincing as it applies to *Così*, however. It is apparent in *Seraglio* that Osmin will not be reconciled to his failure to gain the love of Blonde, Constanze's maid, so it is appropriate that the opera closes as it does. By contrast, Gugliemo soon is to accept Fiordiligi's apparent betrayal of their earlier love. And the canon, which the audience cannot fail to recognize as such, so plainly is it presented, is a form calling for single-mindedness, both musically and dramatically. Gugliemo's subversion of the structure is amusing and effective in its way, but one might wonder why Mozart did not reserve the canon for later, when Gugliemo might have shared both the sentiments and the melody with the others. If the canon is to be highlighted, as it is here, it might seem that it would be located more appropriately in the happy dénouement that is to come.[3]

There is another, far less obvious, reason for Gugliemo's failure to join with the others. He does not take his turn with the melody because "he" cannot. Francesco Benucci is not able to take the tune because it lies beyond his vocal range. Benucci is the singer who took Gugliemo's part in the original production; he is the singer for whom Mozart composed.[4]

It is important not to lose sight of the fact that Mozart penned his operas for particular companies and performers. On September 26, 1781, he wrote to his father about *Seraglio* as follows: "In working out the aria I have . . . allowed Fischer's beautiful deep notes to glow . . . Let me turn now to Belmonte's aria in A major . . . I wrote it expressly to suit Adamberger's voice . . . I have sacrificed Constanze's aria a little to the flexible throat of Mlle Cavalieri."[5] And even if Mozart's own inclinations had not led him to take account of the special talents and predilections of those for whom he wrote, so self-important were the singers of the day that they would have demanded nothing less of him. *Giovanni* was written for the company in Prague, following the earlier success of *Figaro* in that city. When, seven months later, *Giovanni* was produced in Vienna, the performers were not satisfied to accept music written for a company they regarded as provincial. Mozart had to compose additional arias for Don Ottavio and Donna Elvira, and a duet for Leporello and Zerlina, to satisfy the singers' demands.

What resources could Mozart use in accommodating Benucci's compass to the music of the quartet in *Così*? Could he meet the difficulty by using octave transpositions within the tune? No. While octave transpositions work well enough where sequential passages are involved, they would ruin the distinctive character of a melody such as this one. Would the problem be removed if the key were other than A-flat major? No. With the melodic spread of a major eleventh, a change in register would be bound to take the tune out of the range of one of the singers. Besides, so carefully does Mozart treat the tonal centers in the act-finales of his late operas that it is doubtful that many alternative keys could have been integrated into the structure at this juncture. Could the difficulty be avoided by writing the canon at the interval of a fifth, instead of the octave? No. The problem then arises with respect to the range of the singer playing the part of Ferrando.

Such questions may be of technical interest but they overlook the obvious. Mozart could have written a different canon, one that would have allowed Benucci to join with the others. (Probably, he could have written 10 such canons before breakfast.) Ultimately then, this second attempt to explain the course of the canon quartet is no more satisfying than the first. To progress further, we need to understand Mozart's approach as an opera dramatist.

2   Respecting and Transforming Conventional Operatic Structure

The plots of the *opera buffa*, while not so fixed as those of *opera seria*, follow well-established patterns; for example, there is a confused jumble of mistaken identities, neatly unraveled at the end. In the middle of the opera, and at its end, more and more characters are brought on stage, with the sympathetic protagonists in trouble on the first occasion and winning out on the second. Such themes derive from the *commedia dell'arte* tradition, as do many of the stock characters, such as the simple, rough, greedy, but basically good-hearted, male servant.

This dramatic structure inevitably generates a bipartite musical one. Both the middle and the close of the opera see a rise in tension and complexity, as well as a quickening of the pace, as more musical voices are added to the melee. In the final scene, this tension is resolved, as the forces of good win the day. Other aspects of the musical setting draw on established forms. For instance, the typical aria is in *da capo* form – an ABA structure (both for text and music). Dialogue that takes place between arias and ensembles is presented in *secco* recitatives (a stylized representation of speech accompanied by the harpsichord and bass instruments) or, less commonly, in accompanied recitatives (in which the orchestra supports the singer in a style allowing more freedom of rhythm and tempo than is usual in the "numbers"). And the central and closing sections are given over to finales, consisting of continuous music uninterrupted by recitatives.

Meanwhile, the composer and librettist must also conform to other practices and conventions associated with the performance practice. For instance, major characters are each to receive two arias at the close of which they exit the stage, and those with lesser solo roles should be given one such piece. The point in such cases is to provide the singers with vehicles for their skill (in singing, acting, or both) and a chance to milk the audience's applause.[6]

Mozart worked within this framework but did much to transform it. This is apparent, for instance, in his treatment of solos. The aria is effective for dramatically static reflection on a character's inner state and, in the repeated section of the *da capo* form, for vocal display through melodic elaboration. In *Seraglio*, Constanze (or, rather, Caterina Cavalieri, the singer) is indulged with an aria of nearly 300 measures (No. 11), including an instrumental introduction of 60 measures. The mature Mozart might have conceded that this contains "an awful lot of notes" (as Joseph II notoriously complained of *Seraglio*) given the way he treats the form in the later *opera buffa*. There the arias are much shorter. For instance, K. 584 was written originally for Gugliemo, but, finding it too long, Mozart rejected it in favor of No. 15 in *Così*. In some cases the aria is integrated into an ensemble; for example, Nos. 3 and 15 in *Giovanni*. Meanwhile, there is a tightening up of the introductions. The accompanied recitative becomes more prominent and often is merged with a following aria. This device, adopted from *opera seria*, plays an important role in establishing the seriousness of many of the female characters – Anna and Elvira in *Giovanni*, Dorabella and Fiordiligi in *Così*. In the case of the most dominant characters – those who control the action and command the stage for much of the opera – the arias are sometimes downplayed, as is so with those for the Don in *Giovanni* and Susanna in *Figaro*. Mozart did not abandon long *da capo* arias, but he reserved them either for characters, such as Don Ottavio in *Giovanni*, who do not develop and who contribute little to the advancement of the action, or for situations where the dramatic context invites self-consideration, as in Fiordiligi's solos in *Così*. Meanwhile, ensembles increasingly became the focus of attention, both in their number and length.[7] The finales are considerably expanded. This new focus on large-scale numbers brings problems in generating musically integrated structures. The use of quasi-sonata forms in the first act trio and third act sextet of *Figaro*, for example, show Mozart's skill in meeting these demands, but it is in the operas' finales, with their spiraling patterns of modulation and with the controlled inevitability with which pace and breadth accumulate, that his command of musico-dramatic structure is displayed at its most virtuosic.

The point of all this, obviously, is for the composer to take charge of character and dramatic development. Mozart's goal was to create rounded, human characters, revealed mainly through their interactions with others, so that the stories would come to life. And, in achieving this, it is necessary to meld music and drama in a marriage that produces an integrated form responsive to the themes underlying the formulaic narratives on which the plots of such works draw. Already, in quotations offered above, Mozart's awareness of the difficulties posed by this reconciliation are acknowledged. As his letters testify, Mozart charges the librettist with furnishing a book that can be transformed by the composer into music-drama.[8] Da Ponte's success (in *Figaro*, *Giovanni*, and *Così*) in meeting such requirements was no small achievement.

So far I have suggested that Mozart, as opera composer, worked with conventions of the day – practical conventions of performance practice and musical tradition – and that a consideration of this fact is important to a fuller grasp of those works and the composer's achievement in writing them. I have claimed that he was concerned primarily with creating a dramatic whole, populated by believable characters. This is achieved within the limits allowed by the conventions of the genre, sometimes by exploiting their potential and sometimes by working against and overcoming limitations inherent to them. Even if all this is true, it does not yet explain why so majestic a composer as Haydn would express such great admiration for Mozart's operatic exploits.[9] What has been said so far sets the stage for a new story. Mozart plays off the outward, conventional structure in his *opera buffa* against a less obvious musical structure that shapes their dramatic character.

Giovanni begins, after Leporello's first aria, with a frenetic 20 minutes of action the tension of which is electrifying. The Commendatore, Donna Anna's father, dies in defending his daughter's honor, killed reluctantly by Don Giovanni.[10] Anna and Don Ottavio swear vengeance. Then, for the next two hours, nothing much happens. Of course, all sorts of events occur – the Don attempts more seductions, Leporello is beaten, Donna Elvira joins with the avengers but cannot shake free of her infatuation, and so forth – but, although the Don is identified as the murderer before the end of Act I, retribution is never carried through. Finally, when the Commendatore's statue in the graveyard accepts the invitation to dinner, the dénouement is set in motion, proceeding from that point with the irrevocability of a massive door's closing. As a result, the opera has an inverted bow/arch structure that is set off and played against the surface form in which each act builds to a climax at its close. That dramatic structure is built in the music, not only by its generating the pace and pressure of action but also by returning to the brooding menace of the overture's introduction in the final scene. Here, as ever with Mozart's late operas, the underlying dramatic structure tracks the musical structure, so closely does the one control and shape the other.

Why is the lack of dramatic development through the middle parts of the opera not a fault, as is the dramatic hiatus in the last act of *Figaro* (see note 6)? Because that lack of development is a crucial element in the work's structure; it underlines the point that gives the opera its very power. Don Giovanni, as evil personified, is no merely mortal sinner. There is something supernatural about the power he exercises, which renders not only the women but also the men powerless against him. Indeed, Don Giovanni is a vessel through which this force is exercised, since he is as much victim as author of his appetites. This character calls not only on the legends of Don Juan and the Stone Guest but also on that of Faust. Despite the passionate vows of his earthly victims, the Don is immune from their retaliation. Only a force from beyond the grave, the avenging, murdered father, can bring him down.[11] It is this dimension acknowledged in the structure created by Mozart, and it is this dimension that gives extraordinary force to the tale.

If the theme of *Giovanni* is cosmic, that of *Figaro* is domestic and political. The plot concerns the attempt to counter obstacles to the happy marriage of Susanna and Figaro, especially by preventing Count Almaviva from exercising the *droit du seigneur* that he has officially renounced.[12] Beaumarchais's play, adapted by da Ponte for the opera, was banned for its political content, for its indirect criticism of the aristocracy. While Mozart's music explicitly acknowledges the conflict between master and valet, the concern, as revealed in the work's underlying structure, is focused more centrally on sexual politics – and Mozart's vote goes to the women. Susanna may not command the stage in her arias but she dominates the action throughout, as is apparent in the ensembles. She is revealed mainly through duets shared with Figaro, Marcellina, Cherubino, Rosina, and the Count; she appears in all the work's ensembles. The opening duet sets the pattern for the opera's development in that her melody eclipses Figaro's.

Susanna's part draws attention to the division between the sexes, not distinctions of class. As well as mocking Figaro with his own vengeance music ("Di qua non muovo il passo" in the finale of Act IV), she amuses herself at the Count's expense with feigned slips of the tongue (No. 16). Meanwhile, she co-operates as an equal with the Countess. If class conflict is highlighted in the dramatic foreground, it is the strains of sexual politics that create the deeper dramatic form. This dramatic form is generated not by the text of the libretto but by Mozart's treatment, through the musical development of character and the control of pace and emphasis. The manipulative woman who gets her way by clandestine machination is a common stereotype. This, though, is not how Susanna is portrayed. Whereas the woman who fits the stereotype derives her enjoyment from meddling simply for the sake of the exercise of power involved, Susanna is revealed acting as she does in order to retain her autonomy and, hence, control over her own life. Her status and circumstances dictate that she pursues her plans by indirection. For her, scheming is a necessary means and not an end in itself. She emerges from the opera as its most sympathetic character. As such, she is the composer's creation.

Here there is a complex interplay between two structures. The foreground plan is governed by conventions and traditions (social, as well as dramatic and musical); the background structure places Susanna at the opera's heart and provides a dimension that takes the work to a different level. This *musical* form, I have been arguing, is no less a *dramatic* form, created by Mozart. The success of the opera depends on Mozart's breathing life into the work's characters, for there could be no alternative to the surface formula – that is, to the mechanical unfolding of the narrative along boring because predictable lines.

3   Musical and Dramatic Structure in *Così Fan Tutti*

Given what has been argued above, it might be expected that *Così* continues the trend established in *Giovanni* and *Figaro*, with Mozart achieving a musico-dramatic form through the development of character and action, thereby going beyond the surface of stock characters and formulaic plot. Indeed, this is what I will now argue.

In effect, *Così* is a chamber opera with only six characters. The symmetry between the three pairs of men and women allows for a nicely balanced number of duets. Everything *seems* to happen on the surface and it is easy to view the lovers as mirror-image pairs gavotting through the obvious permutations. *Così* offers nothing so throat rattling as is found in *Giovanni*, nor so politically pointed as occurs in *Figaro*. It has a delicacy and subtlety, easily mistaken for effete refinement and fatuousness, which befits an opera whose subject is human character and relationships, rather than the supernatural or blunt sexual politics.

As I hear it, *Così* is about nothing more complicated (and about nothing less important) than difference and similarity, individuality and community, among people.[13] On the surface, it is about couples (men, women, men and women) that mirror each other's images, so that members of the pair might be interchangeable. Despina vies with Alfonso in her cynicism about the other sex; Fiordiligi and Gugliemo match the depth of their love against that of Dorabella and Ferrando; Gugliemo competes with Ferrando as a seducer; Fiordiligi rivals Dorabella in her attraction for her new, honey-tongued suitor; Ferrando is not to be outdone by the complacent arrogance of Gugliemo in assuming the undying commitment of his love's faithfulness; and so on. Yet at this level, the characters can be no more than cartoon-like. They become more than that, though, and the opera is more than a collection of clichés, because each individual is distinctively characterized by Mozart. The opera really would be silly if we could not take seriously the love the couples share for each other at the beginning, and we could not take those loves seriously if there could be no sense of each person's difference from the others. Mozart is at pains to make these characters separate while, at the same time, conceding and playing on their many similarities. Dorabella is more adventurous, more flighty, more easily led, more "romantic" than Fiordiligi, and when Fiordiligi commits herself she does so with a depth and seriousness Dorabella lacks. Gugliemo is the more bitter in betrayal; Ferrando the more superficial. Ferrando is as much like Dorabella, and Gugliemo as much like Fiordiligi, as either is like the other. While Alfonso and

Despina might both be cynics, Despina has a cheerful warm-heartedness contrasting with Alfonso's world-weariness. All this, and more, is established primarily by Mozart's musical treatment, I claim. In their arias (especially) and in the duets, each character receives a distinctive musical personality.

The surface reveals a difference between the sexes – it is the men who are betrayed in their affections by the women. But not far below the surface is the message that the betrayal, if such it is, is mutual, for the men play their lovers false in regarding affections as gifts that might be trifled with, and in risking for the sake of their self-esteem the relationships they had achieved. If women are thus – "così fan tutte" – then men are so, and all have been shown wanting but as no less deserving of love for that fact. If women have a capacity for serious love, they might also love more than one man. If men take conceited pride in being loved, they might also endanger the love they receive. And if such features of human psychology are identified and accepted for what they are, a happy union between the sexes is possible. Their recognition depends on awareness not only of the potential faults of the other and forgiving acceptance of these but, as well, on an acknowledgment of one's own weaknesses. What is needed is knowledge of others as they are, of oneself, and of the human frailty all share.

Earlier I mentioned that the finale coming in the middle of the *opera buffa* pits the protagonists against the antagonists, with the former in danger of succumbing to the latter. In *Figaro*, Susanna, Rosina, and Figaro are opposed by the Count, Marcellina, Bartolo, and Basilio. In *Giovanni*, the Don, as anti-hero, and Leporello, by association, are under attack from Anna, Elvira, Zerlina, Ottavio, and Masetto. The situation in *Così* is instructively different. Alfonso and Despina function as catalysts, not as the lovers' enemies. Instead, Dorabella and Fiordiligi are torn between holding to their pledges and offering comfort to the attractive strangers who (apparently) have taken poison because their affections have not been returned. Meanwhile, Gugliemo and Ferrando devalue the women's seriousness both with their inner lightheartedness, born of misplaced confidence and arrogance, and their outer histrionics. As revealed here, the enemy lies within, not without.

There could be no clearer indication that the danger to be confronted follows from the absence of self-awareness and mutual comprehension. Insofar as *Così* has a deep structure underlying and informing the patina of public action and dramatic form, as I have claimed is true for *Giovanni* and *Figaro*, it is one echoing and reflecting on, while transforming, that surface. The public display of love, disguise, rejection, deception, defeat, exposure, forgiveness, and reconciliation is matched by a psychological journey through which each learns of the desires, attitudes, capacities, and potential present within themselves as well as others. They respond ultimately to these revelations with acceptance and mutual forbearance. The opera ends not with protagonists triumphing over antagonists but with the four main characters coming to appreciate their own virtues and vices, as well as those of others, thereby laying a more secure foundation for rewarding, mutually appreciative, and informed interpersonal relationships. The wheel turns full circle, so that, on the surface, one returns to the point at which the work begins, but the psychological drama created and forwarded in Mozart's music reveals, by contrast, just how far the protagonists have traveled and grown in their understanding of themselves and others.

How do the above reflections provide an insight into the apparently anomalous treatment of the canon quartet in *Così*? Pace and action is not all. As I wrote earlier, the action freezes for the sake of the quartet. Similar moments are found also in *Figaro* – the trio ("Da questo momento") in the finale of Act II – and *Giovanni* – the trio ("Protegga il giusto cielo") in the finale of Act I. Such passages are the more striking for the fact that their occurrence suspends the inexorable dramatic drive established previously. They transcend the context of the moment. They go beyond the platitudinous moral presented by tradition at the *opera buffa's* conclusion. These quiescent passages are reserved for statements that are oblique and personal, I think. They serve as pointers, I claim, to the dramatic significance of the works' underlying musical structures.

In "Da questo momento" in *Figaro*, the Count, Rosina, and Susanna sing of the importance of the Count's learning to appreciate his wife's love. The general theme of the need for, and appropriateness of, respect for the integrity of others as individuals informs the work's structure. "Protegga il giusto cielo," in *Giovanni*, involves a prayer to powers above, implying that protection from the evil abroad in the world can be afforded only by forces of good not available to earthly characters. This encapsulates the theme that underpins and generates the overall, bow structure of the opera, as described earlier.

The canon quartet in *Così* is to be appreciated in a similar fashion, I hold. The proposed toast advocates one's leaving behind the sorrow and regrets of the past. That thought, shared by Fiordiligi, Dorabella, and Ferrando, sets the emotional tone for the disentangling of the plot that follows, yet Gugliemo, who is as much a member of the quartet as the others, remains irreducibly an individual within the structure. How better to reveal in microcosm the subject animating the opera, which sets against the inescapable autonomy of the individual the common need for mutual acceptance and recognition? Had Gugliemo's part been assimilated to the rest, such as might have occurred in a strict canon introduced later when he also comes to accept the situation, that message would have been lost.

To return to the beginning: the suggestion that the dramatic context explains why Gugliemo does not take his part in presenting the canon's theme turns out to be correct, after all, but the route to this conclusion, if its significance is to be grasped, is a much longer one than normally is supposed. This is because the quartet draws attention to the structure that brings life to the stock characters and formulaic patterns in terms of which the particular work conforms to the general type. That structure, which is at the one time both musical and dramatic as a result of the composer's control of action and character in the music, lies below the apparent surface. If that deeper structure is harder to discern in *Così* than are its equivalents in *Figaro* and *Giovanni*, this is because it more obviously imitates the surface pattern, the better to point up the moral and social significance of the tale when it is enacted by individuals invested by the musical treatment with genuine feeling and rounded characters.

Notes

1   The stage directions do not make clear who marries whom, though. (I think it is important that this uncertainty is preserved in performance.) One might speculate about the source of the plot's attraction for Mozart, who seems to have loved the sister of his wife.

2   Peter Kivy, *Osmin's Rage: Philosophical Reflections on Opera* (Princeton, NJ: Princeton University Press, 1988), p. 259. Mozart did write *The Impresario* for characters identified in the way Kivy describes, because in that *Singspiel* he was satirizing the singers and conventions of the day. *Così* is quite different, or so I maintain.

3   Inevitably, Mozart's canon quartet is compared to "Mir ist so wunderbar," the canon quartet in Beethoven's *Fidelio*. In Beethoven's quartet, the characters' thoughts differ considerably, with the result that the musical and dramatic forms do not match. Beethoven may be concerned with the dramatic, but he is not a dramatist in the Mozartian mold. Whereas Mozart attempts the rounded delineation of his major characters, as I later argue, Beethoven is attracted to large, abstract themes, such as the redeeming power of love and the value of political liberty. His characters are props, rather than people.
    The musicologist Edward T. Cone compares the two quartets in these terms:

What is the dramatic relevance of [Beethoven's canon quartet]? Beautiful though it is, it attaches identical music to diverse words sung by a motley quartet. But this is no ordinary ensemble. It is not a conversation but a fourfold soliloquy in which each character comments on a situation that three of them misinterpret. Only Leonora knows the truth, and she must conceal it. Thus the conscious thoughts of the characters – their words – are various. Yet the canonic device implies, through the identity of the melodic lines, that the intuitions of the deceived ones have somehow led them to a subconscious appreciation of the real state of affairs – perhaps not to the truth about Leonora's disguise, but at least of the truth about her character . . . It is interesting to contrast Beethoven's canon with that of Mozart in *Così fan tutte*. As has often been pointed out, Gugliemo's inability to carry his imitative part in 'È nel tuo, nel mio bicchiero' reflects his rage, which makes it impossible for him to mask his true feelings by accepting the words and music of the canon . . . One has the suspicion that Ferrando has enjoyed the whole charade and might not be averse to the change of fiancées! Is this really the case? The answer is not easy. It depends on how successfully music can seem to mask as well as explore a character's true attitudes – and on how one can tell which it is doing. In depicting a character consciously playing a deceptive role, the composer may choose to emphasize either his real subconscious nature or that of his assumed role. Mozart's solution to the problem throughout *Così fan tutte* is typically subtle and ambiguous." (*The Composer's Voice*, Berkeley, CA: University of California Press, 1974, pp. 37–9)

4   Benucci was also the singer for whom Mozart wrote the part of Figaro, and he took the part of Leporello in the Vienna production of *Don Giovanni*. Benucci is mentioned only once in Mozart's letters. On May 7, 1783, he wrote to this father: "Well, the Italian opera buffa has started again here and is very popular. The buffo is particularly good – his name is Benucci."

5   All quotations from Mozart's letters are in Emily Anderson, ed. and trans., *The Letters of Mozart and His Family* (London: St Martin's Press, 1966).

6   In "Musical Understanding and Musical Kinds," *Journal of Aesthetics and Art Criticism* 52 (1994): 69–81, I draw attention to the way such requirements operate against the overall musico-dramatic structure in the last act of *Figaro*. Marcellina and Basilio are there provided with arias, as is their due, but this happens at the expense of the dramatic development. The progress of the plot is halted and the acceleration of musical tension is dissipated. If these arias are cut for the sake of preserving the drama's pace, however, the structural balance between the second and fourth acts is upset.

7   The ratio of ensembles, excluding finales, to arias reveals this. In *Figaro* it is 9:14, in *Giovanni* 10:14, and in *Così* 15:13.

8   When writing *Idomeneo*, Mozart demands many cuts and alterations in the libretto, always looking to the dramatic effect to be obtained – see the letters of November 8, November 13, November 15, November 24, and November 29, 1780; December 9, 1780; and January 3, and January 18, 1781. The following are typical:

The second duet is to be omitted altogether – and indeed with more profit than loss to the opera. For when you read through the scene, you will see that it obviously becomes limp and cold by the addition of an aria or a duet, and very genant for the other actors who must stand by doing nothing; and, besides, the noble struggle between Ilia and Idamante would be too long and thus lose its whole force.

In the last scene of Act II, Idomeneo has an aria or rather a sort of cavatina between the choruses. Here it will be *better* to have a mere recitative, well supported by the instruments. For in this scene which will be the finest in the whole opera . . . there will be such noise and confusion on the stage that an aria at this particular point would cut a poor figure – and moreover there is the thunderstorm, which is not likely to subside during Herr Raaff's aria, is it?

More of Mozart's attitude to the librettist's role is offered in a letter to his father dated October 13, 1781. On July 5, 1783, Mozart writes: "An Italian poet here has now brought me a libretto which I shall perhaps adopt, if he agrees to trim and adjust it in accordance with my wishes." The correspondence with Varesco, via Mozart's father, finds Mozart demanding many changes and suggesting how they should be written – see the letters of December 6, December 10, and December 24, 1783, and February 10, 1784.

9   Joseph Haydn wrote to Franz Rott, Chief of Commissariat in Prague, December 1787:

> You ask an *opera buffa* of me. With the greatest pleasure, if you have the desire to possess some vocal composition of mine all for yourself. But if it is to be performed on the stage in Prague, I cannot oblige in that case, since all my operas are too closely bound up with our personnel, and moreover would never produce the effect which I calculated according to local conditions. It would be quite another matter if I had the incalculable felicity of composing an entirely new libretto for the theatre there. But even in that event I should be taking a great risk, since the *great Mozart* can scarcely have his equal. For if I were able to impress the soul of every music-lover, and more especially the great ones, with my own understanding of and feeling for Mozart's incomparable works, *so profound* and so full of *musical intelligence*, as my own *strong sentiment* dictates, then the nations would vie with each other to possess such a jewel within their encircling walls. Let Prague hold fast to the precious man . . . It makes me angry to think that this *unique* Mozart has not yet found an appointment . . . Forgive me if I stray from my path. I love the man too much. (Quoted in Otto Erich Deutsch, ed., *Mozart: A Documentary Biography*, trans. Eric Blom, Peter Branscombe, and Jeremy Noble, 2nd edn., London: Adam & Charles Black, 1966, p. 308).

10   Whether Donna Anna has retained her virtue never is entirely clear. This topic has inspired at least one novel – Brigid Brophy's *The Snow Ball* (London: Allison & Busby, 1979), first published in 1964.

11   It is difficult to resist speculating about Mozart's psychological state in being attracted to the story. The opera was written immediately following the death of Mozart's father (May 28, 1787 – the first performance took place on October 29), the father who fostered his gifts, but was stern.

12   For a more detailed analysis than I offer here, see Davies, "Musical Understanding and Musical Kinds."

13   A psychologically more complex characterization might be developed, for the opera is equally about the interplay between reason and sentiment, and the balance between the two necessary in a person's character if that person is to be capable of achieving happiness through interpersonal relations.

12

JAZZ IMPROVISATION AND ETHICAL INTERACTION: A SKETCH OF THE CONNECTIONS

Garry L. Hagberg

Not all, but I think a good number, of the available idioms of musical expression place the *product* of musical creativity before the listener. The composer may be present at a performance of what we might here call pre-notated[1] music, but that would be merely a contingent fact about that particular performance. The creative act in such cases, in the first instance, occurred over perhaps many hours, days, weeks, months, or sometimes years prior to what we are now hearing; indeed in such cases the very concept of performance depends for its content on that bifurcation of process from product. Jazz improvisation is an art in which the process itself, in a temporally compressed manner, is presented before the public: one might say here, in a manner consistent with one central theme of American pragmatic thought,[2] that the process *is* the product. It is an art that places not the result of creativity, but rather the very conditions of creativity, on the stage. And those conditions, and the processes that unfold within them, have ethical aspects. In this chapter my modest ambition is to categorize and describe in at least a preliminary way some of those aspects, that moral content. And if I have a slightly more demanding ambition, it is to show something of the way – perhaps the distinctive way (i.e., this feature is, I believe, part of what makes jazz improvisation the art form that it is) – that improvisation simultaneously mimetically represents as well as exemplifies in action the ethical content herein described. And the way in which it does so I believe brings to the fore a matter of some methodological significance for moral psychology. But I will return to those matters after we have seen some of the varieties of ethical interaction as they take place within improvised jazz.

1   Attentiveness

There is, inside the world of collective improvisation, perhaps first and foremost, a pressing and overarching need to *listen*. This is hardly the simple and unremarkable fact that it may initially seem. To listen closely, to stay attuned to the musical movements and gestures of all of those around one, requires – in the higher realms of the art form – a vigilance and discipline, of a kind made possible through mastery of a complex set of learned recognition skills that musicians generically call ear training, that is focused and indeed unrelenting for the duration of the performance. To listen, closely and attentively, is of course one central component of humane acknowledgment: without it one would not so much as know in even the most rudimentary way what to make of the central ethical concept of attentiveness.[3] (Here, even at first glance, one can see that this variety of close listening at once mimetically depicts ethical attentiveness at the very moment that it exemplifies such attentiveness within the improvisational world, but again I will return to this matter below.) To listen closely to a person's unfolding musical thought, and that person's reactions to the thoughts of others within the stream of musical life, is to understand and keep in mind what we might call the causal antecedents that made a given phrase, rhythmic gesture, or melodic motif possible. Such phrases, gestures, and motifs are anything but hermetically isolated moments that emerge *ex nihilo*. On the contrary, they are *developments*, where that very word implies a tracking of the teleology that leads to them. And we similarly hear in them a set of possibilities or potentialities that follow from them, i.e., in grasping them for what they are we hear the musical vectors or lines of development contained within them. To put it simply, if we fail to hear where they came from and where they are (potentially) going, we for that reason fail to hear them for what they are. Almost nothing in the context of improvisational interaction is devoid of this kind of teleological embeddedness. And if it appears devoid of this linear interconnectedness between past, present, and future, then that is almost certainly because we do not yet understand it.

Tellingly, every bit of this describes what it is to listen to a person with a fine and nuanced attentiveness: we do not understand a life, nor do we sympathetically attend to it, by seeing that life as a mere collection of discrete atomistic actions or events occurring sequentially. Such a perspective, taken *of a human being*, would indeed be monstrous. (We might see the movements of a robot that way, and indeed we might marvel at the way in which it seemed to *simulate* teleologically intentional action.) We attend to a life by seeing its teleology, its trajectories of development, where what is now happening came from, and where what is now happening might go. And we achieve such a comprehensive (and indeed comprehending) understanding of a person by *listening* with considerable acuity.[4] Indeed, here (as will happen repeatedly throughout this chapter) the musical case in fact casts light on the ethical: there is something deeply analogous to "ear training" in the realm of humane acknowledgment. Moreover, prosody, as what we might call the musical dimension of verbal interaction, is a significant and powerful conveyer of meaning, and we can be more and less "tone-deaf" to such determinants of significance. Inflection, in music, functions as does prosody in speech, and in contexts of musical improvisation we have an obligation to establish and maintain a close attentiveness to it.

2   Awareness of the Circumstances of Action

The suggestions in the preceding concerning the need to see an action within a broader context in order to so much as see the action for what it is carry an ethical implication that is readily discernible in both moral and musical-improvisational interaction. The attentiveness of which we have just spoken requires an awareness of the larger circumstance within which one acts, within which one reflects, within which one chooses, and within which one engages with co-respondents within a network or web of moral relations. The awareness of this larger circumstance is not the *kind* of thing one gains at a glance – it requires a mindfulness of the labors and projects of others, where those are seen in a way that is woven throughout a life and across the time of the developmental span of a person. That is to say: the anti-atomistic nature of intentional action itself confers an obligation on persons witnessing or interactively engaged with the person undertaking that action to see it in an enlarged frame of reference. Without this we understand neither the action nor the person performing it. This is true in life, and it is true in the mimetic reflection (and enactment) of that life in improvisational interaction.

In an exquisite piece of historic film footage in which we see Billie Holiday listening to the progressively unfolding improvised solo of Lester Young, we see in the subtly changing expressivity of her face[5] the profundity of her comprehension of Young's gestures, his spontaneous choices, the logical implications of the motivic material he puts into place as he progresses, and – perhaps most tellingly – the deep satisfaction that Holiday takes in understanding the utterly masterful, calm, and unhurried way in which Young fulfils those musical-logical implications. In that moment, we see in microcosm the humane content of the distinctive kind of mind-fulness that morally significant intentional action demands. We see it in her attentiveness, the acuity and depth of her listening; in the special pleas-ure which her highly trained ear takes in the sense he is making in response to an underlying ever-shifting harmonic terrain (to which I will return below). We see it in her moment-to-moment facially expressed reactions to Young's rare combination of musical logic ("there you said that, so now – I can see – you say this")[6] and expressive nuances as direct ana-logues of prosody in vocal utterance (to which, as singer, she would of course have been particularly attuned). A person's action is understood against the enlarged background of that person's life-projects, labors, and committed engagements,[7] and the unmistakable depth of understanding and comprehension that is readily discernible in that fleeting moment of jazz footage shows us precisely this ethical fact in beautifully encapsu-lated artistic form.

3   Acknowledging the Autonomy of Others

The two foregoing sections implicitly house another aspect of moral or humane acknowledgment: in seeing another person's actions, choices, responses, and engagements, as they take their place within the expanded frame of that life and its unique developmental teleology, we have to see that life as *that* life, i.e., as one possessing an autonomy from our own interests, drives, ambitions, and concerns. That person as viewed by us may of course become relationally intertwined with all or any of these, and often in intricately complex ways, but the essence of humane acknowledgment is found in our foundational recognition of their auto-nomy or moral independence from us.[8] On one polar extreme, this is precisely what the sociopath, terrifyingly, utterly fails to do; on the other extreme, it is perhaps what the most compassionate, imaginatively sympathetic, and self-sacrificing person does to a very high degree.

It is not difficult to see positions along this continuum portrayed onstage: there are jazz improvisers who can be arrogant, overbearing, self-important, disregarding, condescending, and worse, just as there can be players who are close listeners, mindful of others in the above sense, careful and sensitive contributors, and what we might now call intricate interweavers from a standpoint of, and acknowledgment of, a foundational autonomy. I certainly would not generically place the work of Charles Mingus (when directing his own ensembles from the bass) on the negative side of this continuum – that would be to too-little comprehend that character, the longer-term undertaking and developmental direction of that distinctive experimental ensemble's entire enterprise. But it can be said that Mingus's habit of shouting out to his soloists (indeed here we say, instructively, *his* soloists) to play something else, or to stop playing entirely if he didn't like the content of what they were playing or the implied direction of that playing's unfolding development, does occupy a position that is far from the self-abnegating. On the other extreme we might find, for example, the great guitarist in Count Basie's rhythm section, Freddie Green. His brilliant, original, and utterly masterful accompanimental style was his *entire* contribution – he is not known to have played a single improvised solo. (This incidentally is a far cry from saying he did not improvise. The realizations of his chord-voicings on the fingerboard are, broadly speaking, reminiscent of the improvisational element contained in the baroque figured-bass system of accompaniment – although Green's are considerably more musically complex and often more musically inventive. They also exemplify one kind of autonomy asserted against the actual written chord progressions over which he of course did not have volitional freedom.) If in the history of jazz there is a special case of vigilant and sustained close-listening conjoined to an abiding concern to support the efforts of others while preserving a sense of autonomous independence but where this is muted and made subservient to either a larger enterprise or the undertakings of others, Green is it. And at a thousand stations between those extremes, we find – like life and thus in a mimetically fitting way – players who exemplify some of these virtues some of the time. And like life, the image of perfection in these matters serves as the regulative ideal toward which the best players aspire and against which, in one dimension of their lives as performers, they measure themselves.

4 Respecting Complexity

There is a well-known practice in the world of jazz improvisation that, in students, is (forgivingly) taken as a stage of musical development that serves as a platform to move beyond, and, in professionals, is (unforgivingly) taken as a rather serious aesthetic weakness. It stands perfectly parallel to one quite sharply delineated variety of moral weakness. It concerns the extent to which, on the one hand, harmonic structures, and on the other, persons in their individuality, are taken *seriously*. Some jazz improvisation takes place over rather static harmonic underpinnings where the rate of change in the underlying harmony (players call this "harmonic rhythm") is slow. (Jazz compositions that are constructed upon such static or slow-moving harmonic settings are called modal pieces – the player can successfully improvise over them using just one or a few scales or, consistent with the legacy of ancient Greek thinking about music, "modes."[9]) In such cases, rudimentary or student players will very likely construct improvised lines or phrases using only these simple melodic or modal materials. It is interesting that (frequently but certainly not always) more experienced or advanced players will take such simplified harmonic platforms as invitations to import, within the unfolding improvisation, much greater melodic complexity – where this carries implications of, and thus in a sense superimposes, correspondingly greater harmonic complexity – in a way that moves well beyond the simplified (aficionados of modal writing will say "purified," which of course also carries its interesting moral connotations) harmonic foundation as given.[10] The complexity that such players superimpose is required in more traditional jazz compositions in which the harmonic rhythm is much faster, i.e., where the underlying chords change or progress at a much faster rate (which is of course distinct from a faster tempo). And often, such rapidly changing underlying chords not only change frequently, but change *keys* frequently, thus requiring the player to develop melodic lines and preserve a sense of thematic continuity or coherence over not just changing, but radically changing, terrain. Beyond this, usually the chords that change at this rate have extensions (e.g., a ninth added to a dominant seventh chord) or alterations (e.g., a raised or sharped ninth added to a dominant seventh chord), requiring still further nuance. And it is just here that the aesthetic weakness in question becomes visible.

If one is insufficiently schooled in harmonic analysis and ear training, and insufficiently skilled in, as players put it, blowing over changes, one can get through (in a limited way) the chord changes by what players used to call "shucking," or using hyper-simplified melodic material that does unarguably fit – but only in an untailored, one-size-fits-all way. A simple pentatonic scale (the five notes C-D-E-G-A within an octave in the key of C major or the same simple pitch set but starting on the A in the key of A minor), used in such demanding circumstances, will prevent most readily-audible catastrophes. But it does so at the heavy cost of failing to sufficiently engage with the *complexity* of the harmonic material, the harmonic content of the composition at hand. Indeed, just as we may witness this phenomenon in ethical life, we may see in the aesthetic case a kind of corrosive cheapening that comes in the form of the trivialization of complexity. The pentatonic scale alone, used in this way (and, importantly in connection with context-sensitivity, not in some other cases, where it can indeed be precisely what is called for), functions as, and indulges in, pretence: it pretends that things are much simpler than they in truth are. To the extent that such pretence becomes convincing to the listener, it promulgates deception. And to the extent that such pretence becomes convincing to the practitioner, it exemplifies, and succumbs to the worst temptations of, self-deception. It is no accident that the terminology we use to describe the ethical case applies without modification to the aesthetic. Students of improvisation are, rightly, encouraged initially to play in this way, but then, as quickly as possible, to develop skills of musical discernment and technique that enable a transcendence of these limitations. Just as persons are expected to acknowledge, recognize, and skillfully interact with the complexities of others. Simply put, we find severely truncated narratives of morally complex situations themselves morally offensive: they fail to take complexity seriously.

5 Memory

The more highly evolved practices of improvisational interaction serve to cast into high relief a moral imperative that reasserts itself continually and in contextually variegated ways throughout moral life. That is, the imperative of memory, the obligation to remember, to *keep track*. One might see this as another way of voicing the demand for the kind of attentiveness outlined above, but I believe it deserves its own description.

It was Aristotle who wrote of the great importance for the formal or structural power of a drama of having a beginning, a middle, and an end. This is not, of course, the truism it may appear at first glance to be: a beginning, in Aristotle's sense, is a putting into play of themes that do not in and of themselves urgently call for an elucidation of their antecedents. Any such conceptual urgency would render it impossible to attend to how those themes develop and what might follow from them (owing of course to irrepressible and distracting thoughts concerning what led to them).[11] A middle, by contrast, is a development of those themes where we understand, where we comprehend, their antecedents and where we keep track of those antecedents as we witness the unfolding events of the middle section. And the end, here again distinct from the former two structural elements, is an integration and summing up of those themes in such a way that, as we put it colloquially, no thread is left dangling.

The power of such an aesthetic structure was not lost on the developers of the classical symphony: the sonata-allegro form may be seen as precisely such a structure, if in music rather than in drama (or one might say, perhaps more accurately, that it is just this structure that gives that music its dramatic form). And, significantly for present purposes, this tripartite aesthetic structure was one that for Aristotle stood against and in fact towered over the far weaker episodic structure, i.e., where, as a kind of structural atomism, one thing simply happened after another (as we saw briefly above). If we care for a person, one dimension of that care will be manifested as memory: we will remember the antecedents that led to the themes that are currently in play in that person's life, we will see new beginnings as what they are (if, as the term "new" implies, we see those new beginnings against the backdrop of an earlier "act" or an earlier entire "play"), and we will see middles as developments of themes put into play earlier and leading, perhaps contingently, perhaps inexorably, to subsequent developments. To see a person – a collection of aspirations, attachments, allegiances, hopes, fears, ambitions, regrets, thoughts, second thoughts, and all the rest – in episodic form is to see superficially.

The improviser is in this situation: to develop his or her own solo as it evolves within interactive and progressively changing circumstances involves an obligation to remember what he or she has done to this moment. How one got here informs where one is, where one presently is, is in part determined by what *can* follow, and that is determined thematically, motivically, and harmonically by what came before. A kind of aesthetic amnesia will preclude this mode of engagement, and it will deprive the solo of any significant longer-term form, sense of evolution, or narrative structure (unless the player happens to be the unusual recipient of aesthetic luck in a given case). And the soloist needs to keep one eye, as he or she moves forward, on a rear-view mirror that reflects as well what the other players have done to this point to support, and to interactively develop, that solo. Then each player in the ensemble has a similar obligation to do just the same, but from the point of view of the supporting roles of the bass, the drums, the piano, the guitar, or whatever the supporting accompanying instruments. There is a sense in which, seen from this angle or seen now with these features of jazz improvisation in high relief, this art is an art of memory. To remain in the immediate (this puts the lie to exaggerated notions that jazz is an art exclusively of the moment) is to fail to satisfy a very real demand of memory; it is to remain in an aesthetically amnesiac oblivion.

Aristotle saw that the episodic form (to the extent that it is a *form* at all) is weak, and it is weak for the structural elements it lacks. Life as lived is far more complexly interwoven, more interconnected,[12] more formally structured, and those interweavings and interconnections, in self- or other-understanding, are essential to drama precisely because they are essential in life. To allow episodic perception to occlude the memory-rooted view of the long form with its antecedents and its consequents is, in the forms of attention we give to both persons and players, simultaneously a moral and aesthetic failing. To achieve in full what we might here call the Aristotelian view, by contrast, is a moral and aesthetic triumph. And to maintain an awareness of the importance of this dimension of both human and musical engagement, even if not achieved in full, is nevertheless a moral and aesthetic achievement and a measure of what we are as persons and, within the mimetic improvisational microcosm, as players.

Yet moral philosophers are fond of stating that "ought" implies "can," i.e., that we cannot intelligibly impose normative expectations, or say that someone *should* do something, without that person clearly being *able* to do that thing. So where the ability is lacking, the very possibility of moral responsibility would be removed. What then of an improviser who has not acquired the skills of musical memory sufficient to satisfy the obligations presently described? Memory, as we have known at least since the mnemonic techniques of the ancient rhetoricians, is – or is at least in part – a skill. Do we rightly blame those who, simply put, aren't very good at it? The answer, as Charlie Parker learned the hard way as an aspiring young practitioner of jazz improvisation, concerns second-order obligations. The drunk driver may not be able, while driving under the influence, to steer, brake, judge distance, judge speed, and so forth in the way that he or she would if sober. But the reason that these absent "cans" do not eradicate the "oughts" is obviously that there is a second-order obligation to not get behind the wheel if intoxicated, or to not get intoxicated if one has to get behind the wheel, that runs prior to the driving-without-the-"cans;" that meta-level obligation keeps the "ought" operative. When Parker sat in with an ensemble of extremely professional and accomplished players at a club as a young saxophonist and tried, spectacularly unsuccessfully, to play in doubletime (i.e., twice the speed), the drummer Jo Jones infamously threw one of his cymbals across the stage toward Parker's feet, its crash to the floor serving as a very stern commentary on the semi-competent skill Parker was at that time displaying.

He was not under an obligation to do something then and there on that stage that he clearly could not (yet) do: the second-order obligation was to be aware of the hard-won world-class standards of that ensemble and to not put himself in that position in the first place. So of our present question: like the students with the pentatonic scales above, our moral-aesthetic conventions welcome and encourage growth *as student* – where that student is playing in a context appropriate to student performance. We encourage the development of the requisite skills of musical memory in just this way. But a player posing as a professional and positioning him or herself into a very highly skilled improvisational setting with all the normative expectations that this implies but where such obligations cannot be fulfilled, gets a rather different reaction. It is, instructively, very difficult to definitively say whether this is a moral or an aesthetic fact.

6   Respecting Individuality

There is a variety of moral blindness – the inability to see a person or the details of that person's circumstances for whom and for what they are – that has its direct analogue (or again, indeed, instantiation) in improvisational interaction. Such blindness manifests itself in the form of overhasty judgments concerning the kind of person the person in question is (rather than seeing that person in his or her individuality), or the kind of circumstances the person in question finds him or herself in. In such cases the individualizing details of the person and situation are obscured behind the generic facades the person perceiving them imposes. World-weary, "I've seen it all" attitudes are often frustrating for just this reason: they impose generic templates in front of the contextually specific details and nuances that make the case in question the *individual* case it is. It is here that an obligation, simply put, to *think harder* and to *look closer* arises, where one is called upon to unsettle presumption and presupposition, to reconsider the conventional, to uproot habits of perception and judgment that may fail to properly accommodate, or even acknowledge, the telling detail.

In jazz improvisation, one can all-too-easily negotiate the intricacies and difficulties of challenging harmonic and rhythmic terrain by imposing analogues to such templates, employing what players call "licks" or "riffs" that, while tried-and-true in terms of their efficacy and melodic utility, are nevertheless formulaic responses to intricate harmonic demands. And those formulaic responses not only offer the easy way out: more importantly, they blind one to what may be of great interest in the harmonic passage in question. One can also respond to what one might call the suggestions made by the accompanying players in template-driven, formulaic ways, where one thus sees not the interesting and perhaps unique details of that musical moment but rather only the generic category into which the suggestion falls, or again see (or hear, actually) only the *kind* of suggestion it is. The obligation, of course, is to rise *to the occasion*, and to do so in a way that sees the other players' suggestions for what they are, or that sees the challenging underlying harmonic intricacies for what they are. Like the episodic view above, the lick-based formulaic response is simply weak by contrast to the setting of a courageous example by lifting oneself out of, and then remaining out of, pseudo-inventive ruts. Master jazz players do this all, or at least very much of, the time; there are, fortunately, many examples, but in connection with the present issue one might think of the work of Lee Konitz, who sees the intellectual project represented by building a jazz solo as a challenge of intricate problem-solving, moreover one where the problem represented by the composition is solvable only by seeing all of its details for what they are and avoiding the lapse into generic template-superimposition. Such playing shows courage of a kind that is sustained throughout the piece; it shows a willingness to "unfreeze" or to unlock oneself from patterns of repetition where to stay in them would clearly be the easiest way; and it shows a sustained avoidance of cliché where something that is at once more original and more truly responsive is called for. In moral life, repetitive patterns of perception or of speech (i.e., using a slogan to describe or name a situation or circumstance that itself, as patterned phraseology, blinds) call for something better, something more attuned to the *present* case. The best jazz improvisation (keeping in mind the wholly compatible remarks concerning the demands of memory above) is present in this sense. The most acute moral discernment is present in precisely the same way.

7   Rethinking the Past

It was Iris Murdoch who wrote "Re-thinking one's past is a constant responsibility."[13] That responsibility is closely related to the one we have just considered. Briefly stated, her idea is that, because our self-understanding is a function largely of relational interconnections, of weaving and re-weaving the narratives of our pasts as they lead (in Aristotle's sense above) into the present and project into the future, they are never finished or settled in a definitive way. Relations, as Henry James famously wrote, end nowhere, and thus the very idea of a finalized life-narrative is one that we cannot genuinely comprehend. So what then is re-telling? Adam Phillips[14] has incisively described this as changing the patterns of inclusion and exclusion, so that what was background in one narrative becomes figural in another; what was causally central in terms of life-events in one becomes adventitious in another. One's relations to one's own past, to one's aspirations for the future, and to others, as Murdoch and Phillips see it, are never fixed. And the moral responsibility to tell and re-tell, to continuously interweave, is born of that fact: to live in a stable world of fixity is, for Murdoch, to live in a world of self-perpetuated illusion or self-deception. Jazz improvisation, within the special world of a responsive, attentive, creative, and interactive ensemble is itself an example of the ever-changing lived realities of our interactions with others, our inter-actions with our own pasts, and our creative engagement with our own and others' life-narratives. In jazz, the very idea of a *version* neatly encapsulates this. Moreover, jazz underscores this fact of ethical life – the flux of our moral interactions with self and others – in demanding that an awareness of descriptive-narrative variation (in the form of musical variability and creativity) be sustained throughout the performance. There are forms, idioms, or genres of music in which the exacting re-duplication of prior performances is regarded an achievement and an admirable virtue. Jazz improvisation is not among them. (Note that I am referring throughout to *improvisation* in jazz, not to part-playing, ensemble sections, and so forth, where of course exact reduplication is a virtue as it is elsewhere in music.) Indeed, a pre-ordained fixity in the face of ensemble flux is a clear sign of insufficiency to the task; in jazz such melodic fixity would be received as would, say, a person's repeating the same few sentences within the context of a flowing conversation. Such a person, whatever was taking place, would certainly not be conversing.

We can tell at a glance the very great difference in moral life between a mechanical and a creative response, or between an automatic and a genuinely sensitive reaction, to an ethically significant event. In jazz improvisation this distinction is as important and almost as easily made. In recently released recordings of some studio takes of Charlie Parker we are offered a fascinating glimpse of precisely this kind of difference in action. In addition to the recording of the piece selected for release, we are given the false starts of the takes leading up to the good one, and the details are fascinating. The first one begins with a certain motivic identity, unfolding as it goes until Parker or the producer calls a halt to the take. This is followed immediately by the next take – but with a difference. The next take is now one that is clearly seen *in the light of what just transpired*, so that the approach is subtly different. This too is stopped, followed by another, which is itself seen in the light of its two predecessors, and – most importantly – what is now happening in the ensemble would not have been possible without the previous false starts. Those pasts are acknowledged and, in a sense, integrated into the present "narrative," in such a way that the version now is not only another re-telling, another re-weaving, of the elements in play but also a re-thinking, in precisely Murdoch's sense, of the past of the ensemble (albeit in this case of the very recent past – but then in this way too we have a facet of moral life compressed into real time and represented in microcosm in jazz). And that past resituates what is figural and what is background in Phillips' sense, shifting the patterns of inclusion and exclusion. Charlie Parker, in the context and with the irreplaceable help of that ensemble of extraordinarily accomplished and gifted players, shows in a tightly focused way what it is to fulfill the responsibility to "constantly re-think."

It is also, I believe, of interest that within this category of moral content we can see an image of a distinctive kind of moral striving or aspiration with a striking clarity. Working with one's memories, hopes, desires, fears, patterns of reaction, and so forth one can strive to change for the better: to be, for example, more constant in one's responsiveness to, and indeed more "present" in the preceding sense for, people in difficulty or in conditions of need, whatever they may be. One wants, in short, to take the materials one has, to take the elements that make up what one presently is, and, through a process of rearrangement, make something better. Wanting to be a better player, and working hard to achieve that end, exemplifies such moral striving in artistic form, and seeing it done masterfully on stage represents it and can inspire it. One might here say that this is nevertheless only analogy, only a parallel between the ethical and the aesthetic, and that they do not really intersect at this point in a very significant way. One could say that, but then one would be missing what is also placed before us by this distinctive art – that is, the very real obligations that players can handsomely fulfill to each other in just these terms of striving to be better, to make something better out of the materials and resources one presently has at one's disposal.

8   The Habit of Resourcefulness

Jazz improvisation is an art form that requires one, in perhaps an unusually stringent and demanding way, to draw upon such resources in each moment, and then in every succeeding moment with the same degree of focus and concentration. The jazz pianist Bill Evans has written of the particularly rigorous nature of the discipline, calling attention to this feature and likening it to the art of calligraphy in which one has no possibility of taking a stroke back, of revision – once the ink has touched the parchment one must accept that gesture as now given, as already public, and then work with and from that.[15] Moral life, and particularly moral life *in extremis*, can call upon one to marshal one's resources and to draw upon all that one is. This, of course, is not as simple, nor is it as easy a thing to accomplish, as just saying it suggests. As we have seen in the foregoing, habituated patterns of response, patterns of attention and inattention, and the moral analogues to the formulaic riffs of jazz, all conspire against the achievement. What is required is something akin to the kind of recollection of which both Plato and Wittgenstein, in their separate ways, spoke: we need to get ourselves into a frame of mind in which we can *remember what we know*, where that remembered content will prevent us from lapsing into illusion, into unwarranted generalization, into conceptual confusion.

This capacity to summon resources is indeed, like philosophy and like music (or rather as manifested in the practices of both philosophy and of music), a discipline. In moral life, as Aristotle also argued, we perform actions that are themselves the consequences, good or bad, of the history of choices of predecessor-actions that stand behind, and inexorably lead to, the engraining of those actions into habits that then become, as embedded dispositions to act or respond in one way and not another, an abiding part of our character. He adds that habits formed in the young need not be functions of choices, but rather functions of action chosen for the young person by, say, a parent.

Although a clear parallel obtains here between this kind of moral training and musical training, that is not my central point at present. Rather, the discipline or, broadly speaking, engrained habit of moral resourcefulness is one that we (as volitionally autonomous adults) achieve, and one that we maintain by practice, or by keeping *in practice*. In helping a confidante think through a difficult situation, we need to be mindful of relevant experience from which we have learned. And yet, as discussed above, we need to also be resourceful enough to prevent that from becoming a "template" in the above sense that then blinds us to the idiosyncratic details of this particular case before us or that leads us to see her experience as a mere repetition of ours. In the creative heat of the moment within collective jazz improvisation, an accomplished player will do very much the same: remember what she knows, draw upon that knowledge without descending to mere repetition, use it where needed to find a way through a harmonic thicket, respond to the dialogue as it is unfolding in the full and engaged way that a conversationalist who is in possession of a vast range of intricately recalled experience may do, and see all of this happening in the other players just as it is happening in oneself. It is here again easy to do less well than one would like on this score in both moral and musical life. Ethically, we can fail to recollect all we know in striving to help another better understand and better articulate his or her experience, unwittingly limiting what we perceive of the case to what is contingently available in our presently active repertoire or moral discourse. And aesthetically, we can fail to recollect all we know in striving to contribute to a collective act of creation by unwittingly limiting ourselves to musical materials that are too-readily available. But in the more successful cases, on the moral side we can greatly appreciate the depth of someone's resources as they bring them into focus for us, and on the musical side we can greatly appreciate the capacious grasp of resources that, as we say in such cases of admiration for and recognition of such an achievement of recollection, seem bottomless or endless.

9   Kantian Mutual Respect

Among the contributions Kant made to ethical thought is of course his fundamental distinction between treating someone as an end as opposed to treating that person as a mere means to the furtherance of one's own ends. To put the matter in a way that links this concern to some of those discussed above, one might say that to treat a person merely as a means to the satisfaction of one's own ends is not genuinely to recognize that person *as a person*. In a dialogical conversation, a simple attitude of mutual respect is a precondition of success – and, prior to that, a precondition for a genuine conversation in the first place. Precisely this is true in a dialogical improvisation: it is entirely possible to "talk over" one, or over numerous others, in a musical conversation just as it is in a verbal conversation, and both are instances of the same lack of a foundationally respectful attitude of the kind Kant describes.

Indeed a player, embarking on an improvised solo, can start with the conception of the other players as accompanists of a subordinate kind, such that they are regarded as supportive presences whose supportive role is *wholly* subservient to the providing of the background against which the solo is figural. This, as we say, is more a matter of mere talking *to* (or pejoratively, "talking at") rather than talking *with*, and the dialogue suffers accordingly. And on the other extreme, here again there are a good

number of exemplary cases of the successful and most-engaged "conver-
sationalists" that provide the standard of measurement, but one might
pick out the work of this past decade of Wayne Shorter who has created
an ensemble that is, without exaggeration, perhaps the equal in these
"Kantian mutual respect" terms of anything in the history of jazz. One
might also think of the classic Bill Evans trio with Scott LaFaro, and then
subsequent piano-bass-drums trios that extend and develop this dialogical tradition in small-group improvisation, e.g., Keith Jarrett's trio and
more recently Brad Mehldau's as well. Of course such extraordinarily sophisticated dialogical interaction has its origins in the early call-and-response
tradition (itself a form of mutual acknowledgment). In such highly
advanced dialogical cases (and this starts, or at least comes into new focus,
with the Bill Evans trio) the very concept of accompaniment is reconsti-
tuted by taking so very seriously the musical analogue of the means/ends
distinction: in such circumstances one no longer plays *over*, but now plays
with. In Scott LaFaro's case in particular the bass came to break free of
its historically entrenched subservient role of providing root-and-fifth chord
orientations, with improvised bass lines now weaving themselves within
the improvised melodic piano lines. That emancipation is of a kind that
comes from an acknowledgment, within the musical dialogue, of the end
in itself as well as the accompanimental means.

And another aspect of the Kantian comparison comes to light here as
well: it is not necessary, nor is it a precondition for the legitimacy of the
Kantian principle in moral life, that this principle be verbally enunciated.
Its importance is found in its implementation in practice, within the contexts of humane recognition and engagement. Just the same is true in
the world of improvisatory recognition and engagement. The final live
recordings of Stan Getz with his quartet, playing in Copenhagen in the
last weeks of his life, show a player who sounds unmistakably as if he has
transcended once and for all any lower impulses of musical stardom and
the corresponding aesthetic danger of simply showing off while "talking
over" his subservient "means-providing" ensemble. It is a moment of
rare beauty, in which an ultra-accomplished ensemble of improvisers is
having a final, deeply respectful conversation.

10   Genuineness and Insight

Jazz improvisation is an art in which terms of praise and disapprobation
apply with the force and specificity those very terms do in ethical life. To
be genuine, as in morality, is to be who one is without putting up a false

front, without pretending to be something one is not, without assuming any false mantle of accomplishment. Jazz improvisation is of particular interest here because the demands of the art form tend to *enforce* these virtues: although one can perhaps pretend offstage, one simply cannot stand up on a stage, take a solo, and convince anyone – particularly one-self – that one is what one is not. Self-aggrandizement is not possible *within* the music. False-fronted duplicity is not possible *when playing*. Instruments do not lie, nor, as anyone who has been in a recording studio has been made vividly aware, do recording machines. Indeed, this is an art form that is intrinsically impatient with self-deception. To be insightful, as in morality, is to be one that sees connections, sees rela-tions between things, sees the significance of one thing for another, sees things in special light. The praise we give for being morally insightful is the same praise we give upon witnessing musical insight. To speak with an original voice in ethics is to avoid, or transcend the limits of, the predictable, the hackneyed, the derivative, the mere expression of the commonplace social more. And to have achieved the position of so much as having an original voice in the first place is itself a laudable moral achievement. We witness just the same in improvisational music, and we value an original voice for parallel reasons. One can think of those who achieved a profoundly original voice in jazz improvisation – take Thelonious Monk as an exemplar – and it is clear at a glance that the avoidance of the predictable, the transcendence of the hackneyed, the elim-ination of any trace of the derivative just are the ethical qualities in an aesthetic manifestation that we single out for praise using an evaluative vocabulary that we have already rehearsed to the point of internalized mastery in ethics.

11 Sensitivity to the Context of Discourse

Moral sensitivity can, and often does, take the form of sensitivity to what it is possible, or right, or necessary, or helpful, or fitting, or wise, etc. to say within what Wittgenstein called a language-game, a circumscribed context of discourse. And then these expressive limits themselves have a second-order moral aspect, i.e., a display of moral sensitivity is *itself* the kind of thing that can be evaluated in terms of moral sensitivity. One can in certain settings hear precisely the words of a particularly sensitive person that one needs to hear, and that is a laudable thing; one can also hear words that are sensitized more to what it is fitting (in a superficial or mechanical sense as above, rather like George Eliot's Casaubon in

Middlemarch) to say, and that – particularly where helpful words are needed – is a blameworthy thing. The former is a sign of genuine moral understanding; the latter is a sign of a mere simulacrum of the same. Miles Davis said of Bill Evans that he played the piano the way it ought to be played. This is not a superficial remark or a simple expression of preference. To be able to see what ought to be "said" in the given musical context, the musical language-game, and then to see a deeply nuanced sensitivity attuned exactly to that need or the "ought" that implies its "can" (in the form of the technical skill and musical talent that makes one able to consistently deliver precisely what is needed, and in unfailingly exquisite form), is extremely discerning. It is, in short, a special sensitivity to a distinctive kind of sensitivity. We admire sensitivity at both levels (here, the way Evans plays, and the way Davis sees why what Evans plays is precisely what is needed), and we do so inside the world of musical improvisation once again just as we do in ethical life.

There are probably no fewer musical insensitivities in these terms than there are moral ones, but perhaps one can stand for many: the recent case of the popular saxophonist Kenny G acquiring the rights to a Louis Armstrong recording, playing with it by overdubbing, and then re-releasing it in altered form. It was in part I believe the sense of involuntary post-mortem collaboration of a kind that, one imagines, may well not have happened between the two living collaborators had they been contemporaries[16] that provoked some of the ire. But the trenchant, and sometimes heated, criticism (forcefully articulated by the brilliant jazz guitarist Pat Metheny, among many others) went beyond that: it was a critique concerning what was perceived in this case to be a lack of precisely this variety of moral sensitivity, where – tellingly – that was taken as an immediately aesthetically relevant fact. Or one could express the matter this way: what was "said," while overdubbing in the context of Armstrong's original recording and his original musical genius, was taken to be very much out of place in a way that was by no means a simple matter. It was no less simple than the intricate and complex sets of nested criteria that allow us to discern whether a remark, in a sensitive situation, is wise or not.

12   Excessive Attentiveness

The kind of attentiveness I have described above that shows itself in both moral life and improvisation falls, like most morally relevant actions or modes of engagement and as Aristotle also observed, on a continuum of deficiency to excess. We have seen that one can be insufficiently attentive in many ways and in many contexts. Can one be too attentive? In particularized senses of the term, the answer is yes, and this phenomenon as it occurs within jazz improvisation here again helps cast this moral phenomenon in higher (and thus more visible) relief. In tracking closely the development of the soloist's improvisation one can become too close to the soloist in such a way that the individuality of the soloist is significantly diminished. A somewhat technical case will show how easily this can happen.

A soloist may sequence a melodic motif, i.e., develop a thematic gesture through a series of similar phrases, but steadily increase its harmonic power, its harmonic implications, by adding chordal extension and alteration tones (as discussed briefly above) beyond the set of pitches given in the scale that corresponds to the underlying chord. This may begin by adding a ninth, then a thirteenth, then perhaps a raised ninth followed by a leap from a flatted ninth to a flatted thirteenth over a dominant chord. A pianist or guitarist can quickly kill the power of this gesture – one that has its power by working *against* the given harmonic setting – by following the improvised line so closely that the ninth, the thirteenth, the raised ninth and finally the flatted ninth with flatted thirteenth are all included in the voicings of the chords they themselves are improvising (roughly in the manner of Freddie Green as described above) over the underlying skeletal harmonic progression. The result is that what would have been a melodic sequence with increasing harmonic tension by "fighting" against the dictates of the underlying harmony is rendered powerless in terms of its harmonic implications precisely because it has been integrated into sounded chordal tones. Or to take another brief example, a soloist may move a melodic motif upward by minor thirds in a sequence, but if the pianist hears that first ascending-minor-third step and quickly follows it by voicing a series of ascending diminished-seventh chords (which has notes stacked in the same minor thirds as the sequenced motif) to harmonize the soloist's ascending motif, its power is taken from it and it sounds instead like simply following the underlying harmony almost slavishly. What was played as a powerful departure, in the moment of its creation, is converted into what players call "inside" playing, i.e., into an obedient and chord *following* gesture.

To put the matter one way, one could say that this falsifies what is being said. To put it another way (and more precisely in terms of the present point), it takes a musical idea that possesses its aesthetic identity *oppositionally* and converts it, in a sense against its will or certainly in a manner inconsistent with its character, to its opposite, i.e., a gesture that has its identity *co-operatively*. Still another way to put this would be to say that accompanists who follow the improvising soloist this extremely closely create the misleading aesthetic appearance that it is the soloist who is following, never moving against what the chords dictate, never moving "outside." Indeed, in such harmonically claustrophobic circumstances, one might say that there *is* no "outside" – every effort to move outside is as quickly reconfigured as inside. It is an extremely highly developed skill – one that in itself is entirely laudable – but where it is used to the maximal degree and without moderation, without judgment, that makes this fault possible.

This cloying presence has its direct analogue in moral life, where one is made to feel claustrophobic, or indeed as though one cannot "breathe" in terms of autonomous volition, precisely because the gestures one makes, the stands one takes against something, are as quickly – owing to an overuse of an otherwise laudable sympathetic imagination – integrated into what one is trying to oppose. It turns an autonomous ethical gesture into complicity, an edgy independence into bland agreement. What one wants is a person who, in comprehending fully what is being said, comprehends the assertion of autonomy or independent-mindedness that is being made as part of a remark that is not itself explicitly about autonomy or independent-mindedness. And what an improvising soloist wants is an accompanying player who has the aural acuity, the ear-training skills, to instantly recognize such harmonic implications, but who also has the maturity of musicianship to fully comprehend the character of the gesture as it is made and not falsify it through too-close attentiveness, too-close accommodation, or the musical parallel to an ingratiating solicitousness. And of course, a mere demonstration of technical ability in this regard, a mere demonstration of the very highly trained aural acuity that accomplished jazz improvisers possess that allows tracking to this degree, is as aesthetically objectionable as the person whose desire it is not to respond sympathetically, but rather to display the heightened capacity for a sympathetic response, is morally objectionable. Indeed, sometimes the right thing to do is for players in the rhythm section (usually piano or guitar, bass, and drums) to form a coalition that, in appearing to be oppositional to the soloist, actually gives the soloist precisely what he or she needs: something to play against. Such relational configurations – here in the form of the apparent paradox of working *with* precisely by working *against* – are as interestingly complex in improvised jazz as they are in life. What one wants in jazz is: a player possessing the technique and musicianship sufficient to closely track an improvised solo to this heightened degree all the time, but one who in fact puts that tracking into harmonic and rhythmic action only some of the time – only when it is right. And what one wants in ethical life is: a person possessing a developed moral sensibility sufficient to attend this extremely closely, but who acts on this judiciously – indeed only when such action is what the circumstance calls for.

13   The Diversity of Intentional Action

One finds inside jazz improvisation, as stated at the outset of this paper, an enactment of one aspect of moral life, an aspect relating to the philosophy of mind, that is I believe of considerable methodological significance for ethics in general and moral psychology in particular. And it is at this point – with the dozen previous considerations now in mind – that I move to the somewhat more demanding ambition.

Wittgenstein, in his lectures on aesthetics, said:

> Giving a reason sometimes means "I actually went this way," sometimes "I could have gone this way," i.e., sometimes what we say acts as a justification, not as a report on what was done, e.g., I *remember* the answer to a question; when asked why I give this answer, I gave a process leading to it, though I didn't go through this process.[17]

The fundamental issue here concerns the dangers of – and prior to that the very possibility of – the retrospective falsification of intentional action. The very phrase "intentional action" can all too easily lead one to imagine, in a manner consistent with the Cartesian or dualistic picture of a human being, that any human action of the intentional kind is in truth a dual action: there is the fully formed intention that exists as a mental entity, and then there is the bodily enactment of that intention that follows upon in material form that prior ghostly episode. (The phrase "deliberate action" can do the same: the picture that all too easily comes to mind is that of deliberating within a purely mental realm, prior to the contingent manifestation of that deliberation in embodied action.) Like moral life, jazz improvisation is full of all varieties of intentional action, but also like moral life, that action can be easily misconstrued.

If, in improvising a melodic passage in the moment (but again not *obliviously* in the moment, as discussed above) we play, over the II chord of a II-V-I chord progression (e.g., Dmin7, G7, Cmaj7), a descending line that begins on the ninth scale step, moves down to the tonic, then falls down to the fifth below, then continues down to the third below that, slides down a half-step to the ninth one octave lower than where we started, and then settles on the tonic a step below that, we have fairly uninterestingly outlined a Dmin9 chord (with the ninths, incidentally, functioning as chordal extensions of just the kind discussed in the previous section). But if, as we move to the V chord, instead of playing a line that simply outlines its chordal tones, say the seventh, the fifth, the third, and the root, we move the entire melodic line we just played over the Dmin7 chord up a minor third and repeat it exactly in structure but at that transposition, a host of interesting questions, within the present context concerning retrospective intentional falsification, can be asked. The result of the melodic phrase-transposition is that we get a far more interesting melodic line with far greater harmonic significance that we would have done had we simply outlined the G7. We now get instead a rich set of chordal extensions and alterations (the eleventh and the flatted ninth, among others) that greatly enliven the harmonic implications of the melodic line.

Now, Wittgenstein suggested that we often give an answer that acts as justification, *not as a report of what was done.* Did we, in improvising, think "If we transpose this chord-outlining melodic line up a minor third and play that in place of the diatonically contained (and hence "inside," in the above sense) line that would simply outline a G7, we will have an eleventh and flatted ninth as tension-inducing pitches against the dominant chord that we would not otherwise have had"? The answer – if we are talking about professional players and not students working their way through this out of real time, i.e., note-by-note and thought-by-thought – is neither no nor yes. The right answer is (perhaps frustrating to those who would prefer uniform precision to moral-psychological accuracy) "not exactly." In other words, this *is*, in Wittgenstein's sense, a way we *could* have gone, or a process through which we would have arrived at this result. And this is the process through which we went as students to learn to unpack, to understand, the harmonic implications of this phrase-transposition. And if in a jazz improvisation seminar a student asks why we transposed that line up a minor third as we did, this is, also in Wittgenstein's sense, the justification we will give. It makes the action rational in retrospect – it makes the action one that seems to conform to the dualistic template of ghostly intention followed by embodied action, precisely where that intention is articulated as a sequence of thought that leads to and justifies the ensuing action. But this is how we speak *in retrospect* and when *asked for a justification.* We should remember – here is the matter of some significance encapsulated – that, as Wittgenstein puts it, we "didn't go through this process." Moreover, we should bear in mind that questions asking for a justification, questions of the "Why did you do it?" kind, are hardly unitary in nature: the question as voiced here could well be asking the question of the student in the improvisation seminar, but it could also be the question of a slightly disgruntled fellow improviser who has just used that phrase-transposition idea far too often and feels mocked. Or it could – to take a *very* different kind of case that suggests the vast range of possibility here – be the question of a recently bereaved person on stage who hears that phrase transposition as the melodic trademark of the deceased and feels the quotation to be insensitive in the circumstances. It could be a thousand things, and the answers we give on being asked can be every bit as varied in both content and spirit. Wittgenstein also discussed what he identified as "the power language has to make everything look the same;" such questions look the same because they employ the same words. They are not. And the conceptual picture or template we have of intentional action, especially as in the present discussion where retrospectively imposed, makes all intentional action look the same. It is not. Moral action, dualistically misconstrued, is seen as action that follows hermetic intentional deliberation, where we then ask what principles that ratiocination should explicitly follow and whether the process of reasoning from those principles was sound. Jazz improvisation, seen one way, is itself a corrective against such misconstrual. And seen this way, it is an art form that itself seems to argue for those varieties of moral thinking that focus upon virtue and character, and against those that focus invariably or reductively upon consequence-calculation (utilitarianism) and pre-act ratiocination (deontology).

Improvisers – like moral agents – intend all kinds of things all the time, but, indeed, within the musical analogues to the lived contexts of human life and real human engagements. David Smith, the sculptor, spoke of the great significance of what he called "the direct deed" in sculptural creativity.[18] That direct deed, one imagines, is one that *actually* happened, and not the retrospective re-description of that deed that is tailored, after the fact, to conform to a simplified dualistic intentional template. Nietzsche wrote derisively of what he called the "antecedentia of action,"[19] the retrospectively invented or projected falsifications of intentional action. Jazz improvisation is, or at least can often be, an art form that is utterly in the moment *in this respect*; it is a microcosm of such direct deeds without the falsifications of conceptual templates, without the retrospectively projected antecedentia. And in that, it is at once a representation but also an enactment of intentional life. To attempt to reduce all of the extensively divergent cases of morally significant action in human life to, say, the pre-active contemplation of the universalizablity of the maxim under which we act, or to deliberation concerning the distinction between acting from, as opposed to merely in accordance with, duty, or to the calculation of consequences concerning the greatest happiness for the greatest number, or to a reflective awareness of the obedience of our action to natural law (among many other possibilities throughout the history of ethical theory), is to hopelessly attempt to retrospectively superimpose uniformity on irreducibly great diversity.

The actions undertaken within the special artistic world of the jazz improviser are not, in virtue of such reflections, thus to be regarded random, thoughtless, unprepared, or anything of the kind. To say that would be to stay within the simplified picture of intentional action but to just say that jazz improvisation does not correspond to it, and thus that it is not in any serious way intentional. That would be to miss the point completely: random flux it is not. Rather, it is an art form that itself constitutes a welcome antidote for the trivialization of complexity and impatience with particularity. What, jazz improvisation asks, is happening in *this* moment, with *these* people, in *this* setting, under *these* conditions? Given that *this* musical gesture has just been made in *this* circumstance, what is possible *now*? Jazz improvisation indeed shows within its practice how much attention we should give to the complexities of real moral questions, real moral moments, people, settings, conditions, and circumstances.

At the outset of this chapter I invoked the pragmatists' distinction between process and product, suggesting that an essential part of this art form is that it places the conditions of creativity, in a compressed frame of time, before the listener. That process, on the stage, as we have seen *represents*: it provides a mimetic depiction of the many modes of attention, sensitivity, and humane acknowledgment that we have considered above. But as we have also seen it *presents*: it is a microcosmic world of human beings *actually* interacting with each other, and doing so in a way immune – because it is real action – to the falsifications of retrospective re-description. It is in precisely this sense that it carries perhaps its deepest lesson – in the form of a set of reminders about what life is actually like well beyond its theory-driven simplifications – for moral psychology and thus more broadly for ethical methodology. It is a world within which one player's musicality or musical sensibility can to greater and lesser extents, in at least the dozen respects we have now seen, be understood, comprehended, and responded to by other musicians. And like a number of the issues we have now considered, that too is at once an aesthetic and ethical fact. A musical motif, improvised as an expression of such a sensibility, can be seen in divergent ways, "networked" into contrasting sets of musical relations differently and in a way that is open-ended, into relations that, indeed, end nowhere.[20] That is a profound representation of – and within its own special world, instance of – the genuine, and in an ever-enlivening way, open-ended, comprehension of a human being.

Notes

1   This is not an unnecessary neologism. The common term "notated" is not sufficient to the task: many performances (and particularly improvised ones) are notated, i.e., transcribed, after the fact.

2   A useful collection of such writings can be found in John J. Stuhr, ed. *Pragmatism and Classical American Philosophy: Essential Readings and Interpretive Essays*, 2nd edn. (New York and Oxford: Oxford University Press, 2000). It was John Dewey who brought these issues into aesthetics; I offer a discussion of his aesthetic views particularly in connection with the emphasis on process in "Contours of Experience: The Foundations of Dewey's Aesthetic Thought," in James Conant, ed., *The Cambridge Companion to Dewey* (Cambridge: Cambridge University Press, forthcoming).

3   Martha Nussbaum has called attention to the centrality of this concept for ethics. See, as a start, her " 'Finely Aware and Richly Responsible': Literature and the Moral Imagination," in Anthony J. Cascardi, ed., *Literature and the Question of Philosophy* (Baltimore, MD: Johns Hopkins University Press, 1987), pp. 167–91. This theme is developed throughout a number of her writings; see her collection *Love's Knowledge: Essays on Philosophy and Literature* (Oxford: Oxford University Press, 1990).

4   We might explain what is frustrating at least, and perhaps indisputably morally offensive at worst, about what in some televised contexts has passed for political debate in precisely these terms: it offers the debased spectacle of mutually uncomprehending and humanely inattentive ideologues shouting over each other in the interest of point-scoring.

5   The intricate roles played by nuances of facial expressivity are not always given the attention they deserve in discussions of moral perception and, more broadly, in philosophical psychology. I offer some discussions of this matter in "The Mind Shown: Wittgenstein, Goethe, and the Question of Person-Perception," in Fritz Breithaupt, Richard Raatzsch, and Bettina Kremberg, eds., *Goethe and Wittgenstein: Seeing the World's Unity in its Variety* (*Wittgenstein-Studien*, Band 5: Peter Lang, Frankfurt am Main, 2002), pp. 111–26, and in "The Self, Speaking: Wittgenstein, Introspective Utterances, and the Arts of Self-Representation," *Revue Internationale de Philosophie* 1/219 (2002): 9–47 (in a special issue on Wittgenstein and the Philosophy of Mind, ed. Jean-Pierre Cometti).

6   For a deeply comprehending extended discussion of just this kind of inter-active response, see Ingrid Monson, *Saying Something: Jazz Improvisation and Interaction* (Chicago, IL: University of Chicago Press, 1996).

7   See Michael Krausz, *Interpretation and Transformation: Explorations in Art and the Self* (Amsterdam: Rodopi, 2007) for an analytically acute and humanely rich discussion of this point.

8   I offer an analysis of the moral condition of the character Don Giovanni in just these terms, in "Leporello's Question: *Don Giovanni* as a Tragedy of the Unexamined Life," *Philosophy and Literature* 29:1 (for the symposium Music, Politics, and Morality, April 2005): 180–99.

9   See for example Plato, *Republic*, trans. Richard Sterling and William Scott (New York: Norton, 1985), book 3, especially pp. 95–100. It is instructive that the first discussions we have of the musical modes (in Plato and ancient Greek musical theorists) directly address from the outset the relations between musical content and moral qualities.

10 For a discussion of the aesthetic preference that this practice embodies, see Frances Hutcheson, *An Inquiry into the Original of Our Ideas of Beauty and Virtue* (London, 1729), excerpted in George Dickie, Richard Sclafani, and Ronald Roblin, *Aesthetics: A Critical Anthology*, 2nd edn. (New York: St Martin's, 1989), pp. 223–41; see especially pp. 229–30. Hutcheson discusses the aesthetic criterion of "uniformity amidst variety": here one might say that modal pieces improvised over with only the scalar mode to which they directly correspond offer too much uniformity, where superimposed melodic complexity provides the needed variety.

11 I offer a discussion of this, in connection with the assembly of a life narrative (which a jazz solo can mimetically reduplicate in microcosm) in "Narrative Catharsis," in John Gibson, Wolfgang Huemer, and Luca Pocci, *A Sense of the World: Essays on Fiction, Narrative, and Knowledge* (London: Routledge, 2007), pp. 151–66.

12 I discuss this feature of experience in "Davidson, Self-Knowledge, and Autobiographical Writing," *Philosophy and Literature* 26/2 (October 2002): 354–68 (in which what is called the "bleeding" of the sound of one instrument in a recording studio into the microphone recording another instrument serves as an analogue for human experience).

13 I discuss this matter of the "unfrozen" past in "In a New Light: Wittgenstein, Aspect-Perception, and Retrospective Change in Autobiographical Understanding," in William Day and Victor Krebs, eds., *Seeing Wittgenstein Anew* (Cambridge: Cambridge University Press, forthcoming).

14 Adam Phillips, "The Telling of Selves: Notes on Psychoanalysis and Autobiography," in his *On Flirtation: Psychoanalytical Essays on the Uncommitted Life* (Cambridge, MA: Harvard University Press, 1994), pp. 65–75.

15 See Bill Evans, liner notes for Miles Davis, *Kind of Blue* (Columbia Records, 1959). I discuss Evans' comments, and their significance for the understanding of artistic creativity, in my *Art as Language: Wittgenstein, Meaning, and Aesthetic Theory* (Ithaca, NY: Cornell University Press, 1995).

16 Their being contemporaries is itself admittedly a rather difficult thought, since one cannot imagine Kenny G's music in Armstrong's time. It is,

incidentally, not my intention at this particular juncture to criticize Kenny G's aesthetic choices or his music, but rather to pause to consider the character and tone of the criticism that the Armstrong overdubbing elicited and what it suggests about one variety of the ethical content of this art form.

17 Ludwig Wittgenstein, *Lectures and Conversations on Aesthetics, Psychology, and Religious Belief*, ed. Cyril Barrett (Oxford: Blackwell, 1966). I also discuss this passage and the problem it is addressing, in connection with questions of self-understanding, in "Narrative Catharsis."

18 I discuss this in *Art as Language: Wittgenstein, Meaning, and Aesthetic Theory.*

19 Friedrich Nietzsche, *The Twilight of the Idols*, trans. R. J. Hollingdale (Harmondsworth: Penguin, 1968); see especially "The Four Great Errors," pp. 47–54.

20 I offer a much fuller discussion of the relational conception of selfhood as it has been developed in American pragmatic thought and as it is constituted in part by aesthetic experience in "Imagined Identities: Autobiography at One Remove," *New Literary History* 38 (2007): 163–81.

INDEX